—THE—
WORLD ATLAS OF
HORSE RACING

St Michael

-THE-
WORLD ATLAS OF
HORSE RACING

Julian Bedford

All colour illustrations by
Brian Ceney

All mono illustrations by
Terry McKivragan of Linda Rogers Associates

Designed by Ronald Samuels

This edition published in 1990
exclusively for Marks and Spencer p.l.c.,
by arrangement with
The Octopus Publishing Group,
Michelin House, 81 Fulham Road
London SW3 6RB

Printed in Hong Kong

CONTENTS

INTRODUCTION

Everyone has a favourite racecourse, one for whatever reason they will go back to time and time again. My particular favourite, Cheltenham, will forever remind me of my University days-off at the home of National Hunt racing.

But horse racing is rapidly becoming a global sport. Horses from Europe fly all over the world to compete against the best of America, Australasia and Japan.

It is becoming more and more important to understand the whys and wherefores of international racing. How and where horses race outside one's particular country, the surfaces they race on and the atmosphere of each individual course.

This book explores some the world's top courses and the major races run on them. Although the bias is towards the major racing powers of Europe and North America, I have tried to cover extensively both Australia and Japan where the sport seems to be on the up.

JULIAN BEDFORD

EUROPE

Europe is the cradle of the racing world. Both the thoroughbred itself and the modern sport of racing were born in England and it is still to that country that one turns for equine excellence.

Here the ultimate race is the Epsom Derby, and all other Derbys reflect in the glory of Epsom.

From England the sport spread to Ireland and the rest of the continent, taking a firm hold on the populace. For the spectacle of thoroughbreds competing against each other on beautiful courses is addictive and compelling.

It is the variety of European racing that gives it its uniqueness. No two courses are alike, and over them the full range of distances are used. Whether it be Newmarket's straight mile, or the twists and turns of Epsom, the spectacle is ever changing and ever demanding on the horse.

Chantilly's Chateau provides a magnificent backdrop to the runners as they race at one of France's premier courses.

Newmarket is headquarters, the home of British racing. As Jack Leach said many years ago: 'Newmarket is one of the only places where a man can go racing; elsewhere he merely goes to the races, which isn't the same thing at all.'

Its windswept Heath stages some of the greatest racing in the British calendar and the town is one large centre of the thoroughbred industry. Over 3,000 horses are trained in Newmarket, and if those in the surrounding studs, livery stables and paddocks are added to that number, the equine population very nearly exceeds the human.

Racing at Newmarket spans virtually the whole of the British Flat season, with the early Classics dominating its spring meetings, and the Champion Stakes and the Dewhurst Stakes winding up affairs in October. In between times, racing moves to the more sedate and intimate setting of the July course, whose shady paddock is better suited to the summer heat that occasionally graces the big July meeting.

The Jockey Club

Newmarket's importance in the racing world is not only measured by the races run on the course, but also through its long association with the Jockey Club, the first governing body of the sport. It has ruled the roost in the town since the middle of the last century. To be warned off Newmarket Heath is the final sanction in the racing world and still prevents one from visiting any racecourse.

Formed in 1751 in a bid to impose some discipline on the disorderly world of racing, the Jockey Club has watched over the development of British racing for over 200 years and it is still the ultimate racing

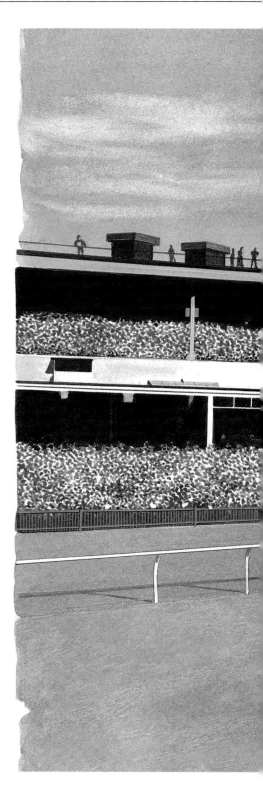

Above: *Newmarket's windswept Heath provides training gallops for the 2,500 horses stabled around the town.*

Left: *The great Eclipse, as depicted by George Stubbs, standing in front of the Rubbing House at Newmarket. Eclipse was not only the first equine champion, unbeaten throughout his career, but is also the tail-male ancestor of most subsequent champions.*

NEWMARKET

The Beacon course spawns two straights, the Rowley Mile, which is used in spring and autumn and the summer's July course. The Rowley Mile is a straight ten furlongs, whose penultimate furlong descends from the Bushes into the dip and then rises to the winning post. The mile-long July course drops gradually until the final uphill furlong.

The magic that is Newmarket. The crowd roar on the horses as they climb through the final furlong of the Rowley Mile course.

Below: *El Gran Senor gallops away from Chief Singer to win one of the greatest 2,000 Guineas in 1984. Ridden by Pat Eddery and trained by Vincent O'Brien, the colt trounced a top-class field with consummate ease.*

Opposite bottom: *Famous colours adorn the Rowley Mile paddock as connections review their tactics before the race.*

authority. Its dominance has often been challenged and sometimes derided, but its prestige has never lessened.

Although members of the Jockey Club first met in taverns in London, the Coffee House in Newmarket's High Street was the recognized home of the body and the present Newmarket offices are on that same site. However, the Jockey Club's main administration offices are now in London in Portman Square.

Men of the stature of Sir Charles Bunbury, Lord George Bentinck and Admiral Henry Rous developed the Club into an organization which laid down the Rules of Racing in 1836. Although at first these applied only to Newmarket, they soon became an accepted code all over the world. It is through the Jockey Club that the racing industry has reached its current shape and position in the world of sport. The ordering of race meetings, the organization of the Pattern committee, which grades races, the official handicapping of horses and the development and introduction of new rules are all overseen by the Jockey Club, whose connection with Newmarket is still fully acknowledged.

Newmarket courses

Newmarket is also the birthplace of the modern sport. The windscoured Heath has been a racing centre since Charles I decided that it would be the ideal place to race his horses. But it was his son, Charles II, who made the course and left it with his horse's name. In 1665 he founded the Newmarket Town Plate, a race which is still run, albeit in a different form. He spent his summers up in East Anglia in the palace built by James I, riding his hack Rowley and racing against his friends. He remains the only British monarch to have ridden a winner on the Flat, twice winning the Newmarket Town Plate, which at the time was perhaps the most important race in the land.

The course used today has changed little over the intervening three centuries. Like a crooked Y, the two courses – the Rowley Mile, named after Charles II's horse, and the July Course – run off the extended Cesarewitch course which stretches back into Cambridgeshire. The Rowley Mile is where the British Flat season really comes to life when the Craven meeting is held in mid-April. The two most significant Guin-

eas trials, the Nell Gwynn Stakes and the Craven Stakes, set the scene for the 1,000 and 2,000 Guineas run over the same course three weeks later.

Newmarket in the spring can be a cold place as winds blown across the continent from Siberia blast the assembled spectators, but all keen racing aficionados are prepared to brave the wintry conditions to see the 'most likely to' horses make their seasonal debuts. Likewise they will return to see the first Classics of the year.

The 1,000 Guineas

The 1,000 Guineas, for three-year-old fillies, is run on the Thursday of the meeting and sets the standard for the whole season. Since it was first run in 1814, the race has thrown up some exceptional winners. The first running of the race was won by Christopher Wilson's Charlotte. As Wilson was at the time one of the most respected men of the turf, and one who reputedly never missed a meeting at Newmarket, Epsom or Ascot, the win was a popular one, although Charlotte herself appears to have been nothing exceptional.

1,000 GUINEAS STAKES

1 mile. Three-year-old fillies, 9st. First run 1814.

Year	Winner	Owner	Trainer	Jockey
1970	Humble Duty	Jean, Lady Ashcombe	P. Walwyn	L. Piggott
1971	Altesse Royale	Col. F. Hue-Williams	N. Murless	Y. Saint-Martin
1972	Waterloo	Mrs. R. Stanley	J.W. Watts	E. Hide
1973	Mysterious	G.A. Pope, jr.	N. Murless	G. Lewis
1974	Highclere	H.M. The Queen	W.R. Hern	J. Mercer
1975	Nocturnal Spree	Mrs. D. O'Kelly	H.V.S. Murless	J. Roe
1976	Flying Water	D. Wildenstein	A. Penna	Y. Saint-Martin
1977	Mrs McArdy	Mrs. E. Kettlewell	M.W. Easterby	E. Hide
1978	Enstone Spark	R. Bonnycastle	B. Hills	E. Johnson
1979	One in a Million	Helena Springfield Ltd.	H. Cecil	J. Mercer
1980	Quick as Lightning	O. Phipps	J. Dunlop	B. Rouse
1981	Fairy Footsteps	H.J. Joel	H. Cecil	L. Piggott
1982	On the House	Sir P. Oppenheimer	H. Wragg	J. Reid
1983	Ma Biche	Maktoum Al-Maktoum	Mme. C. Head	F. Head
1984	Pebbles	Capt. M. Lemos	C. Brittain	P. Robinson
1985	Oh So Sharp	Sheikh Mohammed	H. Cecil	S. Cauthen
1986	Midway Lady	H.H. Rainier	B. Hanbury	R. Cochrane
1987	Miesque	S.S. Niarchos	F. Boutin	F. Head
1988	Ravinella	Ecurie Aland	Mme. C. Head	G. Moore
1989	Musical Bliss	Sheikh Mohammed	M. Stoute	W.R. Swinburn

Neva, the 1817 winner, was the first of many fillies to go on to win the Oaks, but it was the remarkable Formosa in 1868, who first completed the fillies' Triple Crown, of the 1,000 Guineas, Oaks and St Leger. She dead-heated with Moslem in the 2,000 Guineas to boot, a four-timer only equalled once, in 1902, by Sceptre, who was owned and trained by the professional gambler Robert Sievier.

More recent winners of exceptional talent include the Triple Crown winners Pretty Polly in 1904, Sun Chariot in 1942, Meld in 1955, Prince Aly Khan's flying grey Petite Etoile, who was arguably the greatest filly of this century, winner in 1959.

Then there was the Queen's Highclere in 1974 (which is the most recent Royal winner) and Oh So Sharp in 1985.

The 2,000 Guineas

On the Saturday of that meeting, attention is switched to the colts for the second of Newmarket's Classics, the 2,000 Guineas. The longer established of the two races by five years, the inaugural running in 1809 was won by Wizard, also owned by Christopher Wilson, and who was only narrowly beaten in that year's Derby.

The first colt to complete the Guineas/Derby double was Sir Charles Bunbury's Smolensko in 1813, who was made favourite for both races. But the first great winner of the 2,000 Guineas was Bay Middleton. In his short career in the colours of Lord Jersey, he was unbeaten in his six races before being retired to stud by Lord Bentinck, who had bought him for 4,000 guineas only to see his purchase break down with a leg injury.

In 1865 the spoils were taken abroad for the first time when the French-owned-and-bred Gladiateur, the 'avenger of Waterloo', defeated the home team. Trained at Newmarket by Tom Jennings, Gladiateur destroyed the belief that the English thoroughbreds were invincible by adding both the Derby and the St Leger to his Newmarket victory, as well as triumphing

Below: The uphill final furlong awaits the runners of the 1985 Tote Cesarewitch, the second half of Newmarket's famous autumn double. Kayudee, the eventual winner, has just hit the front from Sneak Preview and Jamesmead.

Right: Court and Spark, subsequently disqualified, just gets the better of Master Line in a handicap at Newmarket on Champion Stakes day in 1985. The stands are packed with the crowds awaiting the big race.

in the Grand Prix de Paris, the premier race in France at the time, before 150,000 supporters.

The Guineas, which were for some time seen as stepping stones to Epsom glory, have come into their own this century as the emphasis on stamina has dwindled. Nowadays the Guineas are a natural target for the top two-year-olds of the previous autumn, together with those who have developed into championship potential over the winter.

That they are run so early in the year taxes a trainer's ability to get his charge ready in time and spring is often a worrying time for those whose responsibility it is to turn raw talent into on-course excellence. Numerous are those horses who have been backed all winter to win at Newmarket, but have failed to reach full fitness in time to give their best in the Guineas or even to make it to the post.

The July Course

After one further Rowley Mile meeting following the Guineas, racing switches to the July Course. The major event is a three-day mid-week festival in July, when the atmosphere is more relaxed, though the racing remains as competitive as ever. These three days encompass the Princess of Wales's Stakes, the Cherry Hinton, the July Cup, the July Stakes and the Child Stakes, all top Pattern races offering valuable prize money and prestige, as well as the old and established handicap, the Bunbury Cup, named after Newmarket's first leader of the turf.

The two juvenile races – the Cherry Hinton and the July Stakes – are now run too early in the year to throw up champions consistently, but good fillies of the calibre of Diminuendo and Oh So Sharp, both of

2,000 GUINEAS STAKES

1 mile. Three-year-old colts and fillies, 9st. First run 1809.

Year	Winner	Owner	Trainer	Jockey
1970	Nijinsky	C. Engelhard	M.V. O'Brien	L. Piggott
1971	Brigadier Gerard	Mrs. J. Hislop	W.R. Hern	J. Mercer
1972	High Top	Sir J. Thorn	B. van Cutsem	W. Carson
1973	Mon Fils	Mrs. B. Davis	R. Hannon	F. Durr
1974	Nonoalco	Mme. Felix-Berger	F. Boutin	Y. Saint-Martin
1975	Bolkonski	C. d'Alessio	H. Cecil	G. Dettori
1976	Wollow	C. d'Alessio	H. Cecil	G. Dettori
1977	Nebbiolo	N. Schibbye	K. Prendergast	G. Curran
1978	Roland Gardens	J. Hayter	D. Sasse	F. Durr
1979	Tap on Wood	A. Shead	B. Hills	S. Cauthen
1980	Known Fact	K. Abdullah	J. Tree	W. Carson
1981	To-Agori-Mou	Mrs. A. Munios	G. Harwood	G. Starkey
1982	Zino	G. Oldham	F. Boutin	F. Head
1983	Lomond	R.E. Sangster	M.V. O'Brien	P. Eddery
1984	El Gran Senor	R.E. Sangster	M.V. O'Brien	P. Eddery
1985	Shadeed	Maktoum Al-Maktoum	M. Stoute	L. Piggott
1986	Dancing Brave	K. Abdullah	G. Harwood	G. Starkey
1987	Don't Forget Me	J. Horgan	R. Hannon	W. Carson
1988	Doyoun	H.H. Aga Khan	M. Stoute	W.R. Swinburn
1989	Nashwan	Hamdan Al-Maktoum	W.R. Hern	W. Carson

The stuff that dreams are made of. The winner's enclosure after a Classic is the dream that inspires owners when they buy or breed a horse. Here it's El Gran Senor who is the centre of attention after his 2,000 Guineas triumph.

whom went on to win the Oaks, are recent winners of the Cherry Hinton, although it has been a long time since the July Stakes produced a Classic winner. The Child Stakes and the Princess of Wales's Stakes pit the Classic generation of three-year-olds against their older rivals, whilst the July Cup, the one Group 1 or Championship race of the meeting, is a six furlong sprint, for which the fastest horses in Europe compete.

Sandwiched between the more social festivals of Royal Ascot and Glorious Goodwood, Newmarket's July meeting ex-udes racing for racing's sake. Not for that town the fancy fripperies and the small talk of the places-to-be-seen-at race meetings. No, this is serious stuff. That it is delightful, it is mid-week, and the surroundings at-tractive is all well and good, but as always at Newmarket, the racing comes first.

The racing stays on the July Course until September with a series of Friday night and Saturday afternoon meetings, where the best of the local two-year-olds are un-leashed by the town's powerful trainers. A Cecil or Stoute hotpot will arrive at the course with a fearsome home reputation, be sent off at long odds-on, win hard held and be quoted immediately at 16–1 for one of the following year's Classics, despite whatever the trainer might have to say. For at this

time of the year, everyone is looking for the stars of the future and has come to expect them to be unveiled at Newmarket, much as car salesmen descend on a motor show to see the shape of their future.

Autumn meetings

It is when racing returns to the Rowley Mile at the end of September that the quality of those juveniles is put to the test. Newmarket's autumn meetings stage some of the most prestigious two-year-old races of the season, and those promising colts and fillies of July and August have to prove themselves by making the step-up in class and winning the big prizes. These are the Cheveley Park and Middle Park Stakes, run in that first September meeting, over six furlongs for the speedsters. October's Dewhurst Stakes, over seven furlongs, is now reckoned to be the country's top juvenile race and its winner is nearly always assured of winter favouritism for the 2,000 Guineas and a place at the top of the international ratings.

But, Newmarket's autumn is not just about the juveniles. The Champion Stakes and the two big handicaps, the Cambridgeshire and the Cesarewitch, all receive their fair share of attention, and

have done so for many a decade. The Champion Stakes has been the last major all-aged race of the season since 1877, whilst the two handicaps, known collectively as the Autumn Double, both began in 1839 and were once as important as any of the races run over Newmarket's Heath. Their recent decline is due to the emphasis now put on Group races, the winning of which puts thousands of pounds on to the value of a horse.

Despite increased prize money, all handi-caps have found it increasingly difficult to compete with the prestige of the Pattern system. The end result of that system is to

be seen all round the town, in the studs and stables, but especially at Tattersalls in September when the Highflyer Yearling sales are held. Buyers from around the world descend on the town to pick the best of the British bloodstock, sired as often as not by stallions who proved their merit on the racecourses on the other side of Newmarket.

Newmarket Heath

Newmarket Heath, the straight mile which is reckoned to be the ultimate test of the horse – there can be no excuses on a straight mile, no bends to handle. The field starts seemingly on the horizon to those huddled in the stands at the opposite end of the course. They race towards one, a blur of colours and motion until the binoculars can pick out the details of the struggle. Two furlongs out the track drops from The Bushes – the only noticeable piece of vegetation on the whole Heath whilst a race is being run – before climbing throughout the last furlong to the winning post. That final climb has seen so many races, so many last-gasp struggles, so much history that its perennial greenness seems uncanny.

As the field flashes past the post and into

Leaving the Rowley Mile stands behind them, the field make their way down towards the start.

the form book, you can be forgiven on that timeless stretch of turf for thinking that you have just witnessed the first race held at Newmarket, but if you lift up your eyes and look around and see the thousands in the stands and hear the clamour of the bookies touting up more business, you will realise that you have witnessed what makes one town so important.

DONCASTER

The Town Moor at Doncaster is famous for the oldest of the English Classics, the St Leger, which is named after a popular local sportsman, Lt-Col Anthony St Leger. Run over 14½ furlongs at the September meeting, the race neatly wraps up the three-year-old calendar as it provides a final test of stamina after the Guineas test of speed at the start of the season and Epsom's middle distance crown at the height of summer.

The first two runnings of this race were held on the other side of Doncaster at Cantley Common. It was only in 1778 that the present site became a fixed and recognized venue for racing and that a grandstand, which survived for nearly 200 years, was built for the spectators to watch the great race.

Activities on the Town Moor are not just confined to the St Leger. Since 1965 Doncaster has both welcomed in the Flat season with the March Lincolnshire meeting, which the course inherited from the old Lincoln race course, and watched over its last hours with the running of the November Handicap, another parvenu race that crossed the Pennines from Manchester in 1964. And if that Flat campaign is not enough, Doncaster still finds time during the winter months to host some attractive jumping meetings.

Hard times

It is a sign of the times that both the St Leger and Doncaster have to struggle to remain in the limelight. In days gone by the St Leger was the natural climax to a three-year-old's career, a true test of stamina which would determine whether a horse would develop into a staying four-year-old who could be entered for the prestigious Cup races. Nowadays the thoroughbred is bred to be at his most effective over ten to 12 furlongs and the best of the breed are not expected to attempt any tests of stamina. This has left the St Leger in limbo. The race is still a Classic with the prize money and prestige that accompanies such a title, but it cannot regularly attract the best and unfortunately small fields are usually very normal these days.

Much the same can be said about

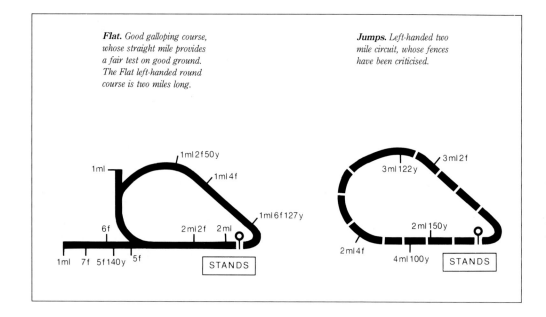

Flat. Good galloping course, whose straight mile provides a fair test on good ground. The Flat left-handed round course is two miles long.

Jumps. Left-handed two mile circuit, whose fences have been criticised.

Doncaster's paddock is packed on St Leger day as the crowds admire the runners for the oldest and longest English Classic.

Left: *Reference Point is clear of his rivals in the 1986 William Hill Futurity. That success earned him the top rating in the International Free Handicap, a rating he justified by winning the Derby in 1987.*

Right: *Steve Cauthen boots home Vague Discretion in a Doncaster nursery on the final day of the '87 Flat season.*

Doncaster: a grand course, with some of the oldest and greatest events in the calendar, but now serving some pretty average fare between the historic peaks, with even these beginning to look somewhat threadbare.

The course itself can give few causes for complaint. A pear-shaped, left-handed course of nearly two miles in circumference, Doncaster is as fair a test of the thoroughbred as one could wish for when the going is good. With a wide straight mile, over which the Lincoln is run, together with the newer round mile, over which the Futurity, now known as the Racing Post Trophy, is run, the course offers the true galloping horse every opportunity to excel over all distances.

There is, however, one drawback. When the ground rides soft, large races over the straight mile become something of a fore-gone conclusion, as those with a high draw face a virtually impossible task. It is that fact which has led to the decline of the Lincoln. For years the race attracted a weight of bets throughout the winter as stables readied their charges for a shot at the first major prize of the new season. But why have a punt if the horse one fancies may be drawn out of contention on the eve of the race?

Without the notorious gambles to keep the contest in the forefront of the public's attention, the Lincoln has slipped into mediocrity. But hopefully the recent injection of prize money by the sponsors, William Hill, and the attempts by the course executive to improve the drainage will return the race to something of its former glory.

Between the opening fanfare of the Flat at the March meeting and the St Leger meeting in September, there is precious little at Doncaster to draw in big crowds. But the St Leger meeting is still a tremendous affair. Four days of high-class racing starts on the Wednesday with the Park Hill Stakes, the fillies' St Leger, and culminates on the Saturday with the Classic itself. In between are the Doncaster Cup, first run in 1766 and the oldest race still run under the auspices of the Jockey Club, the Champagne Stakes and the May Hill Stakes, two cracking good two-year-old races, the Portland Handicap, which is still one of the most competitive sprint handicaps around, and the Flying Childers Stakes, the season's top race for speedy two-year-olds.

St Leger

The St Leger is as steeped in history and controversy as any of the Classics, indeed

ST. LEGER STAKES
1 mile, 6 furlongs, 127 yards. Three-year-old colts and fillies, 9st. First run 1776.

Year	Winner	Owner	Trainer	Jockey
1971	Athens Wood	Mrs. J. Rogerson	H.T. Jones	L. Piggott
1972	Boucher	O. Phipps	M.V. O'Brien	L. Piggott
1973	Peleid	Col. W. Behrens	W. Elsey	F. Durr
1974	Bustino	Lady Beaverbrook	W.R. Hern	J. Mercer
1975	Bruni	C. St. George	H.R. Price	A. Murray
1976	Crow	D. Wildenstein	A. Penna	Y. Saint-Martin
1977	Dunfermline	H.M. The Queen	W.R. Hern	W. Carson
1978	Julio Mariner	Capt. M. Lemos	C. Brittain	E. Hide
1979	Son of Love	A. Rolland	R. Collet	A. Lequeux
1980	Light Cavalry	H.J. Joel	H. Cecil	J. Mercer
1981	Cut Above	Sir John Astor	W.R. Hern	J. Mercer
1982	Touching Wood	H. Al-Maktoum	H.T. Jones	P. Cook
1983	Sun Princess	Sir M. Sobell	W.R. Hern	W. Carson
1984	Commanche Run	I. Allan	L. Cumani	L. Piggott
1985	Oh So Sharp	Sheikh Mohammed	H. Cecil	S. Cauthen
1986	Moon Madness	Lavinia, Duchess of Norfolk	J. Dunlop	P. Eddery
1987	Reference Point	L. Freedman	H. Cecil	S. Cauthen
1988	Minster Son	The Dowager Lady Beaverbrook	W.R. Hern	W. Carson
1989	Michelozzo	C.A.B. St. George	H. Cecil	S. Cauthen

more so since it has been around for three more years than the next oldest, the Oaks. The first man to stamp his mark on the race was Lord Archibald, Duke of Hamilton, who won the race an incredible seven times between 1786 and 1814, a record which is never likely to be surpassed.

The first great horse to win the laurels was Hambletonian, the 1795 winner, who became the Champion of the North and only tasted defeat once in 21 races. He excelled at Doncaster and added two Doncaster Cups to his St Leger success.

Champion in 1800 was the first colt to win both the Derby and the St Leger, but it was another 53 years before West Austra-lian became the first Triple Crown winner, scooping three Classics. This, the ultimate accomplishment of a thoroughbred, has since been achieved 24 times, most recently by the brilliant Nijinsky in 1970 and the filly Oh So Sharp in 1985.

With the introduction in 1961 of the Timeform Gold Cup, Doncaster now hosts the richest two-year-old race in England, and the far-sightedness of Phil Bull in fixing the race has been amply rewarded. It has added an attractive two-day meeting to the course in October and given Doncaster a second Group 1 race.

Doncaster's jumping never quite scales the heights that the Flat fixtures reach, but it does provide good honest fare.

For years Doncaster's original grand-stand stood intact and became the butt of many a joke about the inhospitable nature of the amenities. The stand was finally put out of its misery in 1969, when a splendid new stand, which cost £1 million, was unveiled to give the spectators the comfort they should expect from a top course. With the paddock placed directly in front of the stands, the facilities are now excellent and the course executive, under the leadership of Don Cox, shows a determined and go-ahead attitude to the modern game that should prevent any further slippage by the course.

CHESTER

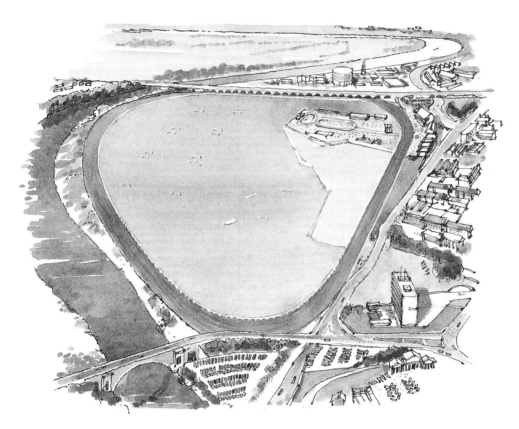

The sharp nature of the course has in some ways been responsible for the relative decline of Chester since many horses are not suited to the greyhound-like nature of racing there. However, Chester, with its beautiful new stand which was opened in 1988 to replace the old Dee stand that had been burnt to the ground, still takes centre stage in the racing world in May.

The principal race of that meeting is the Chester Cup, which has been run in its present form since 1836. But the race can trace its ancestry right back to one of the earliest recorded races run on the English turf: the St George's race. This was first run on Shrove Tuesday in 1541 when the prize was a silver bell. At the height of its popularity in the 19th century, the Chester Cup was second only to the Derby in the volume of betting it attracted. But as is the case with so many staying races, its prestige has declined in recent years.

In addition to the Chester Cup, the meeting also boasts two Classic trials in the Chester Vase, which has an admirable record for throwing up the winner of the Derby, having given us both the great Shergar and Henbit in the 1980s, as well as a decent race for the older horses in the Ormonde Stakes.

The Roodeye at Chester is the oldest and smallest course in England. Delightfully situated outside the Tudor town's old Roman walls on the north bank of the river Dee, Chester's tight left-handed track is not even a mile in circumference, but its three-day May meeting still hosts some fascinating racing.

The charm of the course is inseparable from the charm of the town. Wandering through the streets on the way to the course, one cannot but help thinking that one has been taken back in time and the Roodeye itself, for all its modern amenities and sophistication does little to dispel that thought. The antquity of the course weaves a comforting web around both the spectators and seemingly the horses, as those who have won once at Chester can often run up sequences of victories on the course that they have mastered.

A tight left-handed course that is flat throughout. The straight is only just over one furlong long.

1ml5f88y
1ml4f65y
5f
6f
7f
1ml2f85y
2ml2f97y
7f122y
1ml7f186y

STANDS

Though eccentric by nature, Chester's charm wins through and draws in spectators, many of whom watch from the town's old walls.

Goodwood has to be one of the most picturesque courses in the world. Situated on the South Downs amid glorious rolling countryside, the course picks an undulating path around the side of a hill before straightening up for a four furlong run-in that ends abruptly at the winning post. The July meeting has long been established in both the social and racing calendars as Glorious Goodwood, five days of racing of the highest quality in a relaxed atmosphere that adds to the enjoyment of the spectacle.

Although Goodwood was originally a minor racecourse on the estate of the Dukes of Richmond, the 5th Duke transformed both the quality of the racing and the spectators to make it into a recognized part of the social circuit, aided considerably by the development of the railway network which made for easier transporting of horses from stable to course.

For years the feature races of the July meeting, which was extended to include a fifth day at the beginning of the 20th century, were the Stewards' Cup, a major sprint handicap, and the Goodwood Cup, second only to its Ascot equivalent in prestige. But the vagaries of thoroughbred fashion have now swept the Sussex Stakes to prominence. Under the sponsorship of Robert Sangster's Swettenham Stud, this has become one of the most valuable mile-races of the season.

For betting purposes, however, the Stewards' Cup is still one of the great races of the year and allied with a new mile-handicap, the Schweppes Golden Mile, Goodwood remains the scene of some of the great punts of the year.

Outside the July meeting, Goodwood hosts several attractive cards, including two important Classic Trials in May and a second prestigious mile-race, the Waterford Crystal Mile, at the end of August.

In 1988, it became the first course to host a meeting without the support of the Levy Board, and such a farsighted attitude should ensure that it remains at the forefront of the English racing world.

GOODWOOD

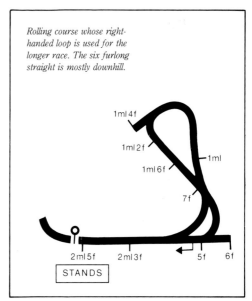

The jockeys pull up their mounts at the end of a race.

Rolling course whose right-handed loop is used for the longer race. The six furlong straight is mostly downhill.

1ml 4f
1ml 2f
1ml
1ml 6f
7f
2ml 5f   2ml 3f   5f   6f
STANDS

Left: *Glorious Goodwood's 'restaurant in the sky' confronts the runners as they race down the course's undulating straight.*

EPSOM

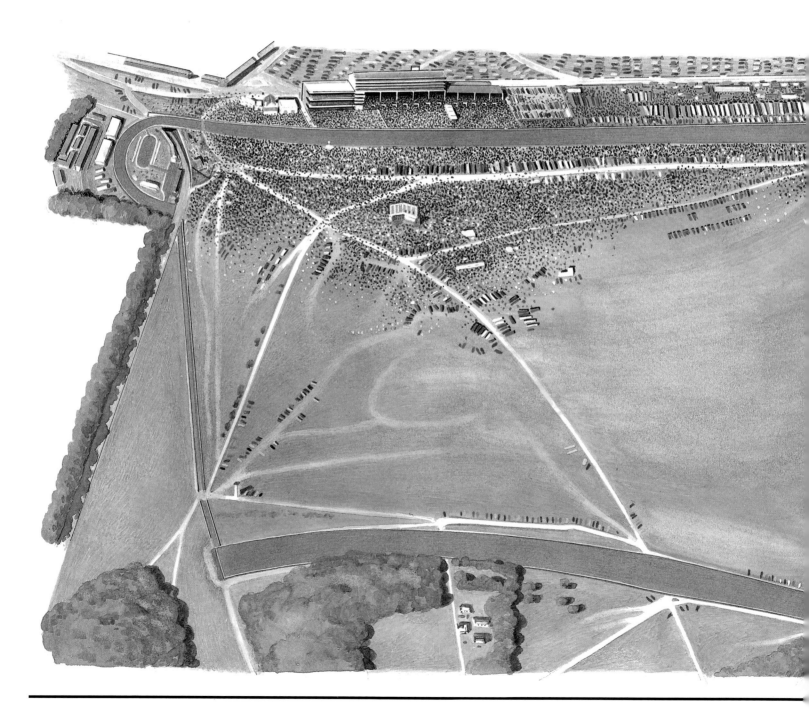

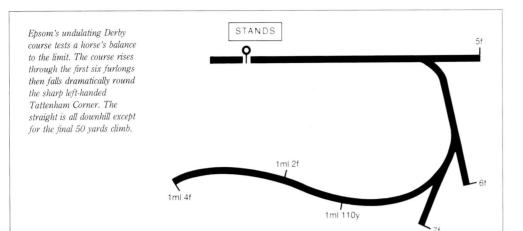

STANDS
5f
1ml 2f
1ml 4f
6f
1ml 110y
7f

Epsom's undulating Derby course tests a horse's balance to the limit. The course rises through the first six furlongs then falls dramatically round the sharp left-handed Tattenham Corner. The straight is all downhill except for the final 50 yards climb.

It's Shergar first, the rest nowhere. The Aga Khan's brilliant but tragic colt leaves the opposition trailing behind to win the 1981 Derby by a record ten lengths.

Epsom means the Derby. Since 1780 this race has developed into the ultimate test of the three-year-old horse. Each year the victor enters the hall of fame and becomes a legend. The Derby is one of the two English races that capture the imagination of the entire nation – offices hold sweepstakes, devout non-gamblers allow their best resolutions to slip for a day as everyone tries to find the winner of what is unquestionably the world's greatest race.

Epsom on the first Wednesday in June is what every owner, breeder, trainer and jockey dreams about when they look at their horse. Will this be the one? Is he going to be the greatest horse of his age? Can he, may he, will he win the Derby?

Lord Derby

Surrounded by the Surrey Downs, Epsom rose to fame through the exploits of the twelfth Earl of Derby, who, when 21, took over the lease of a palatial country house called The Oaks on the outskirts of the town. A keen racing fan, he hosted racing parties at his country seat and acted as a

Diomed, the first winner of the Derby. Owned by Sir Charles Bunbury, he gave his owner compensation for not having the race named after him.

steward at the local meetings. At that time all of Epsom's races were run along the customary lines – heats over two to four miles, matches between individual owners, and in general for older horses – but in 1779 Lord Derby instigated a race for three-year-old fillies over a mile and a half. Twelve fillies lined up for that first running of The Oaks Stakes, named after his house, and Lord Derby took home the spoils himself when his filly Bridget ran out the winner.

Encouraged by the success of the race,

Lord Derby proposed a second contest, this time for colts and fillies over a mile. The name, to be decided by the toss of a coin, was to be either the Derby Stakes, in honour of the host, or the Bunbury Stakes, after Sir Charles Bunbury, one of the early giants of the turf and the foremost racing man of the day.

As luck would have it, the coin favoured Derby, but Sir Charles won the race itself with Diomed, so honour was satisfied. Both events pleased the racing world, and

although the distance of the Derby was increased to 12 furlongs in 1784, the race was soon established as a premier feature of the calendar.

It was the success of the Derby that led to the transformation of Epsom from a minor course favoured by gentry visiting the spa town to one of the leading centres of the thoroughbred world. By the beginning of the 19th century, the Derby had already become *the* race and attracted huge crowds from London to the Downs, where they could watch the race free of charge and enjoy the fun fairs and side shows that had swiftly latched on to the occasion, and sprawled out across the centre of the course.

Derby Day became one big public holiday. Even Parliament took the day off. The great and the good and the world and his wife descended on Epsom in their thousands, at first for the fun of the fair, but gradually for the race itself.

Everyone would have money on the big race and banks of bookmakers plied their trade from the Tattersalls ring all the way up the straight to Tattenham Corner. And so Epsom grew throughout the 19th century. The race, as an occasion, reached its peak in the interwar years when over 500,000 people would congregate on the Downs. Even today when racecourse attendances have dropped well below that benchmark, the crowds are numbered in their hundreds of thousands and are easily the largest of any sporting event.

The course

And what of the course that stages the race? It has been said that the Derby is the best race in the world run on the worst course in the world, but that is unfair. To be sure, Epsom is not the easiest of courses for a horse to perform on, but that is just another of its charms.

From the 12-furlong start the track turns slightly right-handed through the first quarter-mile whilst climbing steadily. It then levels out as it begins the sharp left-handed turn at the bottom of the course which takes the runners through the half-mile of the horseshoe before dropping sharply in the descent to Tattenham Corner, by which time the Derby winner will

have normally come towards the head of the field.

Tattenham Corner, three and a half furlongs from the winning post, is one of the great features in racing – often a place of heartbreak, as when Freddie Head failed to steer the well-fancied Lyphard around the turn in 1972 and nearly ended up amongst the crowds who habitually gather on the far side of the course. Free access is still given to those that watch the race from this point and the thrill of seeing the bluest blood in

Reference Point and Steve Cauthen made all the running to win the 1987 Ever Ready Derby and are seen here out in front as the field make the turn at Tattenham Corner.

racing charging down the hill into the bend will always ensure that there is a healthy gathering.

The course continues to descend gently in the straight until the final 50 yards, which are uphill; often a tense final 50 yards as the leader tries to stay in front and his pursuers are desperately roused in the attempt to overtake him.

Dancing Brave, who was arguably the best horse ever to have finished second in the Derby, became hopelessly unbalanced coming round Tattenham Corner and was almost last as the field turned into the straight. By the time Greville Starkey had gathered the horse together and got him to quicken, victory seemed out of the question.

But Dancing Brave flew through those final furlongs and, with seemingly the entire crowd urging him on, passed horse after horse. One, however, had gone beyond recall and Khaled Abdulla's champion was beaten by Shahrastani by a rapidly diminishing half a length and suffered his only European defeat.

It is whoever comes out on top through that final 50 yards – and there have been much narrower margins of victory than that of Shahrastani and even one dead-heat in 1884 between St Gatien and Harvester – who enters the record books. Roberto and The Minstrel won the Derby, and, whatever their other achievements, it is they who will be remembered and not their victims

EVER READY DERBY STAKES

1½ miles. Three-year-old colts and fillies, 9st. First run 1780.

Year	Winner	Owner	Trainer	Jockey
1970	Nijinsky	C. Engelhard	M.V. O'Brien	L. Piggott
1971	Mill Reef	P. Mellon	I. Balding	G. Lewis
1972	Roberto	J.W. Galbreath	M.V. O'Brien	L. Piggott
1973	Morston	A. Budgett	A. Budgett	E. Hide
1974	Snow Knight	Mrs. N. Phillips	P. Nelson	B. Taylor
1975	Grundy	Dr. C. Vittadini	P. Walwyn	P. Eddery
1976	Empery	N.B. Hunt	M. Zilber	L. Piggott
1977	The Minstrel	R.E. Sangster	M.V. O'Brien	L. Piggott
1978	Shirley Heights	Lord Halifax	J. Dunlop	W. Carson
1979	Troy	Sir M. Sobell	W.R. Hern	W. Carson
1980	Henbit	Mrs. A. Plesch	W.R. Hern	W. Carson
1981	Shergar	H.H. Aga Khan	M. Stoute	W.R. Swinburn
1982	Golden Fleece	R.E. Sangster	M.V. O'Brien	P. Eddery
1983	Teenoso	E.B. Moller	G. Wragg	L. Piggott
1984	Secreto	L. Miglietti	D.V. O'Brien	C. Roche
1985	Slip Anchor	Lord Howard de Walden	H. Cecil	S. Cauthen
1986	Shahrastani	H.H. Aga Khan	M. Stoute	W.R. Swinburn
1987	Reference Point	L. Freedman	H. Cecil	S. Cauthen
1988	Kahyasi	H.H. Aga Khan	L. Cumani	R. Cochrane
1989	Nashwan	Hamdan Al-Maktoum	W.R. Hern	W. Carson

Rheingold and Hot Grove.

Course restrictions introduced in 1985 have ended the life of the long rambling races that wound their way across the Downs - races like the old Great Metropolitan Handicap whose 2¼-mile trip has been cut down to the Derby distance of 12 furlongs, the maximum now possible. Spurs off the main course are used for the starts of seven- and six-furlong races, but the five-furlong course is remarkable in its own right, recognized as being the fastest five furlong track in the world.

The common

Epsom's passage through history has not been the easiest. The course's proximity to London – the reason for its early preferment – has over the last century been the source of many a problem. Being on a Metropolitan Common, Epsom was subject to all the regulations of the old London Commons. This meant that it was strictly illegal to deprive people of free access to any part of the Downs, and that it was also against the law to construct any building, fencing or enclosure.

Common sense will out, however, and the 1925 Act, which introduced these laws, included clauses which had been vigorously championed by horse-loving MPs exempting Epsom from the letter of the law and giving its blessing to the construction of a fine new grandstand, which was completed in 1927.

The year 1925 also saw two other acts that have helped Epsom through the passage of history. The Grandstand Association, the body that controlled the course, bought the freehold of the Downs and the concomitant Lord of the Manor rights to ensure that it was they who called the shots on the course. At the same time it sold the freehold of nearby Walton Downs to the great local trainer Stanley Wootton, who guaranteed its future as the training centre Epsom had become. Wootton, a true philan-thropist, looked after Walton Downs until 1969 when he bequeathed them to the Horseracing Betting Levy Board.

The days when Epsom trainers dominated the racing world have long gone and ascendancy has passed on to Newmarket. The last Derby winner from an Epsom stable was Straight Deal, trained by Walter Nightingall, whose 1942 success was not even at the course, but at a war-time fixture run at Newmarket. However, names like Staff Ingham and Stanley Wootton and more recently Geoff Lewis and Reg Akehurst keep the old traditions keep alive.

With only three meetings held each year, Epsom is notoriously underused. The Spring meeting in April used to be dominated by the two great Handicaps, the aforementioned Great Metropolitan and the City & Suburban, races which were once the subjects of huge gambles, but which are now pale reflections of their former selves. Nowadays the major races are the Blue Riband Trial, named after Disraeli's description of the Derby as the Blue Riband of the Turf, and the Princess Elizabeth Stakes.

The four-day Derby meeting always starts on Derby Day, the first Wednesday in June. The Woodcote Stakes, a once prestigious two-year-old race, starts off proceedings, but really the day belongs to one event only. On the Thursday, the centrepiece of the end is the Coronation Stakes, a race over

GOLD SEAL OAKS

1½ miles. Three-year-old fillies, 9st. First run 1779.

Year	Winner	Owner	Trainer	Jockey
1971	Altesse Royale	Col. F.R. Hue-Williams	N. Murless	G. Lewis
1972	Ginevra	C. St. George	H.R. Price	A. Murray
1973	Mysterious	G.A. Pope, Jr.	N. Murless	G. Lewis
1974	Polygamy	L. Freedman	P. Walwyn	P. Eddery
1975	Juliette Marny	Hon. J. Morrison	J. Tree	L. Piggott
1976	Pawneese	D. Wildenstein	A. Penna	Y. Saint-Martin
1977	Dunfermline	H.M. The Queen	W.R. Hern	W. Carson
1978	Fair Salinia	S. Hanson	M. Stoute	G. Starkey
1979	Scintillate	Hon. J. Morrison	J. Tree	P. Eddery
1980	Bireme	R.D. Hollingsworth	W.R. Hern	W. Carson
1981	Blue Wind	Mrs. B. Firestone	D. Weld	L. Piggott
1982	Time Charter	R. Barnett	H. Candy	W. Newnes
1983	Sun Princess	Sir M. Sobell	W.R. Hern	W. Carson
1984	Circus Plume	Sir R. McAlpine	J. Dunlop	L. Piggott
1985	Oh So Sharp	Sheikh Mohammed	H. Cecil	S. Cauthen
1986	Midway Lady	H.H. Rainier	B. Hanbury	R. Cochrane
1987	Unite	Sheikh Mohammed	M. Stoute	W.R. Swinburn
1988	Diminuendo	Sheikh Mohammed	H. Cecil	S. Cauthen
1989	Aliysa	H.H. Aga Khan	M. Stoute	W.R. Swinburn

the Derby distance for the older horses. The Friday is a quiet day, whilst the Oaks, which, despite being the older of the two races, has never fired the public's imagination in the same way as her younger brother, closes affairs on the Saturday.

Finally there is the two-day August meeting held over the Bank Holiday when the Moet & Chandon Silver Magnum Handicap, better known as the Amateurs Derby, has been the major event.

Royal Derbys

As every Derby winner becomes a part of history, selecting a handful as having been especially brilliant is an invidious task. However, the most popular Derby winner was probably the Prince of Wales' Persimmon, who was beautifully ridden by Jack Watts in 1896 to come home a neck in front of the odds-on favourite St Frusquin. The victory was greeted with unbridled enthusiam by all and sundry, excepting the morose Watts, who, as was his wont, could barely raise a smile. The celebrations that started after the race reached a climax that evening with virtually the whole country joining in, and the parties continued throughout the whole of the meeting. The British Royal family have tasted other Derby victories, but none will ever equal that first, which truly epitomized their involvement in the Sport of Kings. Edward VII won the race twice more: in 1900 when still Prince of Wales with the Triple Crown hero Diamond Jubilee and again in 1909 when Minoru became the only Derby winner to date to carry the royal colours into the winner's enclosure after the world's greatest race.

George V, although he was a keen horseman and reputedly a better judge of a horse than his father, did not enjoy such luck at Epsom. He will be remembered for owning Anmer, the horse under which the suffragette Emily Davison threw herself in 1913, killing both herself and Anmer in the process. Even then the controversy was not finished as a 100-1 shot Aboyeur was awarded the race in the Stewards' enquiry, following the disqualification of the 6-4 favourite Craganour, to become the longest-priced winner ever of the Derby.

Above: *Diamond Jubilee, owned and bred by Edward, Prince of Wales. A temperamental animal, who often tried to savage his jockey, he won the 1900 Derby and Triple Crown for his owner.*

Left: *Edward, the 12th Earl of Derby, whose house parties at Epsom spawned the world's greatest race.*

George VI was not involved with the thoroughbred industry until his accession, but had the privilege of owning the great Sun Chariot, who completed the Triple Crown in 1942, though her Oaks success was in a wartime running of the race at Newmarket.

In the year of her coronation, Elizabeth II had a great chance of another royal victory with Aureole who had been bred by her father, but she had to be content with second place behind Pinza, who gave Sir Gordon Richards his one and only Derby win. The Queen has never been as close to Derby success since, but has twice won the Oaks, with Carrozza in 1957 and again in 1977 with Dunfermline.

The jockeys

Richards, one of the two outstanding English jockeys of the post-war era, had been bedevilled by bad luck at Epsom. Three times he partnered the second horse home, and numerous were the occasions when he was on the favourite or a fancied horse only to see his mount disappoint on the big day.

Pinza was to be Richards' 28th and final ride in the Derby. Having been knighted earlier that week for his services to racing, it was fitting that this recognition of Richards' talents was capped by the one prize he wanted more than any other. Pinza stormed home four lengths clear of Aureole and Richards was led into the winner's enclosure amongst universal applause.

The Epsom fortunes of Lester Piggott, the second great jockey, could hardly be in greater contrast to those of Richards. Piggott was the true maestro of the course and his achievements in the big races speaks for itself: a record nine Derbys and six Oaks in an Epsom career that spanned 34 years from 1952, when he finished second on Gay Time, his first ride in the race, to 1985 when he finished seventh on Theatrical.

Piggott became the youngest jockey to win the Derby this century when, as an 18-year-old, he drove home the 33–1 chance Never Say Die in 1954, and the list of Derby winners he partnered includes some of the finest of the post-war era: Crepello in 1957,

Sir Gordon Richards wins the Derby for the only time in his long career. Pinza, his last ride in the race, breaks Richards' Epsom hoodoo by beating The Queen's Aureole in the 1953 race.

St Paddy in 1960, Sir Ivor in 1968, the immortal Nijinsky in 1970, Roberto in 1972, Empery 1976, The Minstrel in 1977 and finally Teenoso in 1983.

Piggott's mastery of the course was shown by the way he brought Sir Ivor home a length and a half in front of Connaught without letting the horse know that he had even been in a race. Only Piggott could have driven home Roberto. He looked beaten a furlong and a half out when Rheingold had gone a length up. But the 'Long Fellow'

would never accept defeat until the post had been reached and his finish gave Roberto the verdict by the shortest of short heads.

Mahmoud holds the distinction of winning the Derby in the fastest time, whilst Shergar's winning distance of ten lengths is the most emphatic win. But perhaps the greatest of all Derby victors was Sea Bird, whose 1965 triumph had the hallmark of brilliance. Hitting the front one and a half furlongs out, he had only to be pushed out to beat Meadow Court, himself no slouch as

he later proved by winning the Irish Derby and the King George VI and Queen Elizabeth Stakes, by the easiest and sweetest two lengths that Epsom has ever witnessed.

But whatever has happened in the past, it is always the next Derby that holds the attention. All winter, the current crop are keenly dissected to see if they will pass the test. By the time the field have crossed the Downs and arrived at the start, millions of pounds will have been wagered and many millions around the world will be watching.

Unite takes the applause after her victory in 1987 Gold Seal Oaks, but the fillies' Classic has never quite captured the public's imagination in the same way as the Derby.

SANDOWN

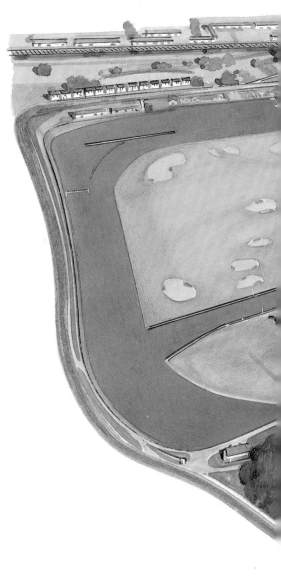

As England's premier park course and as host to two of the great races of the year, the Eclipse Stakes and the Whitbread Chase, Sandown offers practically everything that a racegoer could want. That is attested by the regularity with which the course wins the 'Racecourse Of The Year' award presented by the Racegoers Club, a prize that Sandown appears to share with York to the virtual exclusion of all other courses.

Situated in the London suburb of Esher, Sandown has a remarkably short history for a British racecourse, having been founded as recently as 1875. But the decision by Hwfa and Owen Williams and Sir Wilfred Brett to lay out the course proved to be a successful one almost from the word go. For a start it is one of the best viewing courses in the country, with stands placed on a hill overlooking the course, so the progress of the field is easy to follow throughout the race. Secondly, Sandown was the first course to be totally enclosed.

It had been customary for the public to be allowed to enter all of the course excepting the stands and enclosures free of charge, but Hwfa Williams, with a far-sightedness that was as remarkable as it must have been considered controversial in his day, saw that this state of affairs was ripe for change. So he concentrated on providing superb facilities for the paying customers and complemented those with top-class racing. This combination has been continued by the course administrators ever since and Sandown has an enviable reputation for its course improvements.

That first meeting back in 1875 was a 'mixed' affair – Flat and jumping on the same card – and the course has retained that balance to the present day. The Saturday of the April meeting has without question the finest mixed card in the sporting world, with the splendour of the top chasers competing for the Whitbread Gold Cup balanced by a prestigious Derby Trial, the Guardian Classic Trial and a second valuable Group contest on the level.

The Eclipse

The race, however, that really established Sandown as a premier racecourse was the Eclipse Stakes. Hwfa Williams, encouraged by Leopold de Rothschild, framed the first £10,000 race in the country in the hope of attracting the best of the breed to his new course. This ten-furlong contest was first run in 1886 and was won by Bendigo from a Derby winner St Gatien. From this propitious beginning, the race has developed into one of the country's top ten-furlong races.

In 1903 another Derby winner, Ard Patrick, gave a rare beating to the wonder filly Sceptre in what was a memorable contest. Hailed as the race of the decade, the two champion four-year-olds were pitted against that year's Triple Crown winner Rock Sand, who was made favourite by a huge crowd. Two furlongs out, Rock Sand was under pressure and started to drop out of contention, leaving the filly Sceptre with a slight advantage over Ard Patrick. It was

Spinelle and Motion Picture, on whom Lester Piggott's distinctive style can be seen, fighting it out in a Sandown Maiden.

Flat. *A testing right-handed oval course, whose straight of four and a half furlongs is all uphill. The five furlongs straight course lies inside the oval and is uphill throughout.*

Jumps. *Like the flat course, Sandown's National Hunt track is a testing one mile five furlongs with an uphill finish. The three railway fences in the back straight are close together and can cause difficulties.*

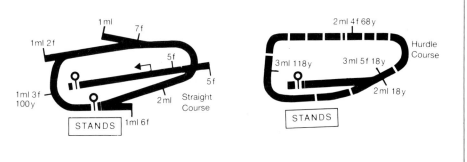

nip and tuck throughout the final furlong, but under a beautiful ride from the champion jockey of that year Otto Madden, Ard Patrick got the upper hand close to home to win by a neck.

The race has rarely slipped from these high standards and since the inception of the King George VI and Queen Elizabeth Stakes over Ascot's 12 furlongs, has become the first half of a prestigious double in which the Classic generation is tested against the older horses. Notable champions to have completed the double are Royal Palace, Mill Reef, Brigadier Gerard, Busted and his son Mtoto.

Considering that Sceptre came so close to winning back in 1903, the fact that it was

nearly 100 years before a filly won the race is something of a surprise. And it took a real champion, Pebbles, to lay the jinx. Her triumph in 1985 was on the way to a second

great ten-furlong victory in the Champion Stakes before she became the only British-trained winner of a Breeders' Cup race to date when she won that autumn's Turf.

Pebbles breaks the fillies' hoodoo by becoming the first of that sex to win the Eclipse, beating Rainbow Quest and Bob Back.

CORAL-ECLIPSE STAKES

1¼ miles. Three-year-olds and upwards. First run 1886.

Year	Winner	Owner	Trainer	Jockey
1971	Mill Reef	P. Mellon	I. Balding	G. Lewis
1972	Brigadier Gerard	Mrs. J. Hislop	W.R. Hern	J. Mercer
1973	Scottish Rifle	A.J. Struthers	J. Dunlop	R. Hutchinson
1974	Coup de Feu	F. Sasse	D. Sasse	P. Eddery
1975	Star Appea	W. Zeitelhack	T. Grieper	G. Starkey
1976	Wollow	C. d'Alessio	H. Cecil	G. Dettori
1977	Artaius	Mrs. G. Getty II	M.V. O'Brien	L. Piggott
1978	Gunner B	Mrs. P. Barratt	H. Cecil	J. Mercer
1979	Dickens Hill	Mme. J. Binet	M. O'Toole	A. Murray
1980	Ela-Mana-Mou	S. Weinstock	W.R. Hern	W. Carson
1981	Master Willie	R. Barnett	H. Candy	P. Waldron
1982	Kalaglow	A. Ward	G. Harwood	G. Starkey
1983	Solford	R.E. Sangster	M.V. O'Brien	P. Eddery
1984	Sadler's Wells	R.E. Sangster	M.V. O'Brien	P. Eddery
1985	Pebbles	Sheikh Mohammed	C. Brittain	S. Cauthen
1986	Dancing Brave	K. Abdullah	G. Harwood	G. Starkey
1987	Mtoto	A. Al-Maktoum	A.C. Stewart	M. Roberts
1988	Mtoto	A. Al-Maktoum	A.C. Stewart	M. Roberts
1989	Nashwan	H. Al-Maktoum	W.R. Hern	W. Carson

The Whitbread

Jumping takes over at Sandown in November and provides cards of a consistently high quality throughout the winter months. The Gainsborough Chase and the Otley Hurdle at the beginning of February are often valuable pointers for the Gold Cup and the Champion Hurdle at Cheltenham the following month, whilst March's Imperial Hurdle and the popular Grand Military Meeting also draw in the crowds.

But Sandown's moment of jumping glory is saved until the very end of the National Hunt season, when attention has again been focussed on the Flat. That is the Whitbread Gold Cup, which has gone into the record books as the first sponsored race in the country. Time after time the race has thrown up glorious winners and dramatic finishes and it annually eclipses the sleeker Flat horses for a day as the elder brethren reclaim the centre stage.

The first running in 1957 was won by Obliged from a field of 24, but it was the successes of the Cheltenham Gold Cup winners Pas Seul in 1961 and Arkle in 1965 that really established the race. Larbawn and the charismatic Diamond Edge are the only horses to have twice won the race, but the biggest cheers have been reserved for two more recent winners. The Queen Mother's Special Cargo was led in to a tremendous ovation following his triumph in 1984, giving that great patron of the winter game her biggest victory to date, but it was the success of Desert Orchid, that most popular of greys, in 1988 that really brought the stands down.

In recent years Sandown has been run by the far-sighted United Racecourses group, who were responsible for the construction of a magnificent new grandstand in 1973 and for introducing a series of very popular mid-week evening meetings in June and July that draw in large crowds from London. It is policies like these, allied with the insistence that the public deserve the best, that has kept Sandown's stands full and its cards competitive. The paddock area is easily accessible from the stands and this encourages newcomers to the sport to go and find out what makes the racing world tick, and, coupled with great horses, that is what will keep the industry thriving.

WHITBREAD GOLD CUP HANDICAP CHASE

3 miles, 5 furlongs, 18 yards. First run 1957.

Year	Winner	Owner	Trainer	Jockey
1970	Royal Toss	C. Handel	C. Handel	R. Pitman
1971	Titus Oates	P. Cussins	G.W. Richards	R. Barry
1972	Grey Sombrero	W. Candwell	D. Gandolfo	W. Shoemaker
1973	Charlie Potheen	Mrs. B. Heath	F. Walwyn	R. Barry
1974	The Dikler	Mrs. D. August	F. Walwyn	R. Barry
1975	April Seventh	Mrs. B. Meehan	R. Turnell	S.C. Knight
1976	Otter Way	O. Carter	O. Carter	J. King
1977	Andy Pandy	Mrs. S. Mulligan	F. Rimell	J. Burke
1978	Strombolus	M. Buckley	P. Bailey	T. Stack
1979	Diamond Edge	S. Loughridge	F. Walwyn	W. Smith
1980	Royal Mail	J. Begg	S. Mellor	P. Blacker
1981	Diamond Edge	S. Loughridge	F. Walwyn	W. Smith
1982	Shady Deal	G. Hubbard	J.T. Gifford	R. Rowe
1983	Drumlargan	M. Cuddy	E. O'Grady	Mr. F. Codd
1984	Special Cargo	H.M. The Queen Mother	F. Walwyn	K. Mooney
1985	By the Way	Mrs. C.E. Feather	Mrs. M. Dickinson	R. Earnshaw
1986	Plundering	Mrs. M. Valentine	F.T. Winter	S. Sherwood
1987	Lean Ar Aghaidh	Mrs. Tulloch	S. Mellor	G. Landau
1988	Desert Orchid	R. Burridge	D. Elsworth	S. Sherwood
1989	Brown Windsor	W. Shand Kydd	N. Henderson	M. Bowlby

'Dessie', the flying grey, has become a standing dish at Sandown in recent years. Here he jumps the last when winning the '88 Whitbread Gold Cup under top-weight.

Like its neighbour Sandown, Kempton can boast of mixed racing of a high quality throughout the year and can guarantee the Londoners who come out to this Surrey suburb, cards that are varied but always interesting.

Although it cannot now match the prestige of Sandown on the Flat, the Kempton executive has at least stopped the decline in the course's fortunes since the Second World War and the future of the course now looks to be both assured and promising.

Kempton could never be accused of being the most beautiful of courses. The stands lack any warmth and, despite recent improvements, have a barren atmosphere, but its proximity to London and the attention paid to the customer will ensure that the problems which the course encountered at the end of the 1960s should never recur.

Kempton's two big Flat races, the Rosebery Stakes and the Jubilee Handicap, may well never recover their former prestige, since the Rosebery is run too early in the year and the Jubilee has suffered the fate of most handicaps, but imaginative use of the mid-summer evening meetings and the growing prestige of the course's one Group race, the September Stakes, suggest that the executive's plans are working.

Kempton's greatest moment comes on Boxing Day when holiday crowds turn out to see the country's best chasers run in the King George VI Chase. The race, which was established to honour the accession of the new monarch in 1937, is now second only to the Cheltenham Gold Cup in its prestige.

Many of the greats of steeplechasing have triumphed here and immortals like Cottage Rake, Mill House, Arkle, Captain Christy and most recently Desert Orchid have completed the Gold Cup – King George double.

But perhaps more interesting are two horses that made the King George their own but failed to win at Cheltenham, Pendil and Wayward Lad. Pendil won the race twice and always looked the supreme chaser around Kempton's tight track. But even he has to take second billing to Wayward Lad, he won the race three times at the beginning of the 1980s and was one of the three horses that contributed to a six-year stranglehold on the race by the remarkable Dickinson family.

KEMPTON

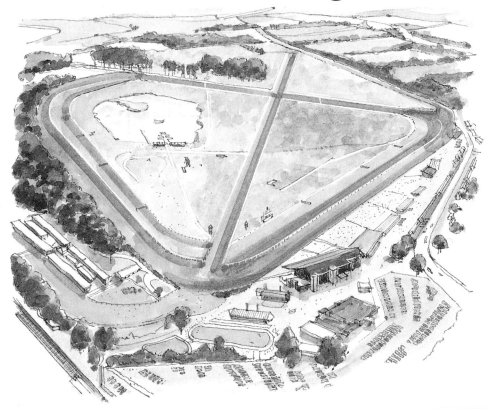

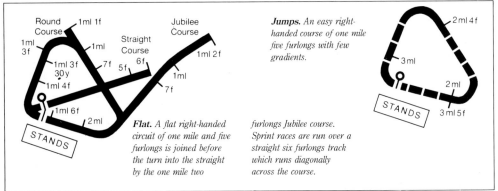

Round Course
1 ml 1 f
1 ml 3 f
1 ml
1 ml 3 f
30 y
7 f
Straight Course
5 f
6 f
Jubilee Course
1 ml 2 f
1 ml 4 f
1 ml
7 f
1 ml 6 f
2 ml
STANDS

Jumps. *An easy right-handed course of one mile five furlongs with few gradients.*

2 ml 4 f
3 ml
2 ml
STANDS
3 ml 5 f

Flat. *A flat right-handed circuit of one mile and five furlongs is joined before the turn into the straight by the one mile two furlongs Jubilee course. Sprint races are run over a straight six furlongs track which runs diagonally across the course.*

Racing in the straight at Kempton, during one of the great British steeplechases, the King George VI Chase on Boxing Day.

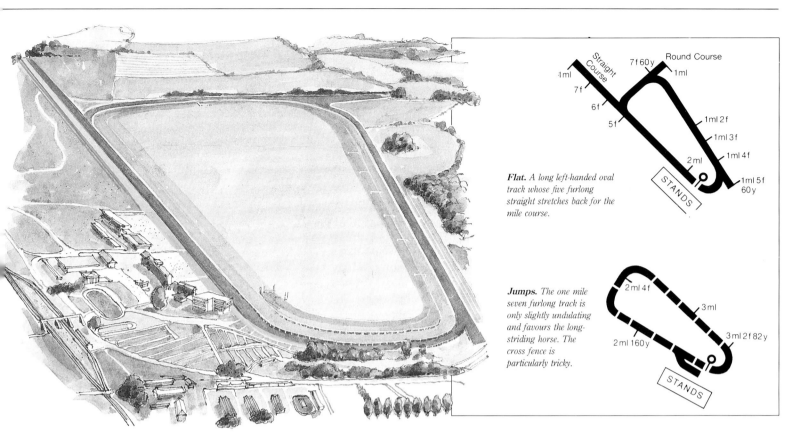

Flat. *A long left-handed oval track whose five furlong straight stretches back for the mile course.*

Jumps. *The one mile seven furlong track is only slightly undulating and favours the long-striding horse. The cross fence is particularly tricky.*

NEWBURY

The proximity of Newbury to the training centre of Lambourn ensures that this charming Berkshire course always stages racing of interest throughout both the Flat and the National Hunt seasons.

A constant stream of high quality juveniles, promising novice hurdlers and proven stars are tested around this fair, flat, left-handed course before hopefully going on to win greater glory elsewhere.

That is not to say that Newbury does not stage any major events, for that would belittle races of the stature of the Greenham, the Lockinge and the Mill Reef Stakes, but simply to acknowledge that rich and important though these contests are, they are only rungs on the ladder to thoroughbred stardom.

Since half the fun of the sport is spotting potential and then watching it blossom, racing at Newbury is never dull and always well attended.

A curious mixture of Lambourn cognoscenti, famed for their liveliness, and the less well-informed fleeing down the M4 from London, pack the two contrasting stands and congregate around the paddock.

The never-ending search for winners is here continued with the aid of the Sporting Life, *Britain's great racing daily, on Newbury's lawns.*

The highlight of the racing year is November's Hennessy Gold Cup, which moved to Newbury after the first three runnings had been held at Cheltenham. Its significance as one of the first major chases of the jumping season and the rich prize money on offer guarantees a top-class field.

The atmosphere of Hennessy Day is one of celebration, as the jumping folk walk proudly onto the stage and show that they too can provide great races and great horses. Newbury welcomes them and given a sunny day when the surrounding countryside is in its full autumn colours, there are few better places to spend an afternoon.

The second running of the race at Newbury in 1961 saw victory falling to the sponsors in the shape of Madame Hennessy's Mandarin, who went on to win the Cheltenham Gold Cup the following spring. Arkle won the race twice, but remarkably also tasted defeat twice, going down to Mill House in 1963 and then losing out to Stalbridge Colonist in 1966.

ASCOT

Right: *Each day of the Royal meeting begins with the Royal procession. The Queen and Prince Philip parade down the Royal Hunt Cup course in a horse-drawn carriage to the applause of the crowds.*

Above: *Ascot's leafy paddock is always packed at the Royal meeting, with the crowd admiring themselves, the horses and the Royal family.*

The Royal meeting at Ascot in June remains one of the centrepieces of the English social calendar and the Royal course blossoms into a multi-coloured carpet of dresses and hats that is for many more important than the racing itself.

Whilst the equine thoroughbreds are performing at the highest level on the turf, equally aristocratic humans are entertaining themselves on the lawns and in the bars of the Royal course as they have been doing for three centuries. It is undesirable and almost impossible to separate these two aspects of the meeting as the one makes the other, and the combination creates a particularly British event.

Queen Anne had the course marked out in Windsor Park and the first meeting was run there in August 1711. For a long time, there was just the one, Royal, meeting, but the coming of the 20th century and the pressures of modern economics have meant firstly more Flat meetings, and secondly the open-ing of a new National Hunt course in 1965.

But for many it is still the four-day Royal meeting that makes Ascot: four days of almost flawless racing that begin with a pageant in the best British tradition as the Queen and the Royal party drive down the straight mile in horse-drawn carriages to the applause of the crowd. But even the Queen has to take a back seat as the racing begins.

The first race is traditionally the Queen Anne Stakes, named after the monarch who began it all, and this ten-furlong event for the older horses is but the forerunner of another 23 races that test every type of horse, from the outstanding stayers to the sprinters, from the top juveniles to the best of the Classic crop, from the handicappers to the Champions.

The Gold Cup

For years it has been the Gold Cup on the Thursday – 'Ladies Day' as it is more

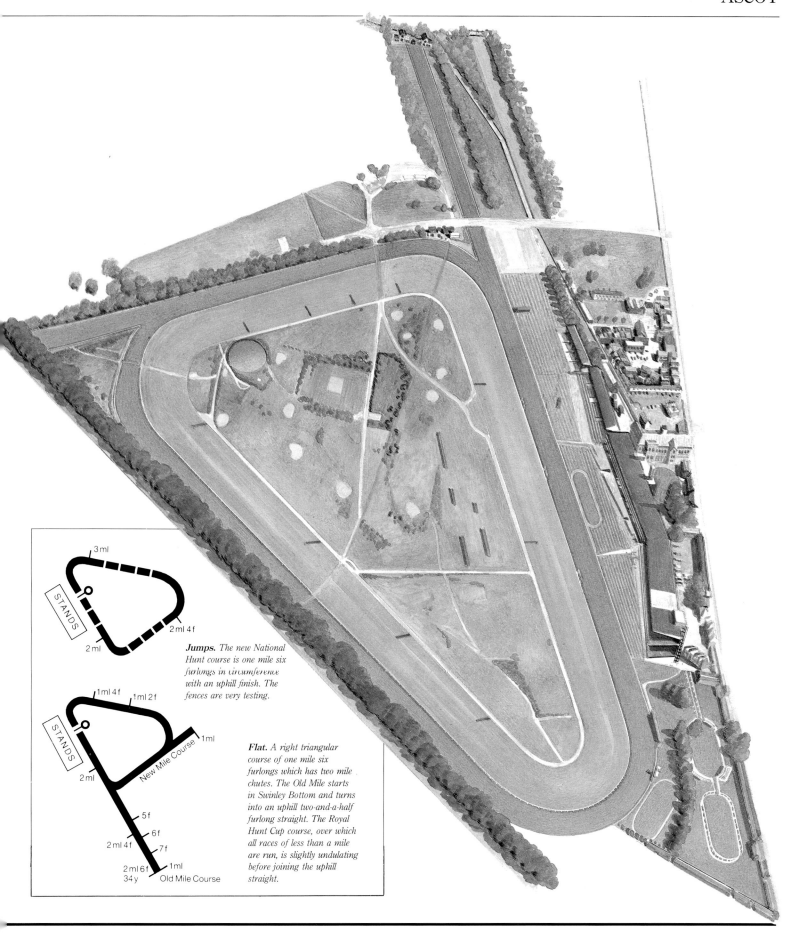

Jumps. *The new National Hunt course is one mile six furlongs in circumference with an uphill finish. The fences are very testing.*

3 ml

2 ml 4 f

2 ml

STANDS

1 ml 4 f   1 ml 2 f

1 ml

STANDS

2 ml

New Mile Course

5 f

6 f

2 ml 4 f   7 f

2 ml 6 f   1 ml

34 y   Old Mile Course

Flat. *A right triangular course of one mile six furlongs which has two mile chutes. The Old Mile starts in Swinley Bottom and turns into an uphill two-and-a-half furlong straight. The Royal Hunt Cup course, over which all races of less than a mile are run, is slightly undulating before joining the uphill straight.*

Top hats and morning suits intermingled with the more glowing colours of the women's costumes pack the stands at the Royal meeting.

popularly known – that has been the centrepiece of attention. This two-and-a-half mile contest is the only remaining Group 1 race for the stayers and has a history that stretches back to 1807.

It was traditionally a contest which the Derby winner of the previous year sought to win to establish himself as a champion four-year-old. Here again the changing face of racing has seen the decline of the true staying blood and a more typical Gold Cup field these days is a small one of dour stayers, who have failed to make their mark over the shorter trips.

In its heyday, the prize was reckoned to be second only to the Derby, and the list of former winners include some of the great horses of the British turf. Champions this century include Prince Palatine, winner in 1912 and 1913; Ocean Swell, the first post-war winner in 1945, and the only horse this century to have won both the Derby and the Ascot Gold Cup; Marcel Boussac's un-beaten Caracalla II; and, more recently, Sagaro, the only horse to have won three Gold Cups and whose third victory over the luckless Buckskin in 1977 led to his being bought by the British Levy Board to stand at the National Stud.

Often a race dogged by controversy and disqualification, the Gold Cup is one of the few Royal Ascot races to have been run elsewhere during the war years. It has also survived a change of name or two.

The visit of the Czar in 1845 and his attendance at the meeting was marked by changing the race's name to the Emperor's Cup, to honour both him and his cousin, Queen Victoria. The race was run under that name for nine years, but the outbreak of hostilities in the Crimea in 1853 per-suaded the authorities that their attempts at diplomacy had not been well received.

Although the Gold Cup still attracts the biggest crowd of the week, it is the racing on the Tuesday and the Wednesday that makes the headlines. The St James's Palace Stakes, the King Edward VII Stakes or the Ascot Derby as it is often known, and the Coronation Stakes for fillies now provide the best of the racing and are little short of the Classics in the quality of fields that they attract.

GOLD CUP

2½ miles. Four-year-olds and upwards. First run 1807.

Year	Winner	Owner	Trainer	Jockey
1971	Random Shot	Mrs. G. Benskin	A. Budgett	G. Lewis
1972	Erimo Hawk	Y. Yamamoto	G. Barling	P. Eddery
1973	Lassalle	Z. Yoshida	R. Carver	J. Lindley
1974	Ragstone	Duke of Norfolk	J. Dunlop	R. Hutchinson
1975	Sagaro	G. Oldham	F. Boutin	L. Piggott
1976	Sagaro	G. Oldham	F. Boutin	L. Piggott
1977	Sagaro	G. Oldham	F. Boutin	L. Piggott
1978	Shangamuzo	Mrs. E. Charles	M. Stoute	G. Starkey
1979	Le Moss	C. d'Alessio	H. Cecil	L. Piggott
1980	Le Moss	C. d'Alessio	H. Cecil	J. Mercer
1981	Ardross	C. St. George	H. Cecil	L. Piggott
1982	Ardross	C. St. George	H. Cecil	L. Piggott
1983	Little Wolf	Lord Porchester	W.R. Hern	W. Carson
1984	Gildoran	R.E. Sangster	B. Hills	S. Cauthen
1985	Gildoran	R.E. Sangster	B. Hills	B. Thomson
1986	Longboat	R.D. Hollingsworth	W.R. Hern	W. Carson
1987	Paean	Lord Howard de Walden	H. Cecil	S. Cauthen
1988	Sadeem	Sheikh Mohammed	G. Harwood	G. Starkey
1989	Sadeem	Sheikh Mohammed	G. Harwood	P. Eddery

Brown Jack

To single out individual races and individual winners is to miss the point of the meeting as a whole. It is above all the occasion that counts. One simply expects to see the best of the thoroughbred world racing at Royal Ascot.

But equine heroes do make their mark.

None more so than the great Brown Jack, who stands alone in the annals of the meeting for winning in seven successive years. The gelding came to prominence by winning Cheltenham's Champion Hurdle as a four-year-old, a triumph spotted by champion jockey Steve Donoghue, who recommended to trainer Aubrey Hastings that he should switch the horse to the Flat.

In that same summer of 1928 Brown Jack won the prestigious handicap, the Ascot Stakes, and his career was then permanently moved to the Flat. Following the death of Aubrey Hastings in 1929, Ivor Anthony took over the control of the gelding, who then went on to win six successive Queen Alexandra Stakes at the Royal meeting. When he, and the ever popular Steve Donoghue who had made certain that he was Brown Jack's regular partner, returned to the winner's enclosure for the last time in 1934, the reception given to the ten-year-old was as great as that accorded to any Derby winner, as both horse and jockey had won the hearts of the racing world.

No horse these days would be expected to match that record, but even in an era when horses were raced much more frequently, Brown Jack's achievements were exceptional and the naming of a race at Ascot's July meeting is a fitting tribute to one of the great characters of the game.

Brown Jack, the hero of seven Royal Ascots, and Steve Donoghue, the jockey who spotted his potential.

Lester Piggott pushes Teenoso clear of Sadler's Wells and Tolomeo in the 1984 King George.

When the pageantry ends on Friday evening, and the last of the human peacocks retire from racing until the following year, the difference between Royal Ascot and the ordinary bill of fare can be seen. The following day's racing – Ascot Heath day as it is known – attracts the usual regulars and the attendance drops from the 30,000 plus during the week to the humdrum average total of four figures. The racing loses its prestige though not its competitiveness and always seems somewhat of an anticlimax after the Royal meeting.

King George

Ascot returns to its full glory for its next meeting, whose centrepiece is England's premier all-aged middle distance race, the King George VI and Queen Elizabeth Diamond Stakes, a race which in its almost 40-year history has become the natural mid-season goal for all 12-furlong horses of quality.

It was introduced in 1951 as part of the Festival of Britain celebrations and the inaugural running was won by Supreme Court, who had not run in any of the Classics, but had won the King Edward VII Stakes over the course and distance. He showed how good he really was by beating a top-class field which included that year's Derby winner Arctic Prince and the top French colt Tantieme.

Derby winners Tulyar and Pinza won the next two runnings, before the Queen's Aureole, who had been second at Epsom, gave the older generation their first success in 1954. By now the King George was a race that attracted the best of all Europe, and the prize went abroad for three successive years in the mid 1950s, including once to Italy when Ribot, the champion of Europe, made his one and only visit to England.

Despite all the greats who have won the race, there is one battle that stands out as being an epic; the confrontation between Grundy and Bustino in 1975, which has been called the race of the century. Grundy came to Ascot as the Derby winner to be pitted against the older Bustino, winner of the St Leger as a three-year-old and the Coronation Cup at Epsom earlier that year.

Grundy v. Bustino

Bustino, whose stamina was assured, had a tremendous pace set for him by two pace-makers, and, once they had done their job, took up the running four furlongs out. Going round the final turn to the sound of the bell that is traditionally rung at Ascot, Bustino under Joe Mercer was four lengths clear of Grundy, who was being ridden by the rising star of the Flat, Pat Eddery. Grundy closed the gap in the straight, but whenever he looked like getting his head in

front, Bustino found a little extra and kept the lead.

Neither lacked for courage nor ability, but only one could win, and inside the final furlong Eddery gained the upper hand and drove the favourite home by a half a length as Bustino, who had given everything that he had without the need of encouragement from his jockey, tired. The pair smashed the course record and even the third horse home, Dahlia, who had won the previous two runnings, beat the old course record.

However, the race took its toll of both the principals. Bustino never raced again,

KING GEORGE VI AND THE QUEEN ELIZABETH DIAMOND STAKES

1½ miles. Three-year-olds and up. First run 1951.

Year	Winner	Owner	Trainer	Jockey
1971	Mill Reef	P. Mellon	I. Balding	G. Lewis
1972	Brigadier Gerard	Mrs. J. Hislop	W.R. Hern	J. Mercer
1973	Dahlia	N.B. Hunt	M. Zilber	W. Pyers
1974	Dahlia	N.B. Hunt	M. Zilber	L. Piggott
1975	Grundy	D.C. Vittadini	P. Walwyn	P. Eddery
1976	Pawneese	D. Wildenstein	A. Penna	Y. Saint-Martin
1977	The Minstrel	R.E. Sangster	M.V. O'Brien	L. Piggott
1978	Ile de Bourbon	D. McCall	R.F.J. Houghton	J. Reid
1979	Troy	Sir M. Sobell	W.R. Hern	W. Carson
1980	Ela-Mana-Mou	S. Weinstock	W.R. Hern	W. Carson
1981	Shergar	H.H. Aga Khan	M. Stoute	W.R. Swinburn
1982	Kalaglow	A. Ward	G. Harwood	G. Starkey
1983	Time Charter	R. Barnett	H. Candy	J. Mercer
1984	Teenoso	E.B. Moller	G. Wragg	L. Piggott
1985	Petoski	Lady Beaverbrook	W.R. Hern	W. Carson
1986	Dancing Brave	K. Abdullah	G. Harwood	P. Eddery
1987	Reference Point	L. Freedman	H. Cecil	S. Cauthen
1988	Mtoto	A. Al-Maktoum	A. Stewart	M. Roberts
1989	Nashwan	H. Al-Maktoum	W.R. Hern	W. Carson

Grundy finally gets past the courageous Bustino to win 'The Race of the Century,' the 1977 King George.

whilst Grundy ran well below par in his next start in the Benson & Hedges Gold Cup and was also subsequently retired.

Ascot takes a back seat during the rest of the summer, but has recently returned to the fore in the autumn with the newly established Festival of British Racing, which is the richest day's racing to be held in England.

First held in 1987, this day was framed by leading breeders as a showpiece for the British thoroughbred, and its first two runnings have been very favourably received by all sections of the industry.

Queen Elizabeth II Stakes

The showpiece of the afternoon is the Queen Elizabeth II Stakes, which is developing into the King George of the milers.

The race, which has been run since 1955, has always been a top-class event and was twice won by Brigadier Gerard in the 1970s. But the additional prize money has attracted even more prestige to the race, and the first two subsequent runnings have seen Milligram hand out a beating to Miesque, that great champion of France, and in 1988 a breathtaking performance by Warning, who smashed a world-class field in one of the best performances of the 1988 season.

To support that race, the card features three further Group races and two valuable handicaps. The Group races include top two-year-old races, the Royal Lodge Stakes and the Hoover Fillies' Mile, which are usually good pointers to the following year's Classics, and the Diadem Stakes.

The success of the Festival has brought problems as well as accolades. The idea was taken from the American Breeders' Cup Series. Seeing how well it had worked at Ascot, the French authorities staged their own version over Longchamp's Arc weekend. Since the two weekends are only a week or two apart, there is a clash between certain races and the international flavour of the racing must be in some danger.

There is talk of a pooling of resources and the promotion of a European Festival, combining racing in Ascot, Phoenix Park in Ireland, where the richest two-year-old race in Europe is staged at about the same time

The Aga Khan's famous horse, Shergar, with Walter Swinburn on board, comes home alone in 1981's King George Stakes.

Chasing has quickly made its mark at Ascot. Here Slalom leads Sir Blake in the 1989 Reynoldstown Chase.

of year, and Longchamp, but national interest has so far condemned – and perhaps always will do so – this idea to the drawing board.

In principle a Championship series with enough prize money to attract the best of the American horses across the Atlantic, before a Breeders' Cup rematch is held back in the States, must be a most attractive idea and one that would do a good deal to enhance and protect the future of European racing.

The course

A course which stages such a feast of racing throughout the summer should have the amenities to match the quality of the fare, and as one would expect, Ascot does. The stands, completed in 1961, and the Royal Enclosure offer the spectator a complete panorama of the course and the numerous bars and restaurants within them offer the less enthusiastic racegoer an equally divert-

ing afternoon. The Flat paddock is a feast for the eyes, especially at the Royal meeting, when the course is at its magnificent best and the outlying bars about the paddock are always busy.

The course itself is a right-handed triangular circuit of a mile and three-quarters with a short straight of only two and a half furlongs. The straight mile course, over which the Royal Hunt Cup is run, stretches out to the gates through which the royal party enter in their carriages at the Royal meeting, whilst the Old Mile course starts at a spur off the main track at Swinley Bottom.

Despite the drop into Swinley Bottom on the far side of the course, Ascot favours the galloping horse, since there are few undulations to the track, which is stiff in nature, especially as the last six furlongs are all uphill. Ascot can look particularly attractive in the autumn when the many trees in Swinley Bottom put their glad rags on, and the course is always immaculate thanks to a hard-working groundstaff.

Compared to the Flat, the jumping game at Ascot is very much the poor relation. The temporary paddock used over the winter is just one half of the Tattersalls enclosure adapted for that purpose and this lends the whole proceedings an air of amateurism. But the racing belies that. Ascot is a tough and testing track, whose fences have acquired a reputation for being particularly unyielding, and the prizes on offer draw both horses and spectators in a plenty.

The first meeting of the season is held in mid-November when the feature event is the H. & T. Walker Gold Cup, a competitive two-and-a-half mile chase, but the best of Ascot's three weekend meetings is held in December when the Long Walk Hurdle and HSS Hire Shops Hurdle are the two feature events. Although its importance on the jumping circuit will never be able to rival that of its Flat racing, Ascot has won itself an impressive reputation as a National Hunt circuit and one which should continue to grow.

YORK

hether York is the Ascot of the North, or whether Ascot is only the York of the South depends solely upon whether or not you were born in God's own county. What is incontestable is that York stages one of the greatest of the English racing festivals: the Ebor festival which is held on the Knavesmire in mid-August.

The Ebor has almost everything one could ask of a meeting. Spread out over three days, the opening Tuesday remains the only day in the English racing calendar on which two Group 1 races are staged: the Yorkshire Oaks and the International, formerly the Benson & Hedges Gold Cup.

The latter was inaugurated in 1972 to provide a spectacular showdown between two of the great champions of the 1970s, Mill Reef and Brigadier Gerard. Unfortunately Mill Reef broke down in a training accident days before the race, making, as was thought, Brigadier Gerard a certainty. But, as it turned out, that year's Derby winner Roberto had different ideas.

Putting in one of the most staggering

INTERNATIONAL STAKES
1m. 2½f. Three-year-olds and upwards. First run 1972.

Year	Winner	Owner	Trainer	Jockey
1973	Moulton	R.B. Moller	H. Wragg	G. Lewis
1974	Dahlia	N.B. Hunt	M. Zilber	L. Piggott
1975	Dahlia	N.B. Hunt	M. Zilber	L. Piggott
1976	Wollow	C. d'Alessio	H. Cecil	G. Dettori
1977	Relkino	Lady Beaverbrook	W.R. Hern	W. Carson
1978	Hawaiian Sound	R.E. Sangster	B. Hills	L. Piggott
1979	Troy	Sir M. Sobell	W.R. Hern	W. Carson
1980	Master Willie	W. Barnett	H. Candy	P. Waldron
1981	Beldale Flutter	A. Kelly	M. Jarvis	P. Eddery
1982	Assert	R.E. Sangster	D. O'Brien	P. Eddery
1983	Caerleon	R.E. Sangster	M.V. O'Brien	P. Eddery
1984	Cormorant Wood	R.J. McAlpine	B. Hills	S. Cauthen
1985	Commanche Run	I. Allan	L. Cumani	L. Piggott
1986	Shardari	H.H. Aga Khan	M. Stoute	W.R. Swinburn
1987	Triptych	A. Clore	P-L. Biancone	S. Cauthen
1988	Shady Heights	G. Tong	R. Armstrong	W. Carson
1989	Il de Chypre	A. Christodoulou	G. Harwood	A. Clark

Ears pricked Diminuendo, partnered by Steve Cauthen, wins the 1988 Musidora Stakes at York's May meeting. The filly went on to record further successes in Epsom's Oaks, the Irish Oaks and the Yorkshire Oaks at this course in August 1988.

performances ever seen on a race course, he ran away from the Brigadier, inflicting on John Hislop's colt his only defeat, and won in a new course record.

Since that running, the race has developed into one of the top ten-furlong races of

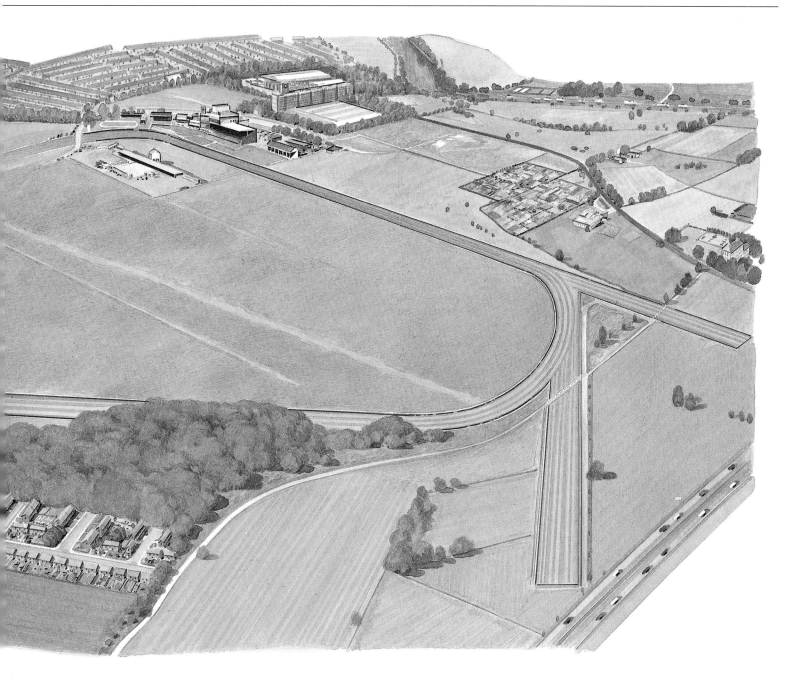

the country, with winners of the class of the great French mares, Dahlia and Triptych, and Classic winners, Wollow and Troy.

The Ebor Handicap, run on the Wednesday, is one of the big betting races of the year and although the days are gone when the best in the land would compete, the winner is still a top-class horse, with recent examples including Jupiter Island, later to gain the Japan Cup, and Protection Racket, who went on to win the Irish St Leger.

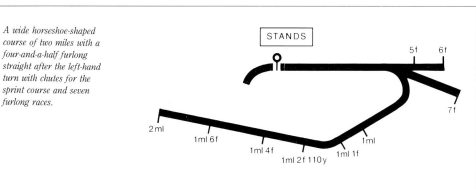

A wide horseshoe-shaped course of two miles with a four-and-a-half furlong straight after the left-hand turn with chutes for the sprint course and seven furlong races.

STANDS

5f 6f

7f

2 ml

1 ml 6 f

1 ml 4 f

1 ml 2 f 110 y

1 ml 1 f

1 ml

1 ml

Right: *The finish of one of the greatest matches in history. Flying Dutchman goes a length clear of Voltigeur to record a historic win.*

Above: *Ajdal, the 1987 Champion sprinter, cements his claim to that title with a brilliant win in that year's William Hill Sprint Championship.*

Gimcrack Stakes

Also on that same Wednesday card is the Gimcrack Stakes, one of the more important two-year-old contests. The winning owner is traditionally invited to give the main speech at the annual Gimcrack dinner in December, an invitation which is still regarded as a great honour.

The third and final day of the meeting sees the running of the William Hill Sprint Championship, formerly the Nunthorpe Stakes, which is the third Group 1 contest of the meeting. From a lowly start as the Nunthorpe Selling Stakes, it has grown steadily in importance throughout its life and is now firmly established as the top five-furlong sprint in the country.

The beauty of the meeting, however, is the combination of these Championship races with the bread and butter events that make the racing world go round. The Selling Stakes that open the Wednesday card is always the scene of great tilts at the ring and the auction of the winner invariably attracts a big crowd as well as the interested parties who actually take a hand in the bidding. The mixture of the great and the small is entrancing and offers everyone a chance of sharing in the atmosphere of this meeting.

The Knavesmire, only 20 minutes' walk from the centre of this beautiful city, is an expanse of common land that has been the home of York races since 1731. It is an unenclosed course, whose flat gradients and friendly turns give a fair test; only when the going turns very soft are there conceivable grounds for excuses. Like Epsom, the course resembles a horseshoe, with the distance starts opposite the stands on the far side of the course.

York's rise to pre-eminence began in 1767 when the Gimcrack Club was founded to honour one of the early champions of the turf, the grey Gimcrack who won 26 races between 1764 and 1771. The Club members organized the York meetings to attract the best of the horses trained in the North.

By the 1840s, the three-day August meeting was beginning to take the shape that we know today. The Ebor Handicap, the Yorkshire Oaks and the Gimcrack Stakes all came into existence and the locals began to appreciate the feast of horseflesh that was annually laid before them.

The Flying Dutchman

In 1851, York was the venue for the most famous match in the history of horse racing, that between The Flying Dutchman and Voltigeur, both Derby winners. The Flying Dutchman had lost his unbeaten record to Voltigeur in the previous year's Doncaster Cup, but both owners had agreed to another contest at York in the following spring.

Interest in the race had grown throughout the winter and a crowd of over 100,000 turned up to see the race of the century. A true head-to-head battle in the best racing tradition, there was never much between the two horses, but in the final furlong The Flying Dutchman, who had been sent off favourite, came to challenge the pace-setting Voltigeur, got the better of him and went away to win by a length.

Nowadays gatherings of that size are a rarity on any racecourse. Derby Day excepted, but York has remained one of the best attended courses in Britain. The magnificent new grandstand, completed in 1965, and the surrounding lawns are always immaculate and the facilities rival those of any other course in the country.

The Dante meeting in May is the first meeting of the year and second only to the Ebor in importance. The feature races of the three-day meeting are the two Classic trials, the Mecca-Dante Stakes for the colts and the Musidora for fillies, both run over the extended ten furlongs. Despite their poor reputation for throwing up Classic winners – to date only four colts have completed the Dante-Derby double – they continue to attract many of the promising spring colts.

During high summer, there are two popular Saturday meetings. The mid-June Timeform charity day always features competitive racing and over its 15-year history, has raised over £1 million.

The John Smith's Magnet Cup Handicap in July is one of the most popular handicaps of the year and attracts another large crowd, but recently the day has won itself a poor reputation for the rowdyism that is threatening the racing world.

York has been most admirably served by its clerks of the course in recent years. Under Major Leslie Petch and his nephew John Sanderson, York was voted racecourse of the year three times in the early 1980s.

York's elegant paddock is always surrounded by huge crowds weighing up the contenders during the Ebor festival.

HAYDOCK

A park course in Lancashire near Warrington, Haydock Park has grown in popularity over the last twenty years, mainly through the hard work of the late clerk of the course John Hughes, who made it his job to improve both the racing and the facilities and pushed Haydock into the top flight of mixed courses in this country.

The Flat meetings, which run from March through to October, are of a consistently competitive quality and, since 1988, the course boasts a Group 1 feature race in the Vernons Sprint Cup, run in September. Other major Flat races include the Lancashire Oaks and the prestigious handicap, the old Newton Cup, which are run on the same card in July.

The steeplechase course is one that is neither daunting nor easy, but one that encourages a good jumper to go for his fences. The meeting at the beginning of March is often a significant pointer towards Cheltenham, and both the Greenall Whitley and the Timeform Chases are valuable races and take some winning.

The one mixed meeting is held on the May Bank Holiday, where the feature race is the Swinton Insurance Brokers Trophy. This is a handicap hurdle over two miles, which is the last major race of the jumping season and is one of the more valuable events of its kind.

A flat oval course of 13 furlongs, Haydock is distinguished by its tight top bend which can become quite hazardous on slippery conditions underfoot. Recent course developments have extended the straight course to allow the six-furlong Vernons Sprint Cup to be run without a bend, and the new grandstand, completed in 1982, has encouraged the public to come in ever-increasing numbers.

Haydock has been a race course since 1899, but has only recently risen into the upper echelons of courses. Given its attractive parkland and the ever more valuable prize money, it should continue to grow in popularity with both trainers and spectators.

Orojoya (nearest), in the famous colours of Robert Sangster, just gets the better of *Primo Domine to win the 1985 Vernons Sprint Cup.*

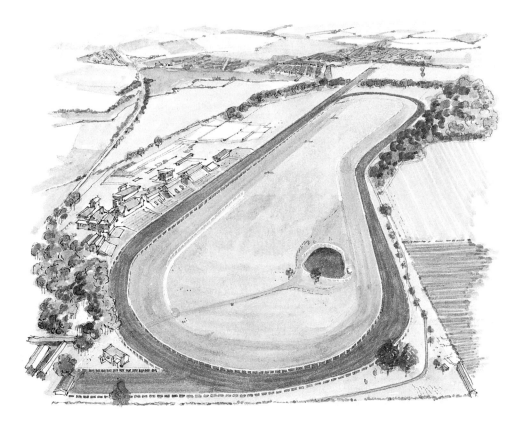

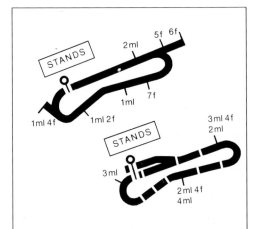

Flat. *Left-handed oval circuit of one mile five furlongs in circumference. The straight has recently been extended to six furlongs, whilst the turn into the home straight is very tight.*

Jumps. *Flat galloping circuit, which boasts awkward drop fences on the chase course. Prone to heavy going.*

The Ayr Gold Cup is the seaside course's major flat race and one of the biggest sprint handicaps of the season. In the 1987 race Not So Silly (far left) gets up close to beat Serve N'Volley.

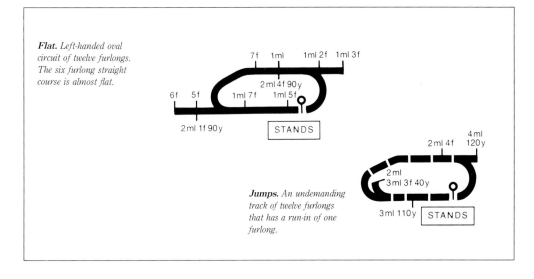

Flat. *Left-handed oval circuit of twelve furlongs. The six furlong straight course is almost flat.*

Jumps. *An undemanding track of twelve furlongs that has a run-in of one furlong.*

AYR

To be called Scotland's most important racecourse is no great honour, given the level of the competition, but Ayr is that and more besides. The current course replaced the old Seafield course, which was closed in 1906, and has made its mark on racing north of the border by hosting both the Scottish Derby and the Scottish National in recent years.

A flat left-handed course of 12 furlongs round, Ayr is a fair course for all types of horses. It has been attracting a better class of runner throughout the last 20 years as improved prize money has drawn the southern trainers north in search of pots and pounds.

The big meeting on the Flat is the four-day Western meeting in September, when the feature race is the Ayr Gold Cup, a six-furlong sprint handicap which has a history

stretching back to 1804. Big holiday crowds come down from Glasgow to watch the top northern sprint handicappers try to hold off the southern raiders in a race that always has a huge field.

The other principal meeting on the Flat is the old Scottish Derby meeting in July. The Scottish Derby had dropped so low in prestige that in 1987 it was decided to combine it with the Land of Burns Stakes, a race for the older horses, in an attempt to get a better field for what has become Scotland's only Group event.

Over the jumps, the Scottish National has been the standard-bearer since its arrival at

Ayr from Bogside in 1965. In its 23-year history at Ayr, only the great Red Rum has added the Scottish National to its Aintree namesake, which is run two to three weeks earlier.

As a spectacle, Ayr cannot hold a candle to Aintree, since the extended four miles of the race require the field to jump round three times and the repetitive nature of both the course and the obstacles can pall on the third time round. But Ayr does provide a valuable service to the Scottish industry and the racing fans of the country and for that reason equally to the industry as a whole.

The famous colours of maroon with a gold disc will always be associated with the National. For they were worn by Red Rum's riders and here the three-times winner jumps the Chair, the biggest obstacle on the course.

AINTREE

Grand National fever envelops the whole country every year some time in early April. For two weeks before the event the papers are filled with the attempts of journalists to find the winner – rather like unravelling a detective story, except, instead of who did it, the question is who will do it? Like no other race, Aintree's Grand National draws the eyes and cameras of the world upon itself.

Sure, it is just another race, but who would want to submit their horses and themselves to an ordeal that has no equal? Four and a half miles over some of the most tortuous fences yet devised by the racing mind to test, fool and cudgel a field into submission.

For some it does not bear thinking about. And yet, as at Epsom, the winner will become a national figure. To have won at Aintree is to have written a small chapter in the history of the British Isles, and those who have done so are no longer mere mortals.

The story began back in 1839 with the first running of the Grand Liverpool Steeplechase. A striking bay gelding called Lottery, partnered by Jem Mason, beat a field of 16 others to win the third running of that race, but the first to be held at Aintree. At that time Lottery was far and away the best chaser in the land. He was often barred from entering run-of-the-mill events because of his superiority, and following his success in 1839, he was asked to do the

Right: *Lottery has gone down in history as the first winner of the Grand National, when, in 1839, he won the first running of the race at Aintree. So good was Lottery in his heyday that he was banned from running in many chases.*

"LOTTERY," THE CELEBRATED STEEPLE-CHASE WINNER. DRAWN BY HERRING.

The Grand National course of two and a quarter miles is unique. The sixteen fences are a true test of a horse's jumping, and the run-in of two furlongs only prolongs the agony.

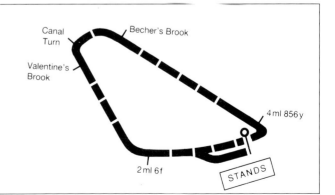

impossible, and carry an 18 lb penalty in the following year's race, a task that was beyond even him and he fell at the stone wall.

The Grand National

That first running was over a course marked out in the nearby fields. The obstacles included a 1.52m (5 ft) stone wall, an ox-fence and a 1.85m (6 ft) brook, all of which had to be cleared twice. A certain Captain Becher fell into the big brook after suffering some interference at the hands of Lottery, and his misfortune has been compounded by having his name attached to the offending obstacle ever since, the now infamous Becher's Brook.

The gallant Captain stayed in the brook whilst the field passed him, caught his horse and remounted, only to fall in the second brook a few fences later. The following year that brook was named after Valentine, an Irish raider who finished third in the 1840 running.

The race has changed considerably over the years, as indeed has the sport of steeplechasing. The more redoubtable fences, such as the stone wall, have been dropped; the open fields that were the bulk of the course have gradually been enclosed and by 1890 the whole race was run on turf.

Since then the distance of the race has been fixed at 4 miles 856 yards and the number of fences has stayed at 30. It is the combination of those two bare statistics that make the race what it is. Longer than any other race over fences, the like of which are not found outside Aintree any more, the Grand National presents any debutants with the unknown and it is this that makes the race so thrilling.

Given the riches bestowed on the race and its renown, there will always be a large field lining up at the start in front of the stands. Thirty odd horses, half of them fancied runners, the rest there to make up the numbers – and perhaps, if Lady Luck is kind to them, cause the upset of the decade – stand chaffing at their bits as they are called into line. The tape is raised and they're off. In front of them is a long, long line of fences that stretch all the way down the back straight until Becher's is met on the corner.

The long gallop to the first fence is frantic, as everyone tries to get a favoured position by the time the field crosses the tan-covered Melling Road, and the innocent-looking 1.37m (4ft 6in) jump, a thorn fence dressed with gorse, always claims its victims. The fallers have often jumped the fence too fast and too well and just buckle up on landing. The list of favourites and fancied horses that have fallen at the first is endless. The great Golden Miller came unstuck there in 1936, whilst more recently both Door Latch and Sacred Path, who were

Above: *With four miles and thirty fences in front of them, you wouldn't imagine that they would be quite so eager to get underway. But every National start is like a cavalry charge as they make for the first.*

Right: *Only the very bold jump the inside of Becher's Brook where the drop is steepest. But after a decade's wrangling over the safety of the fence, from 1990 the famous Brook is to be filled in and the landing side levelled out.*

carrying a weight of the public's money, came to grief.

After that first taste of Aintree, the field settles down and makes its way out into the countryside. The second fence is another plain one, but the third is the first ditch, a 1.52m (5ft)-high fence with a 1.83m (6ft) ditch guarding the front. That too can claim its fair share of victims and scare the living daylights out of both man and beast.

Becher's Brook

The fourth and fifth are two more plain jumps, but the sixth is Becher's Brook. A large crowd is always gathered there, knowing that of all the fences on the course this is where the real action happens. They roar the field on as it nears the jump. Every jockey knows the name of the jump he is approaching.

From the take-off side Becher's looks like another plain obstacle, but on the far side of the 1.47m (4ft 10in) spruce-dressed fence lies a 1.68m (5ft 6in) brook and a drop the far side of that. It has been described as 'the worst view in the world' and 'like looking over a precipice', and as the horse stretches out to rejoin terra firma, his feet find only air. It is the drop as much as anything else that fools the horse. His legs are tensed too soon and when eventually he hits the ground, he can stumble on to his knees and throw his jockey out the front door.

Take off too soon and he might not clear the brook; take off too late or hit the top of the fence and he will never get his legs down in time. Try and save ground by jumping on the inside and the drop is at its most fiendish. Even if the horse survives the jump, he might still be unlucky enough to get brought down by other fallers.

What remains of the field picks itself up and steadies itself for the next fence, another plain one, but one that takes its toll, simply because the horses are apprehensive about jumping again. After all it may be just like the one they had just taken.

It was at the seventh that one of the most remarkable incidents in the history of the race occurred. The year was 1967 and the race had been its usual haphazard self up to this fence the second time round, when it is number 23.

It's a pound to a penny that Rhyme'n'Reason (No 2) is down and out at Becher's. But the gelding picked himself off the floor and ran on to win a dramatic National in 1988.

A loose horse crossed the field as it prepared to jump and a mother and a father of a pile-up ensued. There were horses who had jumped and left the jockeys on the take-off side; there were jockeys who had landed on the far side but left their mounts behind them.

Everything was in total confusion: it was difficult to tell which direction the field was meant to be going as the fence itelf had been totally demolished. Through this mayhem one tailender Foinavon skipped over the remnants of the fence and before anyone else could sort themselves out, the horse had gone clear into an unassailable lead to win at 100–1.

Canal Turn

Next up is the Canal Turn, a stiff 1.52m (5ft) fence which is followed by a sharp left-handed turn. The jockey has to prepare for the turn before he has jumped the fence, pulling out to his right and then jumping diagonally across the fence. If he fails to make the sharp 90-degree turn, he will find only the crowd in front of him.

After the Canal Turn, the field has turned the corner and are heading back towards the stands. But there is still no letting up. The ninth fence is the second brook, Valen-

tine's. A bigger fence than Becher's but without the fearsome drop the far side, Valentine's is still enough of a worry to take its own toll.

Another plain fence is followed by the second open ditch, the 11th of the jumps, and then following a second crossing of the Melling Road, the field turns into the finishing straight for the first time. Two plain fences, which will be the last two on the following circuit, lead up to the Chair, the biggest fence on the course.

Standing at 1.57m (5ft 2in) the Chair looks even bigger, as for once the take-off side is lower than the landing, and it is a narrow fence, hardly half the width of the others. On a slight rise, which makes for problems, the fence is guarded by a 1.83m (6 ft) ditch that beckons like a hungry mouth as the horse makes his leap.

Survive that and the water, which are the only two fences to be jumped but once in the race, and those who are lucky enough, or unlucky enough, depending on one's point of view, to be still on their feet, have to do it all over again.

Come Becher's the second time round, and the likely winner will be beginning to emerge. Four or five horses will have stamped out their claims and will be fighting it out between them. But even after the

The Princess Royal at the unveiling of Red Rum's statue at Aintree in 1988.

final straight has been reached and the last two fences have been jumped, the long uphill Aintree run-in can provide its fair share of drama.

Devon Loch

Without a doubt the fate of the Queen Mother's Devon Loch in 1956 was the most spectacular. A Royal winner looked on the cards, as Devon Loch cleared the last fence some three lengths clear of E.S.B., and was drawing clear when suddenly his legs collapsed, almost throwing rider Dick Francis out of the saddle.

All manner of explanations have been offered – the horse tried to jump the shadow of the water jump, the noise of the crowd cheering home a royal winner had distracted Devon Loch, sheer exhaustion after a fast-run race, though the horse had shown no signs of tiredness – but it is one of those mysteries which will never be resolved.

Then, in 1973, came one of the most dramatic finishes of all time. Crisp, under the top-weight of 12 stone, made almost all the running, and was well clear at the last. But the distress signals were out, and that run-in of 494 yards must have seemed like the full four and a half miles as jockey Richard Pitman tried to coax his mount home. The pair were virtually at a standstill as the lightweight Red Rum passed them just 13.7m (15 yds) from the finishing line to win in the fastest time ever recorded.

Red Rum then proceeded to rewrite the Aintree record books. Winning again in 1974, he was second to L'Escargot in 1975 and to Rag Trade in 1976, before bringing the stands down with an unparalleled third victory on his fifth start to the race in 1977.

An Aintree specialist through and through, Red Rum won the hearts of the nation with his bravery round the course and remains a public figure, opening fetes and making personal appearances, to this day.

There have been many other Aintree specialists, whose feats, though dwarfed by Red Rum, demand respect. Manifesto competed in even more Nationals than Red Rum. He won twice and finished third three times in his eight starts around the turn of the century, when one of his defeats came at

SEAGRAM GRAND NATIONAL STEEPLECHASE			
4½ miles. First run in 1837.			
Year · **Winner**	**Owner**	**Trainer**	**Jockey**
1971 · *Specify*	F.W. Pontin	J.E. Sutcliffe	J. Cook
1972 · *Well To Do*	T. Forster	T. Forster	G. Thorner
1973 · *Red Rum*	N. le Mare	D. McCain	B. Fletcher
1974 · *Red Rum*	N. le Mare	D. McCain	B. Fletcher
1975 · *L'Escargot*	R. Guest	D. Moore	T. Carberry
1976 · *Rag Trade*	P. Raymond	T.F. Rimell	J. Burke
1977 · *Red Rum*	N. le Mare	D. McCain	T. Stack
1978 · *Lucius*	Mrs. D. Whitaker	G.W. Richards	R. Davies
1979 · *Rubstic*	J. Douglas	S.J. Leadbetter	M. Barnes
1980 · *Ben Nevis*	R.C. Stewart	T. Forster	C. Fenwick
1981 · *Aldaniti*	S. Embiricos	J. Gifford	R. Champion
1982 · *Grittar*	F. Gilman	F. Gilman	C. Saunders
1983 · *Corbiere*	B. Burrough	Mrs. J. Pitman	B. de Haan
1984 · *Hallo Dandy*	R. Shaw	G.W. Richards	N. Doughty
1985 · *Last Suspect*	Anne, Duchess of Westminster	T. Forster	H. Davies
1986 · *West Tip*	P. Luff	M. Oliver	R. Dunwoody
1987 · *Maori Venture*	H.J. Joel	A. Turnell	S. Knight
1988 · *Rhyme 'n' Reason*	Miss J.E. Reed	D. Elsworth	B. Powell
1989 · *Little Polveir*	E. Harvey	G. Balding	J. Frost
1990 · *Mr Frisk*	Mrs H.J. Duffey	K.C. Bailey	M. Armytage

the hands of the Prince of Wales' Ambush II, the only Royal winner to date.

Reynoldstown was another to win two Nationals. His triumphs in 1935 and 1936 included the prized scalp of Golden Miller. The second of those wins was a touch fortunate as the buckle on the rein of Anthony Mildmay on the leader Davy Jones broke just as the pair were approaching the last fence and the horse ran out, leaving Reynoldstown clear.

Bob Champion and Aldaniti

There have been few such fairy-tale results as the 1981 race, when an ex-invalid horse Aldaniti, partnered by a jockey who had fought a long hard battle against cancer, Bob Champion, took on the world at Aintree and came home triumphant. That fighting spirit typifies what is needed at Aintree and it does not always come from the English.

The Duke of Albuquerque may not have

Left: *Of all the tear-jerking stories the National has produced, that of Aldaniti and Bob Champion stands alone. Both horse and jockey looked death in the eye before returning to win the 1981 race.*

Above: *Crowds walk the National course before racing. It is only when the fences are seen close up that the enormity of the task can be appreciated.*

been the most stylish of jockeys to have ridden round Aintree. His record in the race cannot match that of Brian Fletcher, Tom Oliver or the five-times successful George Stevens, but he epitomizes the race's lure.

His first ride came in 1952 when he was already 34, and he continued whenever possible until he was banned from doing so by the Jockey Club in 1977. He once completed the course in his 24 years of trying and his eighth place behind Red Rum in 1974 when he was recovering from a broken collar bone, was a triumph of mind over matter.

As each year throws up a plethora of stories, it is impossible to tell every Aintree tale. But behind the scenes of the big race, the course itself has had an eventful life. Ever since Mirabel Topham surrendered control of the course, there has been a question mark over the fate of the National. An annual will it or won't it battle raged over the future of the race until Ladbrokes saved it for the nation at the start of the 1980s and began to repair its lost kudos.

Over the years Aintree had been stripped of its Flat racing, lost its great October meeting and been left with just three moderate days racing at its Spring festival, enlivened only by the three races over the National fences – the National itself, the old Topham Trophy, now called the Glenlivet Trophy and the Foxhunters.

With increased sponsorship having been brought in first by Ladbrokes and more recently by Seagram, those three days have now been turned into a National Hunt festival that is almost the rival of Cheltenham. The best horses are drawn there and not just for the National. Now that the course's future seems assured, there are plans to reintroduce the October meeting and begin to make fuller use of a course that will always be a legend.

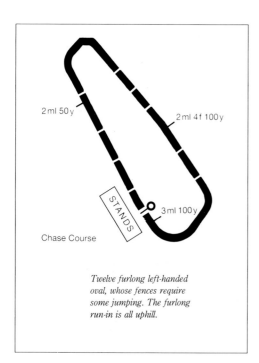

2 ml 50 y

2 ml 4 f 100 y

STANDS

3 ml 100 y

Chase Course

Twelve furlong left-handed oval, whose fences require some jumping. The furlong run-in is all uphill.

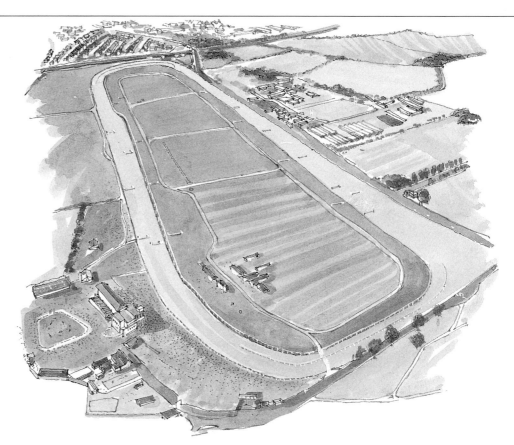

WETHERBY

Wetherby has been one of the success stories of recent National Hunt racing. This attractive Yorkshire course has been developed over the last 15 years into the North's premier jumps course and it hosts as competitive racing as almost anywhere else, with the exception of Cheltenham.

A small left-handed track of about a mile and a half in circumference, Wetherby is notable for the severity of its fences which swiftly punish any horse who tries to take any liberties with the tops of the obstacles. The course favours a long-striding horse who goes for his jumps and it thus attracts some of the best horses in training.

In contrast, the hurdles course, on the inside of the jumps, is much shorter and sharper. With a circuit of only one and a quarter miles, and only two hurdles in the straight, front runners are favoured and can often slip their field.

The racing year at Wetherby starts in mid-October, when the feature race is the Bobby Renton Novices' Chase, the best novices' contest of the season to date. The course is then well used with a meeting once every three weeks, including the late October two-day meeting when the Charlie Hall Memorial Wetherby Pattern Chase is the

Three top Northern chasers battle it out in Wetherby's Charlie Hall Pattern Chase. Forgive N'Forget (far side) jumps up alongside Cybrandium with Wayward Lad tracing the pair.

main race, up to the big Christmas fixture.

Boxing Day at Wetherby is second only to Kempton in importance. The feature races – the Rowland Meyrick Handicap Chase and on the second of the two days, the Castleford Handicap Chase – attract some of the best three- and two-mile chasers in the North. Racing continues apace throughout the winter and spring with the final meeting of the year being held in May.

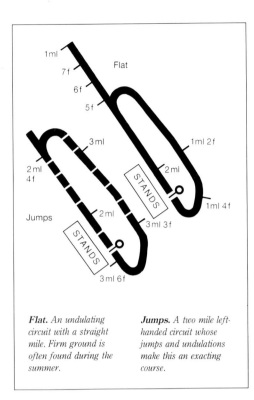

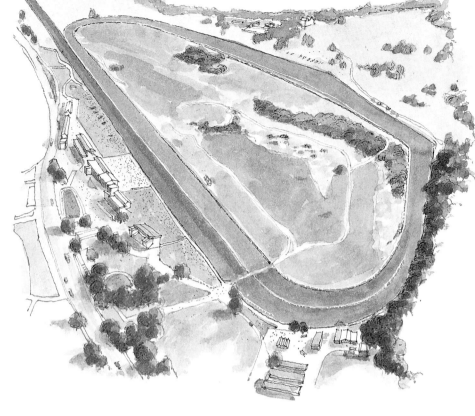

Flat. *An undulating circuit with a straight mile. Firm ground is often found during the summer.*

Jumps. *A two mile left-handed circuit whose jumps and undulations make this an exacting course.*

CHEPSTOW

Chepstow is a beautiful West Country course, just on the far side of the Severn Bridge, that hosts Wales' premier Flat and jumps races: the Welsh Derby and the Welsh National. Unlike its Scottish equivalent, Ayr, it is more renowned for its jumping than for its Flat racing.

The Welsh Derby is a Derby in name only, for it rarely attracts a decent horse and is not much sought after as a prize. The other Flat meetings, staged between May and October, have no other feature race and the frequent hard ground and the lack of sponsors can be blamed for that.

The jumping, however, is of a different nature. Right from the word go, the racing, which starts before the last of the Flat meetings is held, is of a much higher quality. The big guns from Lambourn are tempted over the border and the crowds gather to see the sport. But it is the Welsh National that is the biggest draw.

Recently moved from its traditional February slot to a pre-Christmas meeting because of the likelihood of better weather, the Welsh National is the first of the stamina-sapping tests to be run, but no less important for that. It began its life at Cardiff, but

has been run at Chepstow since 1899.

The undulations of the course make this three-and-three-quarter-mile event a true test of stamina. Surprisingly, though, the race has only just started throwing up top class winners. Both Rag Trade and Corbiere won at Chepstow before going on

Chepstow's undulating straight stretches out into the distance as the field jumps the last at one of the course's big autumn meetings.

to Aintree glory, whilst Burrough Hill Lad capped his Welsh National triumph with success in the Gold Cup.

CHELTENHAM

To the purist, the Cheltenham Festival is the be all and end all of the jumping season. Those three days in March see the annual gathering of the best of the National Hunt horses and spectators and the natural amphitheatre of Prestbury resounds with the hum of the sport's true enthusiasts.

From the din of the crowded Mandarin Bar, which echoes with Irish voices discussing the chances of the next runner from the Emerald Isle, to the two lofty guardians of the paddock, the champions Arkle and Dawn Run, the spirit of the winter game shines out like a reassuring beacon.

It has been a long hard struggle for Cheltenham to reach its now legendary position in the pantheon of jumps racing – and a struggle which for many years it had looked like losing.

Royalty had a hand in its birth, for it was the arrival of King George III at the new spa town in 1788 that first brought the royal sport to this idyllic part of the world.

It was in 1819, some 30 years later, that the first Gold Cup was run. This was a three-mile Flat race held high on the banks

of Cleeve Hill, which overlooks the current course. The meeting proved popular and, within six years, had grown into one of the biggest in the land with up to 50,000 people attending. A grandstand was built up on the hill and all seemed set fair.

An outbreak of puritanism, however, put paid to that. A moral crusade against the evils of gambling took hold of the townsfolk in the late 1820s culminating in the destruction of the grandstand in 1829. Although racing was re-established in 1831 at the current site of Prestbury Park, it did not manage to gain ascendancy over the outraged morals of the locals and between the 1840s and the 1890s, there was no racing in Cheltenham.

They reckon it's the strongest betting ring in the world. Cheltenham at the Festival is awash with punters, both English and Irish looking for someone to accommodate them.

Grand Annual

What did continue in the locality was the lesser sport of steeplechasing at Andoversford, where in 1834 the first Grand Annual Steeplechase, a race that is still a central part of today's festival was held. It was this isolated pillar of the sport that kept racing alive in Gloucestershire until Prestbury awoke from its slumbers in 1898 and, casting off its Flat cloak, began preparing itself to ascend the throne of the jumps game.

It was the purchase of the course by Barry Bingham that turned the tide. He refurbished the course with a new stand and running rails and then opened it to the public. His ideas worked and in 1902 the festival was relaunched. It has grown in stature ever since. What had started as a two-day festival prospered so well that in 1923 a third day was added. The following

year saw the first proper running of the Cheltenham Gold Cup and three years later a similar championship race for hurdlers, called unsurprisingly the Champion Hurdle, was added to the card.

After the interruptions of the Second World War, which curtailed activities, the festival continued on its upward spiral as the National Hunt world began to shake off the shadow of its richer Flat brother and enjoy some boom years of growth. Prize money was up, the number of horses in training grew, and so naturally did the crowds. With the addition of the Queen Mother Champion Chase in 1959, the arrival of the Triumph Hurdle in 1962 from Hurst Park and the novice chase championship, the Sun Alliance Chase, in 1964, the festival became the goal of all jumpers of promise and the quality of the racing was the envy of even the big Flat Festivals.

Golden Miller

The first equine hero of Cheltenham was Dorothy Paget's remarkable Golden Miller, who won five consecutive Gold Cups between 1932 and 1936 and as an 11-year-old was only beaten by two lengths by Morse Code in 1938. Throw in his Grand National success in 1934 and you have arguably the finest chaser ever.

His victory over Thomond II in 1935 provided one of the great finishes for which Cheltenham has become renowned. The pair drew clear of the field after the first

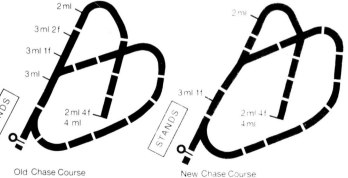

Old. *This left-handed circuit with its severe obstacles and stiff uphill finish is one of the most testing National Hunt circuits.*

New. *Slightly longer than the Old Course, Cheltenham's New Course is used for the Gold Cup. The greater number of fences puts a premium on jumping.*

2 ml
3 ml 2f
3 ml 1f
3 ml
2 ml 4f
4 ml

Old Chase Course

2 ml
3 ml 1f
2 ml 4f
4 ml

New Chase Course

circuit and raced head to head throughout the second. But up the final hill to the finishing line which tests a horse's stamina so throughly, Golden Miller confirmed his ascendancy, sticking his head out in front and winning by three-quarters of a length.

Cheltenham has long been associated with the Irish. Every March they come across the sea in their thousands complete with their best horses and their dreams. They know that they have the champions and they are just waiting for the chance to show the world this by winning at the Festival. After all, they won the second running of the Gold Cup and it has only been through the unkindness of Fate that they have not won every other.

One man more than any other established the role of the Irish at the Festival, and that was Vincent O'Brien. In the postwar years he sent out Cottage Rake to win the Gold Cup three years in succession and then doubled that up by winning the Champion Hurdle with Hatton's Grace three times. With numerous Gloucestershire Hurdle triumphs to his credit too, O'Brien heralded in the golden years which came to a climax with Arkle.

Whether Arkle or Golden Miller was the greatest is an argument that will go on and on, but whenever Arkle ran, there was never an argument. He won – especially at Cheltenham. Arkle first came over in 1963 to take on the supposedly unbeatable Mill House in the Hennessy Gold Cup. Due to a bad error three fences out, Arkle lost that encounter, but he never again let Mill House finish in front of him.

TOTE CHELTENHAM GOLD CUP

3 miles, 2 furlongs. First run 1924.

Year	Winner	Owner	Trainer	Jockey
1971	L'Escargot	R. Guest	D. Moore	T. Carberry
1972	Glencaraig Lady	P. Doyle	F. Flood	F. Berry
1973	The Dikler	Mrs. D. August	F. Walwyn	R. Barry
1974	Captain Christy	Mrs. J. Samuel	P. Taaffe	H. Beasley
1975	Ten Up	Anne, Duchess of Westminster	J. Dreaper	T. Carberry
1976	Royal Frolic	Sir E. Hanmer	F. Rimell	J. Burke
1977	Davy Lad	Mrs. J. McGowan	M. O'Toole	D.T. Hughes
1978	Midnight Court	Mrs. O. Jackson	F. Winter	J. Francome
1979	Alverton	Snailwell Stud Co. Ltd.	M.H. Easterby	J.J. O'Neill
1980	Tied Cottage	A. Robinson	D. Moore	T. Carberry
1981	Little Owl	R.J. Wilson	M.H. Easterby	A.J. Wilson
1982	Silver Buck	Mrs. C. Feather	M. Dickinson	R. Earnshaw
1983	Bregawn	J. Kennelly	M. Dickinson	G. Bradley
1984	Burrough Hill Lad	R.S. Riley	Mrs. J. Pitman	P. Tuck
1985	Forgive 'N Forget	T. Kilroe & Sons	J. FitzGerald	M. Dwyer
1986	Dawn Run	Mrs. C. Hill	P. Mullins	J.J. O'Neill
1987	The Thinker	T. McDonagh Ltd.	W.A. Stephenson	R. Lamb
1988	Charter Party	Mrs. C. Smith	D. Nicholson	R. Dunwoody
1989	Desert Orchid	R. Burridge	D. Elsworth	S. Sherwood
1990	Norton's Coin	S.G. Griffiths	S.G. Griffiths	G. McCourt

Arkle

Mill House was made favourite to confirm that Hennessy superiority at Cheltenham the following spring. But Arkle, under the Irish wizard Pat Taaffe, had his measure. Approaching the third fence, Mill House was under pressure and come the line, the English champion was beaten and all Ireland rose to acclaim their new hero.

Arkle came back and triumphed again in 1965 and 1966. Such was his dominance over his contemporaries that he could have continued his stranglehold over chasing's premier prize for as long as Golden Miller, had he not cracked a pedal bone in the 1966 King George VI, an injury that proved to be the end of his career.

To honour such a champion, a bronze of Arkle stands over the Cheltenham paddock. Across the paddock from him stands a bronze of the Irish heroine, Dawn Run. Charmian Hill's mare is the only horse to date to have won both the Champion Hurdle and the Gold Cup.

To call any one race the best ever is to risk ridicule, but for many people the 1986 Gold Cup was just that. Coming to the last, it looked long odds against a win for Dawn Run. Forgive'N'Forget, the winner the previous year, and Wayward Lad looked to have the measure of the mare, but with Jonjo O'Neill and the whole of Ireland urging her on, Dawn Run ran on and on and took Jonjo, arm raised, past the post and into the record books.

Another staggering Cheltenham achievement was by the trainer Michael Dickinson, who in 1983 sent out the first five home in the Gold Cup, a feat that left every commentator gasping. But Cheltenham is like that:

In the 1964 Gold Cup England could not see Mill House (right) getting beat, while all Ireland were cheering for Arkle (left). But Pat Taaffe knew what he was sitting on and pushed Arkle clear after the pair jumped the last.

Arm aloft the expression on Jonjo O'Neill's face says it all after the Irishman had miraculously driven Dawn Run past Wayward Lad and Forgive N'Forget to win the 1986 Cheltenham Gold Cup.

it encourages the unthinkable and deeds that would be inconceivable elsewhere happen at Prestbury Park.

Cheltenham stages much more than just the Festival. From its first October meeting right through to the hunter chaser evening in May, the racing never slips below top-class. Any horse that clears the stiff fences, handles the undulating course and most importantly runs on up that stiff final hill to win, has accomplished a feat that many others have tried and failed.

WATERFORD CRYSTAL CHAMPION HURDLE

2 miles. First run 1927.

Year	Winner	Owner	Trainer	Jockey
1971	Bula	Capt. E.E. Heathcote	F. Winter	P. Kelleway
1972	Bula	Capt. E.E. Heathcote	F. Winter	P. Kelleway
1973	Comedy of Errors	E. Wheatley	F. Rimell	W. Smith
1974	Lanzarote	Lord Howard de Walden	F. Winter	R. Pitman
1975	Comedy of Errors	E. Wheatley	F. Rimell	K. White
1976	Night Nurse	R. Spencer	M.H. Easterby	P. Broderick
1977	Night Nurse	R. Spencer	M.H. Easterby	P. Broderick
1978	Monksfield	Dr. M. Mangan	D. McDonough	T. Kinane
1979	Monksfield	Dr. M. Mangan	D. McDonough	D.T. Hughes
1980	Sea Pigeon	P. Muldoon	M.H. Easterby	J.J. O'Neill
1981	Sea Pigeon	P. Muldoon	M.H. Easterby	J. Francome
1982	For Auction	F.B. Heaslip	M. Cunningham	Mr. C. Magnier
1983	Gaye Brief	Sheikh Ali Abu Khamsin	Mrs. M. Rimell	R. Linley
1984	Dawn Run	Mrs. C. Hill	P. Mullins	J.J. O'Neill
1985	See You Then	Stype Wood Stud Ltd.	N. Henderson	S. Smith Eccles
1986	See You Then	Stype Wood Stud Ltd.	N. Henderson	S. Smith Eccles
1987	See You Then	Stype Wood Stud Ltd.	N. Henderson	S. Smith Eccles
1988	Celtic Shot	D.E.H. Horton	F. Winter	P. Scudamore
1989	Beech Road	T. Geake	G. Balding	J. Frost
1990	Kribensis	Sheikh Mohammed	M. Stoute	R. Dunwoody

The Curragh's final climb up to the winning post tests a horse's stamina and as the field enters the final furlong, they know there is a lot of racing to come.

The stands at The Curragh loom large over the runners galloping down to the start.

THE CURRAGH

As Newmarket dominates the English turf, so The Curragh holds the ascendancy over Irish racing. And one can understand why. In a country that seems to have been created for the benefit of the horse, the plain of The Curragh in Kildare is greener than anywhere else in the Emerald Isle.

As legend has it, St Bridget was offered as much of The Curragh plain as she could cover with her cloak. Unfurling it from her shoulder, she threw the cloak out to cover the whole of the plain of Kildare. When she gathered it in from her new land, all that had been received was covered in the richest and deepest grass. What is certain is that horses have been raced on The Curragh since time immemorial.

Dating back to the pre-Christian era, the traditional Irish fair, or 'oenach', has long been an important part of life in the land. The most famous of these fairs was the one held at The Curragh of the Liffey, which was presided over by the King of Leinster or, in his absence, by one of his Princes. One would be hard pressed to find a more ideal setting for the racing of horses: the expanse of grassland stretching out into the distance invites a horse to gallop all day and it is only natural that the ancient kings and their lieges tested their skills and the merits of their steeds in such a place.

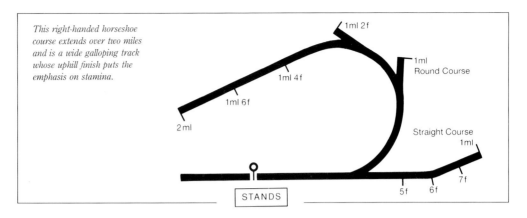

This right-handed horseshoe course extends over two miles and is a wide galloping track whose uphill finish puts the emphasis on stamina.

J. W. Snow pinx.ᵗ   W. B. Scott sculpt.

*First of the great Irish
champions was
Harkaway, who won
over twenty races in
his career and did
much to popularize
Flat racing in Ireland.*

Through the ages this tradition continued; in 1634 the Earl of Ormond matched
Lord Digby in a contest over four miles, a
battle that the Earl won. That first recorded
match suggests the development over the
intervening centuries, a growth that continued throughout the 17th century despite
the suppression of racing under the brutal
excesses of the Cromwellian regime, and
flourished openly under the rule of the
horse-loving Charles II. Whilst Newmarket
under the patronage of Old Rowley grew
into a centre of organized racing, the sport
practised at The Curragh remained very
rough and ready, and the efforts of the

various Lord Lieutenants to tame the contests were of no avail.

Royal Plate

Although a race called the Royal Plate was
instigated, its running was almost ne-
glected and the practice of individuals
matching horses against each other was
considered a much more suitable diversion.
The first race to be recorded at The Curragh
was run in 1741. It was won by Lord
Beesborough's Almazern.
    Shortly afterwards Irish Lass stamped
herself as the first champion of the course

by winning the Royal Plate in 1745 and 1747. She won further glory by beating the English raider Black and All Black in a match over the course in 1749. The event was seen very much as a grudge race between the two countries and a large Irish crowd gathered on the course to see their mare triumph.

By this time The Curragh had turned into the Newmarket of Ireland. The course was not only the racing centre but it had also grown into the training centre. Given that it was none too far from Dublin, this was understandable and slowly the course itself developed. Stands were added to make a day's racing more enjoyable; regular meetings were held and the King's Plate and the Royal Plate grew in importance to become goals for the best in the land.

All that was lacking was the organization, for Newmarket by then had its Jockey Club to order and oversee the proceedings, while the practices at The Curragh were still haphazard and not all the races were run in the Olympian spirit. That was remedied in 1790 when the Turf Club was formed.

Run very much along the same lines as the Jockey Club, albeit from a coffee room in Kildare rather than Suffolk, the Turf Club organized the publication of the Irish Racing Calendar and laid down rules governing the Stewarding of racing. In that first Calendar, The Curragh was allocated five meetings each year, two in April and one apiece in June, September and October.

Even given this rationalization, Irish racing was still very much the poor relation of the British turf and it was to take many more years before The Curragh could consider itself an equal of the top English courses. An attempt by the course in 1817 to copy the English Classics and run an O'Darby Stakes and an Irish Oaks proved to be a failure.

Royal visit

It was the visit of King George IV to The Curragh in 1821 that provided the next real fillip to the course's fortunes. A special stand and banqueting room were built to cater for his legendary love of the life.

All must have passed off well, for on his departure the king presented the course with a gold whip which was to be run for every year. This race, known naturally as The Royal Whip, has survived in a modified form and the present monarch of England, Queen Elizabeth, still puts up some of the prize money.

A greater effort was subsequently made to improve the quality of the horses racing at the course and this, together with the introduction of a better-planned calendar including such races as the Anglesey Stakes, the Peel Challenge Cup and the Northumberland Plate, soon paid dividends with the arrival of champions of the stature of Harkaway.

Harkaway

Harkaway's career got off to a slow start with just one success as a two-year-old, but in the following seasons he came to rule The Curragh with a dominance rarely seen since. Early wins were capped by a stirring success in the Northumberland Plate from the brilliant if erratic Birdcatcher.

Harkaway's record at The Curragh between his debut as a juvenile in the Anglesy Stakes in 1836 and his departure from Ireland in 1838, was 18 victories from 23 starts, with most of his wins requiring him to give pounds of weight away to his rivals.

Having conquered Ireland, he was taken across the water to challenge the best of the British in the hope that he could make more money for his owner.

Owned and trained by one of the first masters of the Irish Turf, Tom Ferguson,

As in England, Irish courses are dominated by the presence of the bookies. Here Peter Fitzsimmons is laying the odds on the '87 Irish Derby.

Above: *Tambourine II gradually gets the better of Arctic Storm as the pair draw clear of their field in the first Irish Sweeps Derby. The stands are a cauldron of noise as they cheer their hopes home.*

Opposite: *Runners make their way across the Sheep Graze in the Curragh's infield towards the Derby start, with the ruins of the castle standing proudly in the background.*

Harkaway's English career was chequered by his owner's desire to make money out of him. To say that all of his seven defeats from his 15 starts were due to being pulled is perhaps an exaggeration, but when Harkaway was allowed to win, he won in style, picking up two Goodwood Cups and a Chesterfield Cup when several Classic winners finished behind him.

That the best of the Irish horses were able to take on all-comers gave encouragement to the Turf Club who were still working hard to improve the quality of Irish racing. But it was not all one-way

traffic as they discovered when they inaugurated the first Irish Derby in 1866.

Despite being pushed as hard as possible by its founder Lord Drogheda, who ruled the Turf Club at the time, the race, run over a mile and three-quarters at The Curragh, attracted few entries. The first two runnings were won by an English owner, James Cockin, who specialized in bringing over good horses from England to clean up the better races at The Curragh.

His Selim was the first name on the victory roster in 1866 and was followed a year later by Golden Plover. Indeed such was Cockin's success in the Plates and big Stakes races that the Turf Club introduced a ruling that banned any horse from running in The Curragh's top races unless he or she had been trained in Ireland for the previous six months.

The distance of the Irish Derby was brought in line with the Epsom equivalent in 1872, but the race still failed to attract large fields. A scale of weights was introduced in 1874 to broaden its appeal, a move that was successful in attracting the interest of the public even if it ruined the Championship status of the event.

The growth of the sport

Public support was, however, what Irish racing needed and the new-look Irish Derby drew the crowds to The Curragh in such numbers that by the end of that decade, the race had become the biggest in Ireland. This, combined with the strength of the now flourishing breeding industry and the arrival of trainers of stature, readied Irish racing for the move into the 20th century.

Those trainers, all of whom were based around The Curragh, were Henry Linde, who worked out of the now famous Eyrefield Lodge, John Moore, F.F. McCabe, who sent out Orby to become the first Irish winner of the Epsom Derby, J.J. Parkinson and Michael Dawson.

None of them baulked at the idea of taking their charges abroad and race them against both the English and the French. Linde enjoyed notable triumphs at Aintree and Auteuil, but it was Orby's success, followed by that of his half-sister Rhodora in the following year's 1,000 Guineas that really made the English take notice.

Following an interval when the First World War and the Irish's own battle for independence overshadowed the battles on the turf, The Curragh returned stronger than ever in the 1920s when it completed its stranglehold on the Irish Classics. All five are run at the course, with the Irish Derby and Oaks being joined by the Irish St Leger in 1915, the Irish 2,000 Guineas in 1921 and the Irish 1,000 Guineas the following year.

This stranglehold ensured The Curragh's continued domination over two new courses, Leopardstown and Phoenix Park, which had sprung up on the outskirts of Dublin at the end of the previous century and which threatened to eclipse for a brief

The stands are packed as the runners for the first Irish Sweeps Derby in 1962 are paraded before the race.

period their older brother.

But the strength of the local trainers and the sense of tradition, which ensured the Turf Club gave the new Classics to The Curragh, looked as if they were misplaced in the inter-war years, when nothing seemed to go right for the course.

The best of the Irish-bred horses found their way to England, only to return to The Curragh to snatch the Irish Derby away from the Irish trainers. The introduction of

AIRLIE/COOLMORE IRISH 2,000 GUINEAS

1 mile. Three-year-old colts and fillies. First run 1921.

Year	Winner	Owner	Trainer	Jockey
1970	Decies	N.B. Hunt	B. van Cutsem	L. Piggott
1971	Kings Company	B.R. Firestone	G.W. Robinson	F. Head
1972	Ballymore	Mrs. J.R. Mullion	P.J. Prendergast	C. Roche
1973	Sharp Edge	J.J. Astor	W.R. Hern	J. Mercer
1974	Furry Glen	P.W. McGrath	S. McGrath	G. McGrath
1975	Grundy	C. Vittadini	P.T. Walwyn	P. Eddery
1976	Northern Treasure	A.D. Brennan	K. Prendergast	G. Curran
1977	Pampapaul	H. Paul	H.V. Murless	G. Dettori
1978	Jaazeiro	R.E. Sangster	M.V. O'Brien	L. Piggott
1979	Dickens Hill	Mrs. J.P. Binet	M.O'Toole	A. Murray
1980	Nikoli	Lord Iveagh	P.J. Prendergast	C. Roche
1981	Kings Lake	Mrs. J.P. Binet	M.V. O'Brien	P. Eddery
1982	Dara Monarch	Mrs. L. Browne	L. Browne	M.J. Kinane
1983	Wassl	A. Al-Maktoum	J. Dunlop	A. Murray
1984	Sadler's Wells	R.E. Sangster	M.V. O'Brien	G. McGrath
1985	Triptych	A. Clore	D.V. O'Brien	C. Roche
1986	Flash of Steel	B. Firestone	D.K. Weld	M.J. Kinane
1987	Don't Forget Me	J. Horgan	R. Hannon	W. Carson
1988	Prince of Birds	R.E. Sangster	M.V. O'Brien	D. Gillespie
1989	Shaadi	Sheikh Mohammed	M. Stoute	W.R. Swinburn

a betting tax drove away the crowds and the fall in attendance was later compounded by the depression of the 1930s.

The one bright light in these years was the success of J.T.Rogers, an Englishman, who had moved to Ireland in the First World War and had been adopted by his new country. He trained Museum, the first winner of the Irish Triple Crown in 1935, and added to that, the two fillies' Classics with Smokeless. As this was one of the few local triumphs of the decade, Rogers was hailed throughout the country.

It has only been since the war that both Irish racing and The Curragh have managed to face the world with equanimity. The Irish Classics were made level-weight-condition races in 1945 to restore true Championship status to them and a huge boost in prize money encouraged owners and breeders, especially the Aga Khan who had first started breeding horses in Ireland after the First World War.

Irish Sweeps Derby

In the post-war years The Curragh has become a rival to any racecourse in the world. The sponsoring of the Irish Derby by the Irish Hospitals Sweepstakes, a feat organized by Joe McGrath, made the race at The Curragh more valuable than Epsom's Derby.

The first running of the new Irish Sweeps Derby in 1962 achieved everything that McGrath could have dreamed when he first set about organizing the sponsorship.

Larkspur, who had been trained by Vincent O'Brien to win at Epsom, and the top French colt Tambourine II were drawn to the course by the big prize on offer, as were a large crowd including all the prominent figures of the European racing world.

In a thrilling race, Tambourine II just held off the challenge of the Irish-trained Arctic Storm to win by a short head and take the Derby to France, but leaving The Curragh with all the prestige. Guinness weighed in with a similar sponsorship deal for the Irish Oaks the following year and the practice has firmly taken hold.

The Irish Derby sponsorship was taken over in 1986 by Budweiser, whose funds again made the race the most valuable Classic in Europe. The first winner of the Budweiser Irish Derby was Shahrastani, who had taken the Epsom equivalent earlier that month. The following year's running of the race was marred by a bomb scare. But thankfully Irish racing, which embraces both North and South, has for the most part escaped the horrors of the civil war. There are many who believe that the infamous kidnap of Shergar was engineered by the IRA, but that will never be known for certain.

At first sight The Curragh enchants one with its multiple tracks and inner and outer circuits, circling back behind the stands and into the green horizon. But the various ways of running the same distance prevent the turf deteriorating through overuse. Recent improvements to facilities have helped shore up a course which was in danger of slipping behind its lesser brethren. But whatever the quality of the amenities, The Curragh leads the way in Irish racing and from its first Flat meeting in March through to November's close of campaign, the courses stage not only some of the best racing in Ireland, but also some of the finest in Europe.

BUDWEISER IRISH DERBY

1½ miles. Three-year-old colts and fillies. First run 1866.

Year	Winner	Owner	Trainer	Jockey
1971	Irish Ball	E. Littler	P. Laillié	A. Gibert
1972	Steel Pulse	R.N. Tikkoo	A. Breasley	W. Williamson
1973	Weavers' Hall	S. McGrath	S. McGrath	G. McGrath
1974	English Prince	Mrs. V. Hue-Williams	P.T. Walwyn	Y. Saint-Martin
1975	Grundy	C. Vittadini	P.T. Walwyn	P. Eddery
1976	Malacate	Mrs. M.F. Berger	F. Boutin	P. Paquet
1977	The Minstrel	R.E. Sangster	M.V. O'Brien	L. Piggott
1978	Shirley Heights	Lord Halifax	J.L. Dunlop	G. Starkey
1979	Troy	Sir M. Sobell	W.R. Hern	W. Carson
1980	Tyrnavos	G.L. Cambanis	B. Hobbs	A. Murray
1981	Shergar	H.H. Aga Khan	M. Stoute	L. Piggott
1982	Assert	R.E. Sangster	D.V. O'Brien	C. Roche
1983	Shareef Dancer	M. Al-Maktoum	M. Stoute	W.R. Swinburn
1984	El Gran Senor	R.E. Sangster	M.V. O'Brien	P. Eddery
1985	Law Society	S. Niarchos	M.V. O'Brien	P. Eddery
1986	Shahrastani	H.H. Aga Khan	M. Stoute	W.R. Swinburn
1987	Sir Harry Lewis	H. Kaskel	B.W. Hills	J. Reid
1988	Kahyasi	H.H. Aga Khan	L. Cumani	R. Cochrane
1989	Old Vic	Sheikh Mohammed	H. Cecil	S. Cauthen

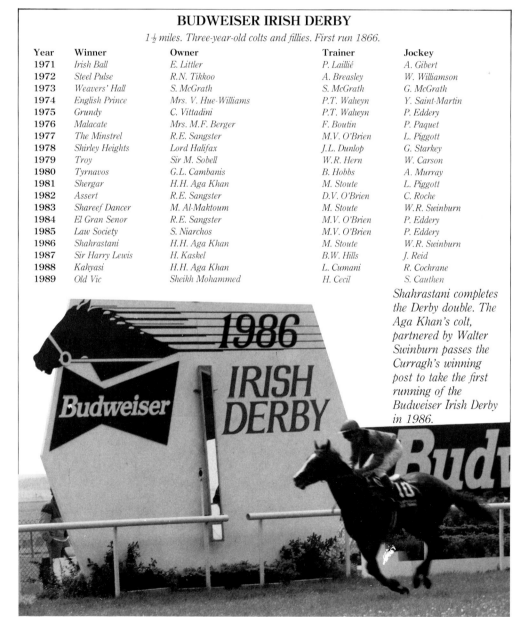

Shahrastani completes the Derby double. The Aga Khan's colt, partnered by Walter Swinburn passes the Curragh's winning post to take the first running of the Budweiser Irish Derby in 1986.

When Dublin decided that it needed a top-class racecourse for its citizens, Leopardstown was built by Captain George Quinn. Completed in 1888, Leopardstown was modelled on Sandown racecourse, which had been such a success in England.

But the very first meeting nearly proved its undoing. The opening of the course was hyped up by the organizers to such an extent that chaos ensued when an enormous crowd turned up. Racecards ran out and the restaurant facilities could not even begin to cope with the demand.

However, Leopardstown survived those early teething problems to stage the Leopardstown Grand Prize, the richest race in Ireland at the time but one that has subsequently fallen by the wayside, and to play host to the then Duke and Duchess of York in 1897.

The course reached its highest profile at the beginning of this century and although it cannot now match the racing at either The Curragh or Phoenix Park on the Flat, it is still Ireland's leading mixed course.

Staging five group races on the Flat, of which the richest is the Derrinstown Stud Derby Trial in May, Leopardstown has at times in recent years had to struggle to draw quality Flat horses to its contests, but has more than made up for that by the improvements in its winter calendar.

The Christmas meeting regularly attracts English raiders, with four days of competitive chasing and hurdling of which

LEOPARDSTOWN

Left: *Though Leopardstown's Flat racing is less distinguished than its jumps, it does not lack for competitiveness.*

Below: *The beautiful Wicklow hills dominate Leopardstown's stands adding to the attraction of the Dublin course.*

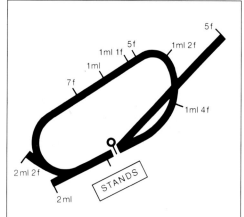

Left-handed circuit of one and three quarter miles with a straight five furlong course bisecting the oval.

The inner chase course has eight obstacles and is a fair test of jumping ability.

the most important races are the Black and White Champion Chase and the Sean Graham Memorial Hurdle. The Ladbroke Hurdle, formerly the Irish Sweeps Hurdle, and the Irish Champion Hurdle, both of which are held in January, whilst the newly founded Vincent O'Brien Irish Gold Cup, one of the richest prizes in chasing, are the other feature events.

Like Sandown, the viewing facilities on this left-handed course are excellent. The superb reconstruction programme that was completed in 1971 has brought the facilities up to a standard that is the equal of anywhere else in Ireland.

Home of the Irish Grand National since its inception in 1870, Fairyhouse began life as the home of the Ward Union Hunt races in 1851. As these were held across natural country, racing proper cannot be said to have begun there until a decade later.

Twelve miles north-west of Dublin, Fairyhouse has watched over its prize possession with great care and nurtured it into a race, which, while it can never rival its Aintree equivalent, outstrips both the Welsh and Scottish namesakes.

Run over three and a half miles round Fairyhouse's right-handed track, the Irish National attracts the best of the Irish chasers and a fair number of English hopefuls, and has seen some epic battles. Ascetic's Silver and Rhyme'N'Reason are the only two horses to have completed the Aintree–Fairyhouse double, but other memorable winners include the great Arkle

in 1964, Brown Lad who chalked up three successes in the race between 1975 and 1978, and Prince Regent, who carried pounds of weight to one win and two seconds back in the 1930s.

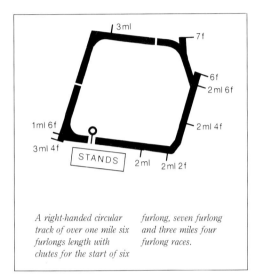

A right-handed circular track of over one mile six furlongs length with chutes for the start of six furlong, seven furlong and three miles four furlong races.

Fairyhouse is not overused as a track and unlike many of the Irish courses does not play host to much Flat racing, although one or two mixed cards are run in September as Fairyhouse shakes off the summer's break. Apart from the three-day Grand National meeting in late March or early April, when other races of importance are the Power Gold Cup, and the Jameson Gold Cup Hurdle, Fairyhouse's major races are the Black and White Handicap Hurdle on December's Saturday card, and the G.V. Malcolmson Memorial Chase at the beginning of January.

Despite the lack of racing, the course always attracts good crowds, who, as one would expect in Ireland, appreciate their racing and are not afraid to go for their bets. A right-handed circuit of nearly two miles in circumference, with minor undulations, Fairyhouse is a good, fair galloping track that tests a horse without being unduly harsh.

FAIRYHOUSE

Fairyhouse's new Jameson Whiskey Stand, opened for the 1989 running of the Irish Grand National, which is sponsored by Jameson.

*More blue-blooded
horses start their
career at Phoenix Park
than at any other
course in Ireland, so a
trip to the Park's
paddock is essential.*

PHOENIX PARK

Phoenix Park, another parvenu to the Irish Turf, has made such an advance in the last 30 years that the Dublin course is now second only to The Curragh in importance. As was the case with Leopardstown, the Park was modelled on a successful English racecourse – in this case Hurst Park, which has since disappeared from the list of British racecourses.

Although the site had previously been used for 'flapping' races – races run outside the jurisdiction of the Turf Club – Phoenix Park was very much the creation of John Peard, the first manager of the course, who supervised the lay-out and framed the races. Initially the course staged Flat racing only, a policy that only The Curragh had maintained, in the face of the love of the Irish for the jumping game, but nowadays some jumps meetings are held here.

Phoenix Park immediately made its mark on juvenile races, a sphere in which its influence has since grown and grown. The first major two-year-old race was the Phoenix Plate, worth 1,500 sovereigns to the winner, and which soon became the most important juvenile race in Ireland. That

prize money is dwarfed by the riches now offered by the course to the winners of the Heinz '57 Phoenix Stakes and the Goffs Cartier Million, two of the richest races run in Europe, but it shows the importance placed by the course on the development of the horse.

The smart set

Phoenix Park was visited by King Edward VII on his state visits to Ireland in 1903 and

Two of the greats of Irish and British racing: Vincent O'Brien, champion trainer, and Lester Piggott, champion jockey, whose partnership in the Seventies proved so successful.

Phoenix Park stages both right-handed and left-handed races. Races of up to six furlongs are run straight across the diagonal, while the home straight of five furlongs is a wide and flat stretch.

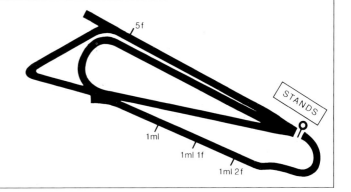

Right: *The field comes out of the back straight at Phoenix Park which basks in its full summer glory.*

Left: *Corwyn Bay, with Stephen Craine aboard, gets up to beat his rivals in the first running of the Cartier Million at Phoenix Park in 1988. Miss Demure and French Pretender fight it out for the minor honours.*

1904. His presence meant that the course quickly became popular with Dublin's smart set, who regarded a day at the Park's races as very much the fashionable thing to do. This incensed the country's racing purists, but delighted the other Dubliners who left the city for the nearby racecourse, and the social status of the racecourse has remained high ever since.

It is in the recent past that Phoenix Park has made such strides. Under that public relations genius Jonathan Irwin, the course, well funded by the Racing Board and other Irish racing luminaries, has come into its own.

A succession of high-profile developments, has led to Phoenix Park becoming the talk of all Europe. There is a continual stream of high-class animals making their way to the course and the standard of the maidens at the course often puts Group races to shame.

Phoenix Park prevents The Curragh from holding a complete monopoly on Irish Group 1 races by hosting two major races. The first is the Phoenix Stakes, which, under the sponsorship of Heinz, has become one of the top juvenile races in the country, whilst the other is the Phoenix Champion Stakes, which, since its first running in 1984, has quickly taken its place as one of Europe's leading ten-furlong prizes and fits very neatly into the calendar of top races.

The Million

A more interesting and even more recent development is the Goffs Cartier Million, the brainchild of Jonathan Irwin. Picking up on an idea born in Brisbane, Australia, Irwin has framed a race just for those horses sold at the Goffs Million Sale the previous autumn, and for which the prize money is a staggering one million Irish punts. The first running of the race in October 1988 attracted not only an impres-

PHOENIX CHAMPION STAKES

1¼ miles. Three-year-olds and up. First run 1984.

Year	Winner	Owner	Trainer	Jockey
1984	Sadler's Wells	R.E. Sangster	M.V. O'Brien	P. Eddery
1985	Commanche Run	I. Allan	L. Cumani	L. Piggott
1986	Park Express	P.H. Burns	J.S. Bolger	J. Reid
1987	Triptych	A. Clore	P-L. Biancone	A. Cruz
1988	Indian Skimmer	Sheikh Mohammed	H. Cecil	M. Roberts
1989	Carroll House	A. Balzarini	M. Jarvis	M.J. Kinane

offered fresh ways to enjoy his leisure time, is of paramount importance to every course. New races must be framed, the best horses must be attracted to the course, new days must be used, and in all these respects Phoenix Park is doing its best.

Sunday racing

Sunday racing was introduced to the course in 1987, and has proved to be a huge success, with big crowds drawn to the afternoon featuring the Heinz Phoenix Stakes, whilst the introduction of the Goffs Cartier Million looks as if it will attract more people into both ownership and attendance. But beneath all the blurb and the specials, the day-to-day management and racing must continue to service the industry as a whole.

Few courses in Ireland offer its spectators a service to rival The Park's and it is particularly commendable that the course is always seeking to attract newcomers to the sport. For though Ireland has gone into history as a great racing country and one of the foremost breeding centres in the world, it is still a small land and to be able to maintain one of its premier industries, the racing side of that industry has to continue to thrive.

The course itself is both left-handed and right-handed. An elongated oval which is bisected by a straight six-furlong course, the majority of the races are run right-handed, but the eleven-furlong course sends the field going the reverse way round the oval. The quality of the turf has been improved considerably in recent years, and the going is rarely too unfriendly. This, combined with the fairness of the track with its long five-furlong straight, gives a horse every opportunity to find its stride and balance.

That the stock of Phoenix Park is still on the upgrade is certain, and that the course deserves such growth is also true, but there has been a drop in the quality of the horses running in Ireland. The biggest favour the course could do to Irish racing is to ensure that racing here remains competitive and that the years when British-trained horses looted all the major prizes, as is the case at present, soon become a shameful memory.

HEINZ 57 PHOENIX STAKES

6 furlongs (5f to 1982). Two-year-olds.

Year	Winner	Owner	Trainer	Jockey
1971	Celtic Twilight	S. McGrath	S. McGrath	G. McGrath
1972	Marble Arch	N.B. Hunt	T.G. Curtin	T.P. Burns
1973	Noble Mark	Dr. J. Torsney	S. Quirke	D. Hogan
1974	Lady Seymour	E. Loder	P.J. Prendergast	C. Roche
1975	National Wish	Dr. J. Masterson	H.V.S. Murless	J. Corr
1976	Cloonlara	J.A. Mulcahy	M.V. O'Brien	T. Murphy
1977	Perla	Sir T. Antico	J. Oxx	R. Carroll
1978	Kilijaro	N. Robinson	D.K. Weld	W. Swinburn
1979	Smokey Lady	Mrs. W.F. Davison	D.K. Weld	W. Swinburn
1980	Swan Princess	M. Brand	B. Swift	M.L. Thomas
1981	Achieved	R.E. Sangster	M.V. O'Brien	P. Eddery
1982	Sweet Emma	Mrs. J. Ward Ramos	K. Prendergast	G. Curran
1983	King Persian	S. McAleer	L. Browne	M.J. Kinane
1984	Aviance	R.E. Sangster	D.V. O'Brien	D. Gillespie
1985	Roaring Riva	W. Gaff	D.R. Laing	R. Cochrane
1986	Minstrella	E.P. Evans	C. Nelson	J. Reid
1987	Digamist	K. Abdullah	J. Tree	P. Eddery
1988	Superpower	Mrs. P.L. Yong	W.A. O'Gorman	W.R. Swinburn
1989	Pharoah's Delight	Al-Deera Bloodstock	J.P. Hudson	R. Cochrane

sive field, but also numerous members of the racing world curious to see whether this idea would take off.

A closely fought contest was won by Corwyn Bay, who at a stroke won more prize money than any European-trained two-year-old had ever approached. This satisfied Irwin, even if the attendance at Phoenix Park that day did not. Enough press publicity was generated to keep the sponsors and the racecourse quiet and the race has spawned an equivalent race for fillies which will be run for the first time in 1990.

The course also attracts the best of the mighty Vincent O'Brien's juveniles and the master of Ballydoyle rates the course to be as fair as any in Ireland on which to introduce his youngsters and school them in the arts of racing. That itself, given O'Brien's stature in the Emerald Isle, is a healthy recommendation for the course and one that has been taken up by many a trainer, so the maidens at Phoenix Park are as competitive as many of the more valuable prizes.

With the secondment of John Sanderson, who enjoyed such success as Clerk of the Course at York in England, to help bolster the disappointing crowds, Phoenix Park keeps a healthy eye on its future success. The racing world is becoming increasingly cut-throat and the necessity of continuing to attract the spectator, who is forever being

Above: *The sea in the background, the sand in the foreground and the horses racing. Laytown's strand racing is now the only one of its kind left in Europe.*

Right: *The finish is marked out by flimsy railings and a wall of people. But the temporary arrangements do not detract from the spectacle.*

Left: *As the runners gallop down towards the start the crowd move to take up their positions at the finish.*

Right: *Of course any race meeting needs the bookies and they too come down to the sands for the Laytown summer meeting.*

LAYTOWN

The racing at Laytown is unique in Europe: there is no course, no railings, indeed the only permanent building is the concrete lavatory. And it is only in the three hours or so before racing starts that Laytown begins to look anything like a racecourse. That is because it is the only survivor of the once numerous strand courses around the coast of Ireland. Once a year, at a time dictated by the tides, Laytown welcomes the country's top jockeys and trainers for an afternoon or evening of seaside fun.

This is no donkey derby either. The faces that you see as you parade up and down the beach are those that you would find at any of Ireland's more prestigious courses. The jockeys' silks will be as familiar, if a little damper, as ever and the jockeys are the best that the country can offer.

So what if a horse leaves the track to take both himself and his hapless partner for an unauthorized swim, or if the punts that you win are covered in sand? That is all part of life's rich tapestry and one that is worth experiencing. For racing is not just a million pound industry that requires the elite to strike their poses in the most elegant surroundings, it is also about the fun of the relationship between man and steed and nowhere is that more evident than at Laytown.

Racing on Laytown's beaches has been an annual event for over a hundred years. According to the locals, the first races were organized by the parish priest before his bishop took a dim view of this spiritual guidance of his flock. But the idea had taken hold at this stretch of shoreline 40 miles north of Dublin, and and the practice was continued by the Delaney family.

A track is marked out on the sand with poles, then harrowed and finally raced on. The preparations for the spectators are much grander, with lines of marquees flowering on the sand, bookmakers staking their pitches, bars and cockle sellers plying their wares and enough people to make a carnival atmosphere.

With any distance up to two miles being possible, the races are varied in both nature and running, with puddles and flotsam and jetsam to be avoided, but there is never any shortage of runners, and whilst they may not be of Classic standard, all the top stables in Ireland like to be represented in what is as much a celebration of the roots of racing as a serious fixture.

Up to 10,000 turn up for the one-day carnival and disport themselves around the beach. But given everyone's desire to be in at the business end of the race, the jockeys can find themselves riding their finish into a veritable wall of people, and it is astonishing that no one is ever hurt. Be that as it may, Laytown races will continue to be run under the watchful eye of the Irish authorities and will continue to give fun to thousands for as long as the tides wash along the coast of Ireland.

GALWAY

As well as beach races, Ireland specializes in the country festivals, which have their roots in the old horse fairs. Of these, Galway is perhaps the most celebrated and the week-long meeting which the west coast course stages at the end of July is further evidence of the roots of the whole sport.

As with the similar fairs of Killarney and Tralee, racing is but part of the entertainment that Galway provides. Tourists, who have but little interest in the horses, will come to Galway to enjoy the atmosphere of the mystical West of Ireland; there, when Festival comes, life is one of horse trading, horse racing and the partying that is the natural end to every one of the six days.

The Ballybrit course was opened in 1869, but the fair and the racing pre-dated such organization by many centuries. However, the local MP, Lord St Lawrence wanted to set up a proper show and laid out the course complete with 'a rattling double bank similar to the Punchestown bank', fly fences and a flat track. Stands were built to accommodate the expected crowd of tourists. Although the improvements were not universally popular with the locals, who saw no reason to change what had worked so well in the past, St Lawrence's designs were favourably received by those who were drawn to Galway by his advertising.

To be truthful, not much has changed since. The entrancing combination of the locals and trainers from the East of Ireland, those who know the score and those who have dropped in for the first time, jockey around the course, drinking in this marvellous occasion.

The big day of the festival is traditionally the Wednesday, when the Galway Plate is staged. This race, which has been in existence for as long as the course itself, is the most important chase to be staged during the Irish summer season, when the chasers have to take a back seat to their Flat brothers, and it consistently attracts a decent field.

The racing on all six days – the sixth has only been recently added – is full of excitement, a balanced mixture of both Flat and jumps. Galway will always prove popular with the crowds who still cross Ireland for this summer's fare.

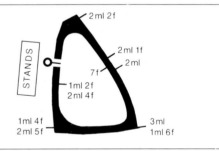

Sharp right-handed circuit of one and a quarter miles in circumference, which is used for both Flat and National Hunt racing.

Top: *The Festival attracts large crowds, many of whom come for the fun of the fair, but stay and enjoy the racing.*

Left: *The major event at Galway's July Festival is the Galway Plate. Down by the start the runners take a good look at the first fence.*

STANDS

1000m 1200m

Racing is conducted on both a turf and a wood-chip surface round Ovrevoll's left-handed circuit, whose three turns are used for a variety of distances.

OVREVOLL

Scandinavian racing suffers by having to live in the shadow of the local trotting industry, which is much more popular and thus much better endowed. However, Denmark, Sweden and Norway all stage some good Flat racing during the summer and always attract runners from the more established racing nations to some of their contests.

Although Ovrevoll, on the outskirts of Oslo, is not the most attractive of courses, which is disappointing given the natural beauty of both the country and the city, its racing is always competitive and enjoyable. Its strong ties with England are obvious when a glance down the racecard will reveal numerous ex-English horses and jockeys who have taken to performing across the North Sea. Ovrevoll stages one of the most important Scandinavian races in the Oslo Cup, whose annual running at the end of September tempts some of the better

English handicappers out to Norway for a shot at the rich prize.

Run on a surface of wood shavings which can confound those unfamiliar with the kick-back over a distance of a mile and a half, the Oslo Cup gives the locally trained

horses a chance to race against the best of Denmark and Sweden as well as runners from Germany, France and England.

The supporting card on Oslo Cup day includes a valuable sprint handicap, which has often proved to be much more to the locals' liking, given the relative strength of their sprinters, who often pick up decent races abroad during the season.

The Norwegian Grand National, whilst in no way threatening Aintree's race as a spectacle, is another good race that can more than hold its own on the Scandinavian circuit. Again international competition is welcomed by Ovrevoll, which is 'twinned' up with Stratford in England and promotes this association with the Stratford-upon-Avon Hurdle on the supporting card.

Racing at Ovrevoll way back when; the Norwegian course captured in its Thirties clothing.

The Czechoslovakian Pardabice is a hybrid of steeplechasing and cross-country. From the latter discipline, comes the Moat, seen above, which soaks both horse and rider.

PARDUBICE

If there is any spectacle in the racing world that can match Aintree's Grand National, it has to be Czechoslovakia's Pardubice, which stands in the middle ground between racing and cross-country riding. A fiercesome test for both man and horse, the race is run over a cross-country track of about four and a half miles with 30 obstacles to be traversed, including two formidable jumps: the daunting Taxis and a huge water jump called the Moat.

Pardubice itself is a small town some 90 miles east of the capital Prague in northern Moravia, the centre of the country's thoroughbred industry.

Every October some 50,000 Czechs will gather at different spots along the course and at the finish to admire the brave men from Czechoslovakia, Hungary, Russia and occasionally Western Europe, including England's Chris Collins who indeed won the race, trying to make their mark in this ordeal.

In nearly every year since the race was first run in 1874, there have been some dramatic incidents and most of these have occurred at the Taxis. This hedge-cum-ditch requires a horse to cover 7.31m (24 ft) in the air and was the scene of such a notorious pile-up in 1984 that the Poles, who had competed in every running, vowed that they would never come back.

The Czechs too have since insisted on all their runners taking part in qualifying races before being allowed to enter in the real thing and there are moves to lessen the dangers of the course. But the race itself is growing in popularity. The prize money is being boosted all the time in an effort to attract more runners from the West and the 100th running in 1990 is hoped to be a showpiece for the sport in Czechoslovakia.

Right: *The field gallops across country between obstacles and takes a well-earned respite from the fearsome tests to which they are subjected.*

Below: *The fearsome Taxis rivals even Becher's Brook as an obstacle. The prodigious leap required to negotiate the fence will often unbalance the horse on landing.*

ST MORITZ

Winter racing with a difference. The holiday resort of St Moritz boasts the novelty of racing on ice and snow. The quality may not make a Derby, but the spectacle is unique.

Though the racing in Switzerland could never aspire to greatness, and the quality of the thoroughbreds in the country is poor compared to her neighbours, the ice racing on the frozen lake at St Moritz always attracts plenty of interest.

The town awaits the deepest frost of the winter before opening up a tight six-furlong circuit around its lake. Runners from both the main Swiss training centres and from nearby countries are boxed up by intrepid trainers, who fancy a crack at the most unusual day's racing in the world.

As the horses are literally racing on a sheet of ice covered by a blanket of snow, they have to be specially shod. The run-of-the-mill aluminium racing plates would be worse than useless in these conditions, and a specially studded shoe is the best grip that the ingenious Swiss have found.

Even that can fail the runners, who race at good speeds round the tight track and many a Swiss franc has disappeared into a bookmaker's pocket on one or another corner as a fancied runner loses his grip.

When racing is scheduled, a wooden grandstand goes up for the local burghers. A couple of tents serve as changing rooms for the jockeys and the weighing in and out room. Bars are opened, stalls set up and a

crowd of winter sportsmen, who have abandoned their skis for the afternoon, congregate.

The racing itself is a sight to behold. Set against an imposing backdrop of the Alps, the horses and jockeys in their silks stand out in brilliant contrast to their surroundings. And that is how the day should be remembered: as a spectacle rather than as a test of the thoroughbred.

Below: *The perfect marriage, ski racing at St Moritz combines the winter sports for which the town has become famous and its own special horse racing.*

Right: *Remarkably even hurdle races are held on St Moritz's frozen lake.*

BADEN-BADEN

Baden-Baden is by far the most popular racecourse in Germany. Nestled between the Rhine, that source of all German romance, and the Black Forest, the spa town has been a host to horses and their followers since the first meeting in 1858. This was run under the aegis of the French Société Sportive d'Encouragement, because the German Jockey Club, then based in Berlin, did not take the place seriously.

As with many other courses, the reason for the building of the racecourse was to provide an adjunct to the town's major attraction, the Casino. The franchise for the latter was held by a Frenchman, Edouard Benazet, who decided that his guests needed some innocent entertainment during the daylight hours before the Casino's evening diversions began.

Although the racing was successful, it fell victim to international politics. The Franco-Prussian war of 1870–71 concerned precisely that part of the world – the Alsace–Lorraine–Bavarian border – and racing was discontinued until that particular dispute had been settled. The outcome naturally meant that the French authorities could not easily continue running the track, so the Internationaler Club was born and that body still organizes the racing.

Baden-Baden hosts two festivals, the long-established Autumn meeting, and the more recent Spring meeting. Although it has been the success of the more international Autumn meeting that has brought

Left: *Baden-Baden glistens in the late summer sun and the Rhine-side course is surrounded by greenery that makes it so attractive.*

Right: *The old-fashioned charm of Baden-Baden with its packed stands and top-quality racing makes it Germany's most prestigious course.*

the track to worldwide prominence, the late May/early June meeting is making rapid progress and looks like sharing in the success of its older brother.

The spring meeting

In six days of racing stretched over two weekends, the big races of the meeting are the Badener Meile on the opening Sunday and the Grosser Preis der Badischen Wirtschaft (German race names are rarely known for their brevity). Sandwiched in between are an important Deutsche Derby trial for local horses only, and two valuable Listed races, one for sprinters, the other for stayers, that both draw horses from abroad.

The charm of the course is often best appreciated at this less busy meeting. The racecourse is situated some eight miles west from the centre of the town near the village of Iffezheim. Behind the course lie the rolling Rhenish vineyards, which are clothed in their first leaves, whilst the daunting splendour of the Black Forest lies in front, once more fresh with new life.

The course has often been compared to Deauville. Of course there is no sea and no sands, but the same relaxed holiday atmosphere prevails. One is not just there to race, but also to enjoy the antiquity of the course and the buildings.

Gerald Bocksai punches the air in triumph as the great German champion Acatenango gets up to beat Moon Madness and Winwood (on the rails) in the 1987 Grosser Preis Von Baden.

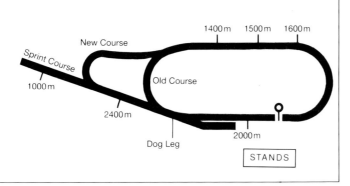

Left-handed track of 2000 metres in circumference with a three furlong straight. The six furlong sprint course has a dog-leg at halfway.

The course opens early in the morning and as you have breakfast in the stands, you can view the horses being exercised on the course, surely the best way for a racing man to come to grips with the early hours.

When racing returns in late August, the grapes have ripened and the Rhine flows in its full summer glory. The racing too is that much richer, with a six-day feast of top-class racing awaiting those who make the trip to the spa town.

The major race of both the meeting and

GROSSER PREIS VON BADEN
2,400m. Three-year-olds and up.

Year	Winner	Owner	Trainer	Jockey
1971	Cortez	Gestüt Zoppenbroich	S. von Mitzlaff	O. Langner
1972	Caracol	Gestüt Fahrhof	S. von Mitzlaff	O. Langner
1973	Athenagoras	Gestüt Zoppenbroich	S. von Mitzlaff	H. Remmert
1974	Marduk	Countess M. Batthyany	H. Bollow	P. Remmert
1975	Marduk	Countess M. Batthyany	H. Bollow	P. Remmert
1976	Sharper	A. van Kaick	A. Hecker	W. Carson
1977	Windwurf	Gestüt Ravensberg	H. Gummelt	G. Lewis
1978	Valour	G. Ward	R.F.J. Houghton	J. Reid
1979	M-Lolshan	E. Alkhalifa	R. Price	B. Taylor
1980	Nebos	Countess M. Batthyany	H. Bollow	L. Mader
1981	Pelerin	Sir P. Oppenheimer	H. Wragg	G. Starkey
1982	Glint of Gold	P. Mellon	I. Balding	P. Eddery
1983	Diamond Shoal	P. Mellon	I. Balding	S. Cauthen
1984	Strawberry Road	R. Stehr	J. Nicholls	B. Thomson
1985	Gold and Ivory	P. Mellon	I. Balding	S. Cauthen
1986	Acatenango	Gestüt Fahrhof	H. Jentzsch	G. Bocskai
1987	Acatenango	Gestüt Fahrhof	H. Jentzsch	G. Bocskai
1988	Carroll House	A. Balzarini	M. Jarvis	B. Raymond
1989	Mondrian	Stall Hanse	U. Stoltefoss	K. Woodburn

the season is the Grosser Preis von Baden on the closing Sunday. With a history going back to the 19th century, the race has long been a major feature on the international calendar.

International competition

French, Italian and British champions figure on the roll of past winners, as well as many of Germany's great champions. The race is certainly one of the most important international events in the country. Indeed in the 1980s, only the two great German champions Nebos and Acatenango, together with the wonderful Strawberry Road, have prevented a British clean sweep.

Ian Balding has been particularly successful, winning the race three times.

Perhaps the most remarkable triumph happened in 1984 when the Australian filly, Strawberry Road, came out on top. The filly, who had been stabled in France, had her prep race in the Oettingen-Rennen, in which she came second. But by post time for the big race, she was fully acclimatized to Northern conditions and proceeded to demolish a quality field. Although she never again scaled those heights in Europe, her win will always be prized by the Internationaler Club for showing just how wide an audience the festival can reach.

As all the Group races at the meeting are now open to all-comers, it is not unusual to

The world-famous colours of Paul Mellon are seen at the head of affairs as the field turn out of the home straight.

find horses from ten or more nations stabled at the course during the meeting. The Golden-Peitsche for the sprinters in particular is a cosmopolitan melting pot. The fastest horses in Scandinavia come down from the North; the French, Swiss and Italians travel across the continent, and a strong British raiding party makes sure that the Germans have a difficult task in keeping the prize within their own country.

The international flavour of the racing reflects the character of Baden-Baden. The style of the architecture in the town proper is Franco-Italian, whilst English is to be heard everywhere. The stock of the spa

town has risen considerably since the intrepid Monsieur Benazet began his adventure. Edward VII, when Prince of Wales, was a frequent visitor to the town, and to this day European notables are often in evidence.

The yearling sales

The day before the Grosser Preis sees Germany's one international yearling sale. Considering the huge prices paid elsewhere and the quality of the German bloodstock, the sales always seem to be a real bargain for those interested in stoutly bred horses.

But that strength in stamina makes for the weakness in the market. Too much stamina scares away commercial breeders and trainers who are looking for a sharper type of horse. That should not, however, deter would-be buyers who are at the meeting, because the stock of the German thoroughbred is definitely in the ascendancy now that traumas of the Second World War and the division of the nation have begun to fade.

Indeed those horrors seem far away when one takes one's place in the stands at Baden-Baden. The luxury of the viewing facilities, the quality of the restaurant and the pleasure of the racing combine to make a most enjoyable day.

The new stand, finished in 1978, provides spectators with every luxury they could expect on a racecourse and combined an excellent view of the racing. All in all there is little that one could fault about both the course and the welcome provided by the Bavarians, who flock to the course in greater numbers than to any other German racecourse.

The tight left-handed track is always in immaculate condition, it is fair - though the dog-leg in the straight, a furlong and a half out from the finish can cause some scrimmaging, and the extraordinary jumps course is a bonus. Wandering around both the inside and the outside of the Flat track in a figure of eight, the latter features a wonderful bank in the depths of the country. The best of the German jumpers are to be seen at both the May meeting, when the Bader-Preis, Germany's richest hurdle race, is run, and in September when the Altes-Badener-Jagdre, a premier steeplechase, is the feature race.

COLOGNE

Cologne has become the centre of the German racing world since the division of the country following the Second World War. The loss of the Berlin-Hoppegarten course and training centre set the nation's racing back many a year, as did the loss of a substantial part of the country's breeding stock. But those losses are being put right at Cologne, which is helping to re-establish German racing on the European circuit.

Home of the Direktorium fur Vollblutzucht und Rennen, the German racing authority, which combines the functions of a Jockey Club, Levy Board and Racecourse Association, Cologne is also the centre for the country's great training establishments.

Cologne has the honour of staging the country's richest race, the Puma-Europa-Preis. Since the first running in 1963, the

race has fallen to Germany, Russia, with their champion Anilin who won the race three times, France and England. The course's second big race is the Mehl-Mulhens-Rennen, the German equivalent of the 2,000 Guineas, which gives Cologne a taste of the Classics. But all of the 23 days racing at Cologne are of a high standard.

Within the last 15 years, substantial improvements have been made to both the course and facilities. The final bend of the flat right-handed track, which had proved troublesome on soft going, has been rebuilt with a slight camber, whilst the old stands, that had not offered too much in the way of comfort, have been refurbished to a far higher standard.

Below right: The river Rhine lazes through the background behind Cologne's racecourse.

Central to the major training stables it is one of Germany's most used courses.

Left: The runners leave the paddock at Cologne.

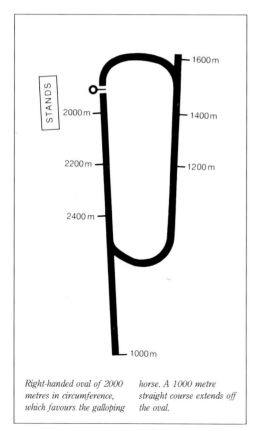

Right-handed oval of 2000 metres in circumference, which favours the galloping horse. A 1000 metre straight course extends off the oval.

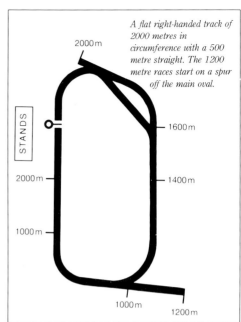

A flat right-handed track of 2000 metres in circumference with a 500 metre straight. The 1200 metre races start on a spur off the main oval.

HAMBURG

Not the most delightful of the German racecourses, Hamburg stages only one meeting each year. But those seven days of racing include the Deutsches Derby.

Hamburg has only succeeded in keeping the Deutsches Derby through its industrial wealth, for the race has been run in a town which has no trainers, no horses and, the late June/early July meeting apart, no racing since 1869.

With a lucrative sponsorship deal from Holsten Pils, the Deutsches Derby, which, like the other German Classics is closed to foreign-bred horses, is still the prize that all good three-year-olds are aimed at. It also captures the imagination of the German public and attracts a greater volume of betting than any other race in the country and for that reason alone, can claim pride of place in the German calendar.

The course itself needs a good deal of work before it can claim a stature equal to its chief attraction. Poor crowds on all days other than the Derby, depressing stands and amenities do sway the casual visitor.

The soil is not well drained, which, allied to the local climate, makes for heavy going. However, the current president of the racecourse, Franz-Gunther von Gaertner, is working hard to improve both the track and the facilities in the hope that Hamburg will

Above left: *Hamburg's big day each year is Deutsches Derby day. The runners for the 1972 event, won by Athenagoras, parade in front of the stands.*

Left: *Hamburg has come in for its fair share of criticism, but the course can provide some splendid contests.*

be able to rival Baden-Baden and Cologne.

Outside the Deutsches Derby, which is run on the final Sunday of the meeting, Hamburg stages two other Group races, which are open to foreign horses and which do draw an international field. The Grosser Hansa-Preis on the opening Sunday is always a competitive race, which, despite being recently downgraded, throws up

some useful winners, whilst the new Sprinter-Preis looks like establishing itself as an important European sprint.

Just five miles outside one of Germany's biggest, and certainly its richest cities, Hamburg should be able to offer more than it does and it is to be hoped that the current policies will bear fruit and reward the executive for their hard work.

CAPANNELLE

Arguably Federico Tesio's finest hour, leading in Nearco after the colt's superb victory in the 1938 Derby Italiano. The colt went on to the Grand Prix de Paris and was unbeaten in 14 races.

Capannelle, home of the Italian Derby, is the larger of Italy's two principal racecourses. This suburban course to the south-west of Rome has flourished as the home of the Jockey Club Italiano since 1881.

Since Rome had just been made the capital of Italy, it was only natural Capannelle was picked to be the stage over which the Derby Reale, Italy's premier race, was to be enacted. That, allied to the presence of the Jockey Club, has proved sufficient to attract several other of the country's top races.

Racing in Italy was at that time a poor relation to the major powers of France and Britain. It is solely due to the work of one great man, Federico Tesio, that Italy climbed into the international bracket in the 1920s and 1930s and following his demise in 1954, the quality of horses racing in Italy has again declined.

Although Tesio had his stud at the Razza Dormello on the shores of Lake Maggiore in Lombardy, and trained at the second of Italy's great tracks, San Siro, the overall impact of the man on the country's racing was such that Capannelle and the Derby Italiano were both brought into the international limelight by his genius.

Tesio's triumphs

Tesio's record at Capannelle included a staggering 22 Derby Italiano wins, 13 Premio Parioli, the Italian 2,000 Guineas, and 18 Premio Regina Elena, their 1,000 Guineas. His runner in any of the three Italian Classics to be run at Capannelle was regarded as the one to be beaten throughout the 40 years when Il Mago, the Wizard, was at the height of his powers.

Not surprisingly, the first winner of the Derby Italiano to go onto international glory was one of Tesio's horses, Apelle, who, though not the first of his to race abroad, subsequently won the 1928 Coronation Cup and the Sandown Anniversary Cup in England.

In the 1930s two great horses rose to

fame through their Derby Italiano successes. Dontello II, winner in 1937, was unbeaten in Italy, but had little luck in running when beaten in that year's Grand Prix de Paris. The legendary Nearco, successful the following year, was unbeaten in all his 14 starts, winning the Premio Parioli at Capannelle before his Derby triumph and succeeding where Donatello II had failed with a victory in the Grand Prix de Paris, after which he was retired to stud in Newmarket.

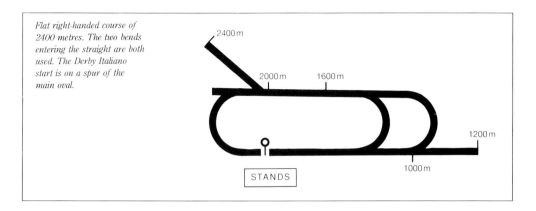

Flat right-handed course of 2400 metres. The two bends entering the straight are both used. The Derby Italiano start is on a spur of the main oval.

Nearco

That Derby Italino triumph of Nearco had to be seen to be believed. The colt had looked the complete horse on his debut at San Siro the previous July, and he had gone from strength to strength with every race. On his arrival at Capannelle for that race in May 1938, he was hailed as the greatest of the Tesio stable to date.

He did not belie that reputation in the race. He made all the running to win in a canter, but it was the power and the grace in that hollow victory that won the accolades. The rest of the field appeared to be running through treacle as Nearco left them in his wake and, after a mile, the colt had such a tremendous lead that his jockey, Gubellini, gave him a pull to stop him wasting his energy.

Quite simply, the animal was awesome. Nearco's influence on the thoroughbred is such that he is regarded as perhaps the most significant stallion of the 20th century. His influence on the breed is still felt today through the success of his male line, with champion sires like Northern Dancer and his dynasty, Mill Reef and Seattle Slew all tracing their pedigree back to the Italian champion.

The crowds who flocked to Rome racecourse and the general interest in the sport grew to an unequalled peak in those years leading up to the Second World War.

But the war took its toll. When the Italian government surrendered in 1943, racing in Rome, which had temporarily become separated from the Milanese training centre, came to a virtual halt during the Allied occupation. The Derby Italiano was run at Milan, where racing continued almost as normal under the German authorities.

Post-war decline

When the reunification of the country came in 1945, the Italian Jockey Club, who had been left out of the Milan scene, resumed their place as the controlling body. But the damage had been done.

Despite Tesio's continued success, racing failed to regain its former popularity, and the years following his death were marked by the decline of the Italian thoroughbred, though the successes of Ribot and Molvedo both at home and abroad prolonged the Tesio tradition into the 1960s. It was a lack of investment in bloodstock that led to the gradual deterioration and as the quality of locally bred and trained horses slipped, more and more prizes started to go abroad.

This in turn led to a protectionist policy being introduced by the Jockey Club. The leading races were all closed to foreign-trained horses and the stock of the Derby Italiano and other leading races at the course fell.

However, top international jockeys continued to travel to Italy to ride in the Classics and Lester Piggott, as could be predicted, chalked up three Derbys. That

Opposite: *Tisserand (far side) holds off the late challenge of Carroll House to become only the second Italian-bred winner of the Derby Italiano since the race was opened up to all-comers in 1981.*

Jockeys in Capannelle's glass tunnel which takes them from the weighing room into the paddock.

policy was reversed in 1981 and the deterioration in the protectionist quality was highlighted by the success of English-trained colts in the first two open runnings. And even those Italian horses who have won this decade have been bred abroad.

The prize money at the Capannelle is enormous, easily big enough to draw top horses from all over Europe to compete for their races. English trainers like John Dunlop and Ian Balding have become familiar names at the Capannelle for both the Classics and races like the Premio Presidente della Republica, whose history is even older than the Derby, going back to 1878.

The course has the equine stars and the trainers but it lacks real atmosphere that other top courses can produce. The crowds are not large – only 10,000 odd will turn up on Derby day – and are almost silent during the proceedings unless a hot favourite get beaten. The anemities are a combination of the very modern and the dilapidated, and improvements would be welcomed.

A flat right-handed circuit with a four-furlong run-in, Capannelle is a good galloping circuit that is only used during the spring and the autumn, for the scorching heat of the Roman summer makes racing impossible. The course is always liberally watered to prevent the going becoming too firm, and the use of the sprinkler often produces soft going even when the sun is shining.

DERBY ITALIANO
2,400m. Three-year-old colts and fillies.

Year	Winner	Owner	Trainer	Jockey
1971	Ardale	C. Vittadini	M. Benetti	G. Dettori
1972	Gay Lussac	Scuderia Cieffedi	S. Cumani	S. Fancera
1973	Cerreto	Scuderia Alpina	S. Cumani	L. Piggott
1974	Suffolk	Scuderia Aurora	E. Camici	M. Cipolloni
1975	Orange Bay	C. Vittadini	M. Benetti	B. Taylor
1976	Red Arrow	Scuderia Diamante	A. Pandolfi	W. Carson
1977	Sirlad	Razza la Tesa	G. Benetti	A. di Nardo
1978	Elgay	Razza Ascagnano	F. Boutin	G. Doleuze
1979	Marracci	Razza Dormello-Olgiata	F. Boutin	M. Depalmas
1980	Garrido	Razza Dormello-Olgiata	F. Boutin	M. Depalmas
1981	Glint of Gold	P. Mellon	I. Balding	J. Matthias
1982	Old Country	Mrs. O. Abegg	L. Cumani	P. Eddery
1983	My Top	Scuderia Siba	A. Botti	P. Perlanti
1984	Welnor	Scuderia Concarena	G. Benetti	L. Piggott
1985	Don Orazio	Lady M. Stable	F. Jovine	M. Jerome
1986	Tommy Way	Scuderia Erasec	J. Dunlop	W. Carson
1987	Zaizoom	F. Salman	P. Cole	T. Quinn
1988	Tisserand	Az. Ag. All. La Madia	M. Vincis	V. Mezzatesta
1989	Prosutori	A. Balzarini	M.A. Jarvis	M. Roberts
1990	Prosutori	A. Balzarini	M.A. Jarvis	M. Roberts

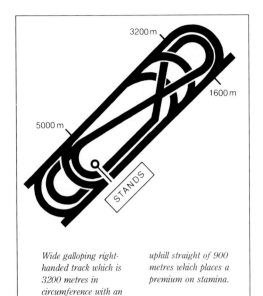

3200 m

1600 m

5000 m

STANDS

Wide galloping right-handed track which is 3200 metres in circumference with an *uphill straight of 900 metres which places a premium on stamina.*

SAN SIRO

I f Capannelle takes pride of place in the Italian calendar for the stranglehold it has on the country's Classics, San Siro plays a much more significant role in the country's day-to-day racing. It is at San Siro that the future champions take their first tentative steps on a racecourse, and it is at San Siro that the true Italian racing aficionado spends his afternoons.

Since Milan only joined forces with the Romans and others in 1861 on the creation of the kingdom of Italy, the racing that took place in the city before that date could hardly be called official.

It took the formation of the Italian Jockey Club in 1881, for the Milanese authorities to organize the city's racing. A strict calendar, to encompass both San Siro and Capannelle, was introduced to build a structure within which the Italian Classics and other Championship races took place.

The old San Siro course was founded in 1889, with races such as the Premio del

Left: *San Siro's stands are packed for the 1980 running of the Oaks d'Italia, which is now the course's sole Classic.*

Above: *Federico Tesio, known as Il Maggio, leading in his Donatello after the colt's triumph in the 1937 Gran Premio di Milano.*

Nearco and Ribot

It was the natural development of the Tesio bloodlines which had only been in operation for 20 odd years at the time of the San Siro changes that led to the subsequent arrival of champions of the stature of Nearco and Ribot. For even by the time these changes in the calendar were made, Tesio was known to the Italian racing world as a masterful trainer and breeder.

The realignment was prompted as much by the general manager of the course, Mario Locatelli, who contributed greatly to making the standard of racing at San Siro between the wars so high, as by the Jockey Club. Both Locatelli and Tesio realized that it was only by such changes that Italian racing would continue to improve.

Tesio had his rivals at San Siro, but never equals. The de Montel stable came closest to matching 'Il Mago', and the 1920s and 1930s saw rival gangs at San Siro, one supporting the Tesio red-on-white colours, the other favouring de Montel's black. The Tesio fans were the more excitable, greeting each and every success with tremendous enthusiasm, whilst de Montel's supporters were drawn from the establishment, and rather looked down on the rowdy opposition.

The whole atmosphere of San Siro was built on these contrasts and rivalries. The triumphs of de Montel's giants Ortello and Orsenigo, winners of the Premio del Jockey Club, the great filly Erba, whose duels with Tesio's Delleana dominated the 1928 season, and Ortona, had to balanced against Tesio's victories at San Siro in the 1920s with Scopas, Crananch and Neroccia.

That rivalry died out with the war, but while it existed, San Siro was the most exciting course in the world to visit. The feud, although always friendly, produced an atmosphere that is still evident in Milan and is in complete contrast to the staid proceedings in Rome, where raised passions are rare.

San Siro's programme begins each spring in March, but really comes to life with the Derby and Oaks trials, the Premio Emanuele Filiberto and Premio Baggio, before the course stages its only remaining Classic the Oaks d'Italia, in late May.

Commercio and the Premio Chiusura as the standard-bearers of the quality races. Quality was not at a premium and the racing had a very provincial air to it.

San Siro was, however, completely revamped in 1920 to put the course on to a more international footing. It was redesigned to make it a tougher test for the thoroughbred and the training facilities at San Siro were improved to help the locals reach the top of the European ladder.

The rise to prominence was helped by the involvement with the course of Federico Tesio, whose stable was north of the city but who trained his stars at San Siro. It is debatable whether it was the punishingly tough calendar introduced at the time that helped Tesio to produce the champions he did, but it is more likely that the structuring of the races had little effect other than to introduce more great races to the country.

GRAN PREMIO DI MILANO

2,400m. (since 1974). Three-year-olds and up, colts and fillies.

Year	Winner	Owner	Trainer	Jockey
1971	Weimar	Scuderia Aurora	E. Camici	S. Atzori
1972	Beau Charmer	G. Weisweiller	J.C. Cunnington	F. Head
1973	Garvin	Scuderia Fedelglas	A. Pandolfi	V. Panici
1974	Orsa Maggiore	Scuderia Metauro	U. Pandolfi	G. Dettori
1975	Star Appeal	W. Zeitelhack	W. Zeitelhack	G. Starkey
1976	Rouge Sang	D. Wildenstein	A. Penna	Y. Saint-Martin
1977	Sirlad½	Razza la Tesa	G. Benetti	A. di Nardo
1978	Stuyvesant	Gestüt Schlenderhan	H. Jentzsch	B. Taylor
1979	Sortingo	Z. Yoshida	G. Benetti	S. Atzori
1980	Marracci	Razza Dormello Olgiata	F. Boutin	M. Depalmas
1981	Lydian	Ecurie Aland	Mme C. Head	M. Depalmas
1982	Terreno	G.A. Oldham	F. Boutin	C. Asmussen
1983	Diamond Shoal	P. Mellon	I. Balding	S. Cauthen
1984	Esprit du Nord	R.F. Scully	J. Fellows	G.W. Moore
1985	Shulich	Razza la Tesa	U. Pandolfi	S. Dettori
1986	Tommy Way	Scuderia Erasec	J. Dunlop	W. Carson
1987	Tony Bin	All. White Star	L. Camici	M. Jerome
1988	Tony Bin	All. White Star	L. Camici	P. Eddery
1989	Alwuhush	H. Al-Maktoum	J. Dunlop	W. Carson

The Gran Premio

June's Gran Premio di Milano, formerly the Premio del Commercio, is San Siro's most prestigious race of the season. Although for years it was run over 15 furlongs, the distance was reduced to 12 furlongs in 1972 to reflect the change in emphasis from stamina to speed.

Despite this switch being greeted with considerable hostility, it has now been recognized as inevitable and a move that has strengthened the Italian calendar. A similar fate befell that other great staying race of the European calendar, the Grand Prix de Paris in 1987, and the day of the distance race seems to have gone.

After the Gran Premio, San Siro takes a midsummer break until September for an autumn campaign in which Milan rather than Rome stages the major contests: the Gran Premio d'Italia, the Gran Premio del Jockey Club and the Gran Criterium. The loss of the St Leger Italiano to neighbouring Turin in 1988 has taken away the course's second Classic, but the race has lost so much prestige recently that the departure was not widely mourned and the standard of racing has not been unduly affected.

The drop in the quality of the Italian thoroughbred during the 1960s and 1970s affected San Siro as much as any other course. The number of home-bred horses fell as did the number of horses in training.

The course has, however, worked hard at recovering its lost prestige in the years since 1981 when the races were reopened. The course executive now welcomes the challenge of the foreigners, even if it does mean that the cups, the glory and the lira leave the country. That bold approach seems to be working as an increasing number of the major and rich races run at San Siro stay at home, thanks to the new crop of Italian wizards like Alduino Botti.

GRAN PREMIO DEL JOCKEY CLUB E COPPA D'ORO

2,400m. Three-year-olds and up, colts and fillies.

Year	Winner	Owner	Trainer	Jockey
1971	Weimar	Scuderia Aurora	E. Camici	S. Atzori
1972	Tierceron	Razza Dormello Olgiata	Marchesa Incisa	M. Andreucci
1973	Sang Bleu½	C. del Duca	R. Pelat	J. Taillard
1974	Authi	J. Wertheimer	A. Head	F. Head
1975	Laomedonte	Scuderia Cièffedi	S. Cumani	G. Dettori
1976	Infra Green	J. Pochna	E. Bartholomew	G. Doleuze
1977	Stateff	Scuderia Lady 'M'	D. Tettamanzi	S. Atori
1978	Stone	A. Palvis	L. Turner	G. Doleuze
1979	Scorpio	G. Oldham	F. Boutin	M. Depalmas
1980	Pawiment	Gestüt Moritzberg	C. Seiffert	O. Gervai
1981	Konigsstuhl	Gestüt Zoppenbroich	S. von Mitzlaff	P. Alafi
1982	Friendswood	N.B. Hunt	L. Turner	M. Jerome
1983	Awaasif	Sheikh Mohammed	J. Dunlop	L. Piggott
1984	Gold and Ivory	P. Mellon	I. Balding	S. Cauthen
1985	St. Hilarion	A. Christodolou	G. Harwood	G. Starkey
1986	Antheus	J. Wertheimer	Mme C. Head	G.W. Moore
1987	Tony Bin	All. White Star	L. Camici	C. Asmussen
1988	Roakarad	Sc. Gabriella	E. Camici	J. Heloury
1989	Assatis	K. Abdulla	G. Harwood	G. Baxter

Above: *The field turn out of the home straight in the 1987 Gran Premio di Milano, which was won by Italy's greatest performer of recent years, Tony Bin.*

Right: *San Siro's long broad straight favours the galloping horse, which is reflected by the quality of horses that are stabled and raced at Milan.*

The course itself is a tough right-handed circuit. The long turns and the straight that seems to go on forever search out any suspect stamina. The facilities are that much better than those at Capannelle, and with its lively atmosphere San Siro is always the more exciting of the two courses to visit.

Longchamp is the jewel in the crown of French racing and the jewel of Longchamp is the Prix de l'Arc de Triomphe which in its 60-year history has come to dominate the European racing calendar.

Traditionally run on the first Sunday in October, the Arc is now accepted as the official all-aged middle distance championship of Europe. The Derby winners, the older champions and the other pretenders line up for Longchamp's exacting 12-furlong trip to try to find out who will go down in history as the best of that year.

Longchamp, however, offers much more to its racing public than just the Arc. Throughout its spring and autumn seasons, the best of the French horses compete for some of the richest prizes in the European calendar and have to try to repel the numerous foreign invaders who are lured to the course in search of the Franc.

Although a younger course than Chantilly, Longchamp's longer seasons soon enabled the course to take the top slot from the home of the Prix du Jockey Club. The rise was helped by the poor quality of the turf at the other Parisian racecourse, the Champs de Mars, where the Eiffel Tower now stands. The State, which ran the racing at the Champs de Mars, recognized that their course was not ideal and agreed to let Longchamp stage the autumn meeting that it had previously held on the Champs de Mars.

The Société Sportive d'Encouragement, the governing body of French racing, gave its blessing to the construction of a racecourse in the Bois du Boulogne, a large park just to the west of Paris in 1854. Lacking the funds to finish the grandstand, the Société had to borrow money from its own members to complete its ambitious project.

Gladiateur and the Grand Prix

Longchamp was fortunate enough to inherit one of France's oldest and most prestigious races from the former course. The Grand Prix began life in 1806 and by the 1850s had become the top Parisian prize. The name was changed to the Prix Gladiateur in 1869 to honour the first French-bred winner of the Epsom Derby. With this race in its grasp, Longchamp was always going to be a success.

The first meeting was held on 27 April 1857. The Emperor Napoleon who came by boat, the then traditional way of reaching

The right-handed ovals of Longchamp have three separate turns, the outermost of which gives the course a circumference of one mile six furlongs. A straight five furlong course runs parallel to the home straight on the far side of the course.

Action at Longchamp. The slow pace at which races are run in France often results in a blanket finish.

LONGCHAMP

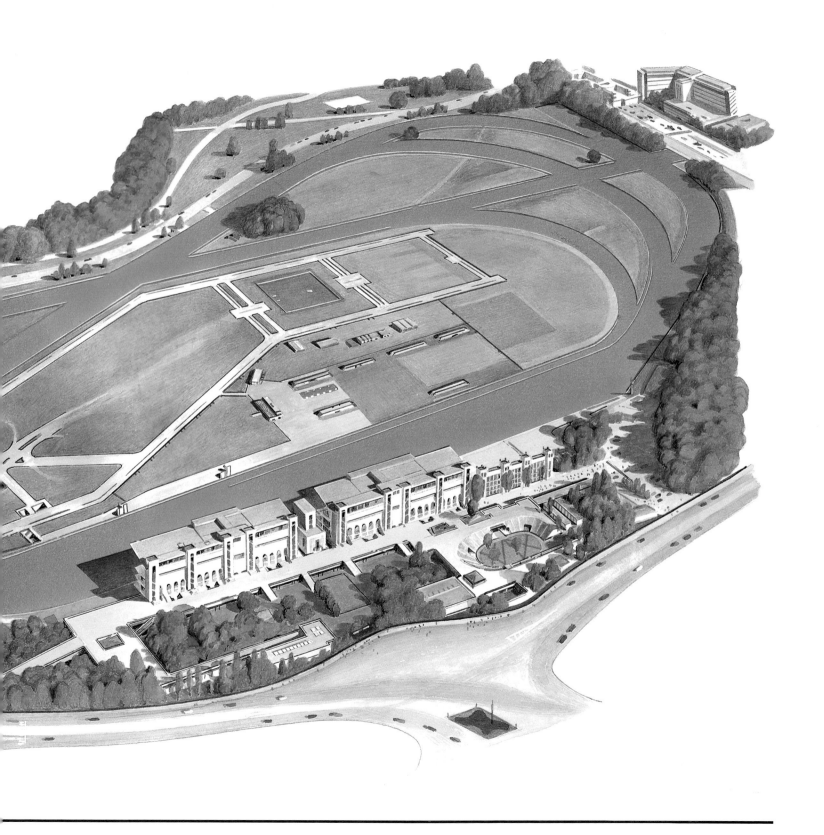

Gladiateur scores his greatest French triumph in the 1865 Grand Prix. The colt, nicknamed 'The Avenger of Waterloo' had earlier become the first foreign-bred winner of the Derby.

the course, was amongst the crowd of almost 10,000. Five races were held, the second of which was won by Miss Gladiateur who later became famous as the dam of the great Gladiateur.

Six years later the Grand Prix de Paris, the first of the great Longchamp races, was inaugurated. For many years the race was one of the highlights of the Parisian social calendar and the grand procession of carriages from the centre of Paris out to the Bois du Boulogne excited almost as much interest as the race itself.

Zola, in his novel *Nanou*, gives his own typically naturalistic interpretation of the scenes. The great and the good were admitted to the 'pavilion', whilst their mistresses and lackeys sat in their carriages 'unnoticed' by their betters.

Of the early winners of the Grand Prix de Paris, which should not be confused with Grand Prix, none was more famous than the great Gladiateur. A French-bred colt who had been sent to Newmarket to be trained by Tom Jennings, he won the 1865 2,000 Guineas on his first outing as a three-year-old before going on to win the Derby.

Immediately after his Epsom success

Gladiateur made his first appearance in his native France, and a crowd of 150,000 watched the 'avenger of Waterloo' win the Grand Prix with the greatest of ease. He went on to win three more races in England, including the St Leger, to become only the second horse to win a Triple Crown, before returning to take the French St Leger.

Gladiateur won three more races at Longchamp as a four-year-old, including the four-mile Grand Prix de l'Empereur on his final start and was undoubtedly the first great hero of the French turf, although it is arguable that his greater successes, amongst them a 40-length victory in the 1866 Ascot Gold Cup, were all achieved in England.

The Pari-Mutuel

In the year of Gladiateur's Grand Prix success, another Frenchman made a significant impression on French racing. Pierre Oller invented the Pari-Mutuel system of betting which is the only one used in France. Basically it is a pool system, in which the total money wagered is divided by the number of winning tickets and the dividends paid accordingly. The course or the governing body takes a cut from the total pool, which is then reinvested in the racecourse or the available prize money and so all the proceeds stay in racing.

This has long been the main form of betting in France, the United States and the majority of other racing countries, England and Ireland excepted. It has ensured that the French prize money is the highest on offer anywhere in Europe. Although the Tote operates a similar system in England, the continued popularity of the bookmakers, makes the amount of money gambled on the Tote miniscule in comparison to its French counterpart.

However, there are persistent grumbles about the slowness of the French system which seems to crack up when confronted by a crowd of any size. On a big day like the Arc when the English cross the Channel in large numbers, an afternoon's racing at Longchamp can be spent in one long queue after another, firstly to put a bet on, then to try to pick up one's winnings afterwards.

The Classics

As the shape of the Longchamp seasons took on a more complete form, so the other Classics were added. In 1883 the Prix d'Essai des Poulains and des Pouliches, the French equivalents of the 2,000 and 1,000 Guineas, were introduced to perform a similar role for the French Classic crop.

With the strength of both its spring season, built round those two Classics run in May and the Grand Prix always run in June, and the autumn season when the major events are the Prix Royal Oak, the Prix Gladiateur and the Prix de la Foret, firmly established, Longchamp packed in the crowds. At the turn of the century it was not uncommon to find over 100,000 at Longchamp on Grand Prix day and despite the troubles of the First World War, French racing continued to thrive in the 1920s.

In 1920 the Société held the inaugural running of the Prix de l'Arc de Triomphe. The plan was to hold a race of comparable status to the Grand Prix in the middle of the autumn season that would attract the best of all Europe to Longchamp for an end-of-season championship.

Marcel Boussac was one of the great French owners of this century, whose French Classic triumphs spanned over fifty years from Ramus' Jockey Club success in 1922 to Acamas' win in that same race in 1978.

CIGA PRIX DE L'ARC DE TRIOMPHE
2,400m. Three-year-olds and up, colts and fillies.

Year	Winner	Owner	Trainer	Jockey
1971	Mill Reef	P. Mellon	I.A. Balding	G. Lewis
1972	San San	Comtesse M. Batthyany	A. Penna	F. Head
1973	Rheingold	H.R.K. Zeisel	B.W. Hills	L. Piggott
1974	Allez France	D. Wildenstein	A. Penna	Y. Saint-Martin
1975	Star Appeal	W. Zeitelhack	T. Grieper	G. Starkey
1976	Ivanjica	J. Wertheimer	A. Head	F. Head
1977	Alleged	R. Sangster	M.V. O'Brien	L. Piggott
1978	Alleged	R. Sangster	M.V. O'Brien	L. Piggott
1979	Three Troikas	Mrs. A. Head	Mme C. Head	F. Head
1980	Detroit	R. Sangster	O. Douieb	P. Eddery
1981	Gold River	J. Wertheimer	A. Head	G.W. Moore
1982	Akiyda	H.H. Aga Khan	F. Mathet	Y. Saint-Martin
1983	All Along	D. Wildenstein	P.L. Biancone	W.R. Swinburn
1984	Sagace	D. Wildenstein	P.L. Biancone	Y. Saint-Martin
1985	Rainbow Quest	K. Abdullah	A.J. Tree	P. Eddery
1986	Dancing Brave	K. Abdullah	G. Harwood	P. Eddery
1987	Trempolino	P. de Moussac	A. Fabre	P. Eddery
1988	Tony Bin	All. White Star	L. Camici	J. Reid
1989	Carroll House	A. Balzarini	M. Jarvis	M.J. Kinane

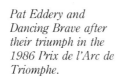

Pat Eddery and Dancing Brave after their triumph in the 1986 Prix de l'Arc de Triomphe.

The first Arc

The idea worked like a dream. The first running saw horses from both Italy and England competing against the best of the French and the result proved to be a wonderful international combination. Evremond de Saint-Alary, one of France's leading owner/breeders of the time, won the race with Comrade, who was trained in England by Peter Gilpin and ridden by the Australian jockey Frank Bullock.

The prize which had tempted all the horses to Longchamp was a staggering 172,425 old francs. The success of the race continued with home victories intermingled with another success for England and Ortello's triumph for Italy in 1929, but for one reason or another the race failed to attract international interest in the 1930s and became a largely home-grown affair.

The Second World War caused its own interruptions and the race was abandoned for two years before being run twice outside Paris at Le Tremblay. But after the war the race once again became the focal point of Europe's autumn. England gained their third success in the fourth post-war running when the Aga Khan's Migoli beat the home hope Nirgal.

Tantieme, reckoned by some to have been the best French horse ever, won the race twice – in 1950 when he also won the Poule d'Essai des Poulains and in 1951– but

Three Longchamp Champions. Akiyda after her triumph in the 1982 Arc; her jockey Yves Saint-Martin, the finest French jockey; and her owner His Highness the Aga Khan, whose CIGA hotels now sponsors the race.

the honour of the best ever Arc winner must lie between three great colts: Ribot, the unbeaten Italian colt, who won the race in 1955 and 1956; the astonishing Sea Bird, who left his field for dead in 1965; and Dancing Brave, who won so brilliantly in the 1986 race.

New look

In recent years the Arc's success has so far outstripped that of the Grand Prix that the old favourite of Paris became a second-class race which could not attract any of the best of the Classic crop.

In 1986 the Société Sportive d'Encouragement decided to alter the conditions of the race to restore it to its former glory. The best horses were no longer being bred to stay the two-mile trip and the move to cut it to ten furlongs has been a success even

though many people in the racing industry deplored the change.

In its three subsequent runnings, both the size of the field and its quality have grown and the race looks like once more becoming a spectacle that can thrill the whole of Paris, despite the fact that the 'whole of Paris' now only numbers 10,000 rather than 100,000.

Regardless of the diminishing crowds at Longchamp, the standard of the facilities remains high. The original stands were completely rebuilt in 1903, and since then there have been continual improvements to the viewing facilities. In 1962 a fantastic new stand was built all around the old rococo one, which was demolished once the new stand had been completed in an architectural operation of outstanding complexity.

The course itself is a right-hand oval

Pat Eddery on Detroit passes Argument and Ela-Mana-Mou to win the 1980 Arc. The Irishman's record of four Arc successes is only matched by that of Yves Saint-Martin.

Like father, like daughter, Alec Head was a leading trainer in France from the mid-Fifties until 1984, since when his daughter Criquette has taken over the reins.

with three separate tracks, the largest of which allows races of 11 furlongs to be run on one circuit of the course. The straight five-furlong course bisects the oval on the far side of the course, which means that viewing of the sprints is particularly difficult.

Otherwise the races are relatively simple to read if one is armed with the knowledge of which track is going to be used. The two finishing posts in the straight have been known to confuse some foreign jockeys and the course is one on which past experience is a great help.

Yves Saint-Martin

Yves Saint-Martin who ruled the French jockeys' roster for 20 odd years between 1962 and 1987, was a master at Longchamp and a great favourite with the crowd. His record of four Arcs, 12 Guineas and four

DUBAI POULE D'ESSAI DES POULAINS

1,600m. Three-year-old colts.

Year	Winner	Owner	Trainer	Jockey
1970	Caro	Comtesse M. Batthyany	A. Klimscha	W. Williamson
1971	Zug	W.R. Hawn	J. Cunnington	J.C. Desaint
1972	Riverman	Mrs. P. Wertheimer	A. Head	J.C. Desaint
1973	Kalamoun	H.H. Aga Khan	F. Mathet	H. Samani
1974	Moulines	J. Kashiyama	R. Carver	M. Philipperon
1975	Green Dancer	J. Wertheimer	A. Head	F. Head
1976	Red Lord	J. Wertheimer	A. Head	F. Head
1977	Blushing Groom	H.H. Aga Khan	F. Mathet	H. Samani
1978	Nishapour	H.H. Aga Khan	F. Mathet	H. Samani
1979	Irish River	Mrs. R. Ades	J. Cunnington, Jr.	M. Philipperon
1980	In Fijar	M. Fustok	M. Saliba	G. Doleuze
1981	Recitation	A.E. Bodie	G. Harwood	G. Starkey
1982	Melyno	S. Niarchos	F. Mathet	Y. Saint-Martin
1983	L'Emigrant	S. Niarchos	F. Boutin	C. Asmussen
1984	Siberian Express	M. Fustok	A. Fabre	A. Gibert
1985	No Pass No Sale	R.C. Strauss	R. Collet	Y. Saint-Martin
1986	Fast Topaze	M. Fustok	G. Mikhalides	C. Asmussen
1987	Soviet Star	Sheikh Mohammed	A. Fabre	G. Starkey
1988	Blushing John	A. Paulson	F. Boutin	F. Head
1989	Kendor	A. Bader	R. Touflan	M. Philipperon

DUBAI POULE D'ESSAI DES POULICHES

1,600m. Three-year-old fillies.

Year	Winner	Owner	Trainer	Jockey
1970	Pampered Miss	N.B. Hunt	J. Cunnington, Jr.	M. Philipperon
1971	Bold Fascinator	W.P. Rosso	W. Williamson	J. Fellows
1972	Mata Hari	Comtesse M. Batthyany	A. Penna	J. Cruguet
1973	Allez France	D. Wildenstein	A. Klimscha	Y. Saint-Martin
1974	Dumka	C. Bauer	J. de Chevigny	A. Lequeux
1975	Ivanjica	J. Wertheimer	A. Head	F. Head
1976	Riverqueen	Mrs. A. Head	C. Datessen	F. Head
1977	Madelia	D. Wildenstein	A. Penna	Y. Saint-Martin
1978	Dancing Maid	J. Wertheimer	A. Head	F. Head
1979	Three Troikas	Mrs. A. Head	Mrs. C. Head	F. Head
1980	Aryenne	D.G. Volkert	J. Fellows	M. Philipperon
1981	Ukraine Girl	Mrs. J.R. Mullion	R. Collet	P. Eddery
1982	River Lady	R.E. Sangster	F. Boutin	L. Piggott
1983	L'Attrayante	Mme. C. Thieriot	O. Douieb	A. Badel
1984	Masarika	H.H. Aga Khan	A. de Royer-Dupre	Y. Saint-Martin
1985	Silvermine	Mrs. A. Head	Mrs. C. Head	F. Head
1986	Baiser Vole	R.E. Sangster	Mrs. C. Head	G. Guignard
1987	Miesque	S. Niarchos	F. Boutin	F. Head
1988	Ravinella	Ecurie Aland	Mrs. C. Head	G.W. Moore
1989	Pearl Bracelet	Ecurie Fustok	R. Wojtowiez	A. Gibert

Grand Prixs compares favourably with that of Lester Piggott, the English maestro of the same era, and he is held in the same awe by the French press as Piggott was in England.

Longchamp holds a stranglehold on the Sunday (the major day of the week) racing in France from April through to the end of May, during which time it stages not only the first two French Classics, but also the major trials for the Prix du Jockey Club and Prix de Diane. After the Chantilly interlude at the beginning of June, Longchamp stages just one more Sunday meeting, that of the Grand Prix de Paris, before the midsummer break.

When the racing returns to the course in September, the eight-day meeting is of an even higher quality. Races like the Prix du Moulin du Longchamp, named after the famous windmill that stands within the course, the Prix Vermeille, the fillies' Arc, top juvenile races, like the Prix du Salamandre and the Grand Criterium, the Prix Royal Oak, the third French Classic to be run at Longchamp and the Prix de la Forêt will all attract foreign runners, but it is the newly formed Ciga weekend that is the highlight.

The Aga Khan

The Aga Khan, whose father and grandfather were both been major figures in European racing, decided to set up a French racing festival to rival the Breeders' Cup. His Ciga hotels group now sponsor two successive days' racing, built around the Arc, when ten Group races are run. The first running in 1988 was a huge success with runners from five countries being drawn by the wonderful prize money on offer.

The Sunday, Arc day, is still the more important of the two and the three Group I races on that day – the Arc itself, the Prix Marcel Boussac for two-year-old fillies and the Prix de l'Abbaye de Longchamp for the sprinters – are all championship races.

Considering the distance involved in travelling to America for the Breeders' Cup and the ever contentious issue of medication, which is permitted in America but banned in Europe, the Ciga weekend, allied to the Festival of British Racing at Ascot, looks assured of growing in stature and will soon rival its American counterpart. And that it is held at Longchamp is only fitting, given the course's standing as one of the leading European racecourses and one which has always seen racing of the highest quality.

MAISONS-LAFFITTE

Maisons-Laffitte began life as an offshoot of a property development. A French banker, Jacques Laffitte, decided that this was the way to attract people to a new development he was creating on the banks of the Seine to the west of Paris. Finished in 1887, Maisons-Laffitte was taken under the wing of the Société Sportive d'Encouragement, who initially rented the course, and then in 1895 bought it outright to promote it as the flagship of their racing empire.

The importance of the course lay in its straight ten-furlong track which exceeds even Newmarket in length. On that straight, major Classic trials have been held, and every April, all the English press and bookmakers come to Maisons-Laffitte to watch the Prix Djebel and the Prix Imprudence, the races in which the French candidates for the British Guineas are tested.

Like most Parisian courses, Maisons-Laffitte takes a midsummer break, but at its final July meeting, the course stages the Prix Robert Papin. This top-class two-year-old race, despite falling a little from its original high standards, has been won by many of the great French horses. In 1970 it was the scene of a tremendous encounter between My Swallow and Mill Reef.

The major races of the course's autumn

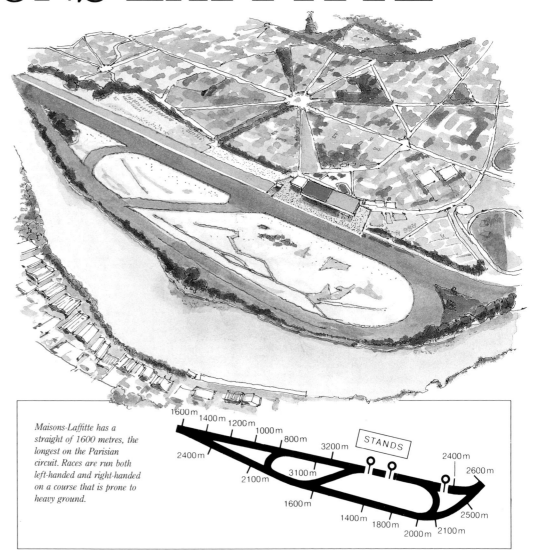

Maisons-Laffitte has a straight of 1600 metres, the longest on the Parisian circuit. Races are run both left-handed and right-handed on a course that is prone to heavy ground.

Maisons-Laffitte cannot compete with Longchamp, but the Seine-side course has the longest straight in France as well as an excellent restaurant.

season are La Coupe de Maisons-Laffitte and the Criterium de Maisons-Laffitte, two Group 2 races that pull in the spectators. Since Maisons-Laffitte is on the banks of the Seine, the course is prey to very heavy going, or even water-logging in early spring and late autumn, and meetings have occasionally to be switched from here to Saint-Cloud. In general, however, the course offers a very fair test of the horse, although the three separate finishing posts can sometimes fool an unwitting jockey into riding his finish too soon and then losing out come the correct post.

Evry is very much the newest of the courses on the Parisian circuit. Completed in 1972, the course was built to supersede the old Le Tremblay course, which was converted into a general sports complex in 1965. The governing body of racing at Le Tremblay, the Société de Sport de France, was forced to go elsewhere to stage their racing and elected to go to Evry.

This choice was somewhat controversial as the town, a large new development, is 20 miles south of Paris and a good 50 miles away from the major training centre, Chantilly. Many professionals were far from happy, but the planning and thought that went into the construction of the course has converted all the doubters and Evry now attracts bigger fields than any of the other Parisian courses.

All possible care was taken in the laying out of the course. Over 30 miles of drainage pipes were installed a metre under the ground to ensure good going and special soil was imported. There are three separate tracks built within the left-handed oval, and a straight course which runs diagonally across the course. Again attention was paid to the design of the course and Evry is reckoned to be one of the fairest galloping tracks in the country.

The grandstand has been brilliantly designed and executed, and the planners left open the option of increasing the viewing area if demand ever required such a measure. Facilities are of the highest standard and the whole course shows the potential of the modern racing world.

Allowing for its recent arrival on the scene and the brief held by the governing body – to promote apprentice and amateur races and juvenile events – it is not surprising that no great races are run at Evry. The Grand Prix de Evry is the course's big day, but the cards are always well-balanced and of interest, and the course has proved a successful addition to Parisian in particular, as well as French racing as a whole.

EVRY

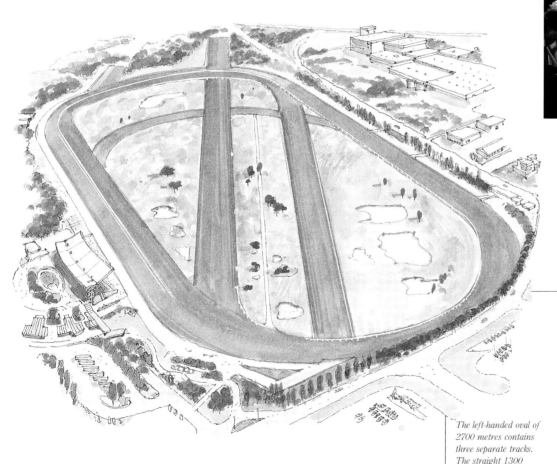

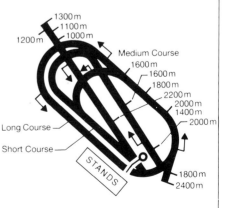

Above: *The eternal ritual before a race. Jockeys in Evry's weighing-in room take to the scales before they go out onto the course.*

The left-handed oval of 2700 metres contains three separate tracks. The straight 1300 metre course runs diagonally through the oval.

1300 m
1100 m
1200 m
1000 m

Medium Course
1600 m
1600 m
1800 m
2200 m
2000 m
1400 m
2000 m

Long Course

Short Course

STANDS

1800 m
2400 m

CHANTILLY

The Chateau provides a superb backdrop to Chantilly's finishing straight.

O n one's first visit to Chantilly's racecourse, one's eyes are immediately drawn to the magnificient château that stands opposite the stands. That grand folly, built by the Prince de Condé, is a symbol of what Chantilly is: a home to the French racehorse.

The slightly dotty Prince believed that he was to be reincarnated as a horse. He therefore built himself a stable in which he felt he would be kept in the manner to which he was accustomed. The château, called Les Grands Ecuries, is no more than a grand stable which can hold 250 horses.

Chantilly was picked by the members of the newly founded Société Sportive d'Encouragement as an ideal place to hold races and the first meeting was arranged for the 15 May 1834.

The publicity was dealt with by the mayor who said: 'The favourable season, the beauty of the landscape and the originality of the show should ensure that Chantilly on 15 May will be the rendezvous of all the rich farmers of the neighbourhood. The notables of the capital will also want to witness this important trial and we hope that some day Chantilly, like Epsom, will have its Derby, a race which will make all important foreigners aware of this most exceptional of French sites'.

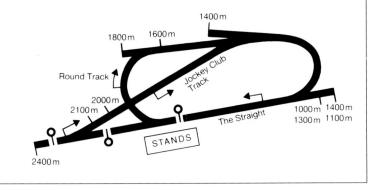

Chantilly's right-hand course is a good galloping track of 2600 metres in circumference. Races of up to 1400 metres can be held on the straight using the furthest of the three winning posts.

Prix du Jockey Club

The mayor proved to be a good tipster, for in 1836 the first running of the Prix du Jockey Club, the French Derby, was held at Chantilly. Seven years later the Prix du Diane, the French equivalent of the Oaks joined her older brother to make Chantilly the most important centre of racing in France.

Recognizing this fact, the Duc d'Orleans moved all his racehorses to Chantilly to be trained there by the Englishman George Edward. This move began a trend and by the middle of the 19th century, Chantilly had become the foremost training centre in the country, a position it still holds.

Indeed there are as many horses in training at Chantilly as there are at its British equivalent Newmarket. With strings of the quality of the late Francois Mathet, the Head family, Francois Boutin and the current leading light André Fabre, there is little wonder that the Chantilly gallops, notably La Piste des Aigles, are as well frequented by those looking for inside information as Newmarket's windswept Heath.

Chantilly has never allowed itself more than one month's racing a year. Like Epsom the course is not overused even though it happens to be a very fair, if exacting, test of the horse – something one could not say about Epsom.

The grand folly of Les Ecuries makes a magnificent backdrop to Chantilly's racing. The stables were built by Comte du Conde who believed that he would be reincarnated as a horse.

Criquette Head supervises her string in the Chantilly Forest. The town is France's largest training centre and the forest surrounding the Chateau and racecourse is criss-crossed with gallops.

June at Chantilly

Racing only comes to Chantilly for the month of June when, apart from the two Classics, the major races to be staged are the Prix du Chemin de Fer du Nord and the Prix Jonchere, and they are merely supporting races on the most important days.

The lack of racing on the course has often been a cause of complaint for the trainers, who have to box their horses to all the other Parisian tracks. There has recently been a proposal that the traditional Deauville August meeting be replaced with an extension of Chantilly's brief racing season, but it seems unlikely that the calendar will ever be changed.

There is little doubt, however, that Chantilly is one of the most delightful courses in the world to go racing at. On Jockey Club day, a spectacular feast of entertainment is laid on between the races, but a bigger crowd is present for the fillies' race, which has been sponsored recently by Hermes. The link with the Parisian fashion world has proved a popular one and the crowd outdo even Royal Ascot in their finery.

However, the size of the racecourse means that only a small crowd can ever gather to watch the races. Ten thousand is just about the maximum Chantilly can hold, but one always gets the feeling that one is amongst an exclusive crowd as one watches what could be the next Tourbillon, the first truly great Jockey Club winner, pass the post.

As French racing has been concentrated around one small area, so has the owner-

PRIX DU JOCKEY-CLUB LANCIA

2,400m. Three-year-old colts and fillies.

Year	Winner	Owner	Trainer	Jockey
1970	Sassafras	A. Plesch	F. Mathet	Y. Saint-Martin
1971	Rheffic	Mrs. F. Dupré	F. Mathet	W.B. Pyers
1972	Hard to Beat	J. Kashiyama	R. Carver	L. Piggott
1973	Roi Lear	Mrs. P. Wertheimer	A. Head	F. Head
1974	Caracolero	Mrs. M.F. Berger	F. Boutin	P. Paquet
1975	Val de l'Orne	J. Wertheimer	A. Head	F. Head
1976	Youth	N.B. Hunt	M. Zilber	F. Head
1977	Crystal Palace	Baron G. de Rothschild	F. Mathet	G. Dubroeucq
1978	Acamas	M. Boussac	G. Bonnaventure	Y. Saint-Martin
1979	Top Ville	H.H. Aga Khan	F. Mathet	Y. Saint-Martin
1980	Policeman	F.E. Tinsley	C.G. Milbank	W. Carson
1981	Bikala	J. Ouaki	P. Biancone	S. Gorli
1982	Assert	R.E. Sangster	D.V. O'Brien	C. Roche
1983	Caerleon	R.E. Sangster	M.V. O'Brien	P. Eddery
1984	Darshaan	H.H. Aga Khan	A. de Royer-Dupré	Y. Saint-Martin
1985	Mouktar	H.H. Aga Khan	A. de Royer-Dupré	Y. Saint-Martin
1986	Bering	Mde. A. Head	Mme. C. Head	G.W. Moore
1987	Natroun	H.H. Aga Khan	A. de Royer-Dupré	Y. Saint-Martin
1988	Hours After	Mise. de Moratalla	P-L. Biancone	P. Eddery
1989	Old Vic	Sheikh Mohammed	H.R. Cecil	S. Cauthen

The pageant that precedes a Classic always includes a parade. Chantilly does it with typical French style and here the 1982 runners are led past the stands.

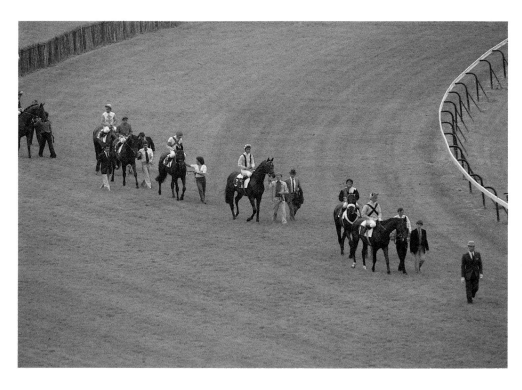

ship of the horses been concentrated in the hands of a few giants of the turf. For many years it was the late Marcel Boussac and the Aga Khan whose strings dominated the big races. Other major owners include names like Dupre, Wildenstein, Rothschild, Wertheimer and Lagardere, all of whom have seen their colours carried to success at Chantilly.

Boussac

Boussac was without doubt the biggest and the most successful. His string won 12 Jockey Clubs and five Dianes between the success of Ramus in 1922 and that of Acamas in 1978. More recently the race has been farmed by the current Aga Khan who won three of the five Jockey Clubs between 1984 and 1988.

This concentration of power in the hands of the few is uniquely French and although it may lead to repetition, it has not harmed the strength of the country's racing, for the Chantilly trainers have long managed to launch successful raids on the top prizes across the Channel.

Apart from the grand folly, Chantilly is surrounded by woods, lakes, the real Château, acres of gallops and thousands of horses. The course is a sharp right-handed one with a stiff uphill finish that really tests the field's stamina. The most unusal feature of the course is that the home straight, which extends a long way past the winning post, can be used in either direction for the running of five-furlong sprints.

The course has not received the attention which has been lavished on other French courses and the facilities are somewhat primitive judged by the high French standards, but the place and the racing are full of atmosphere.

PRIX DE DIANE HERMES

2,100m. Three-year-old fillies.

Year	Winner	Owner	Trainer	Jockey
1971	Pistol Packer	Mde. A. Head	A. Head	F. Head
1972	Rescousse	Baron de Rède	G. Watson	Y. Saint-Martin
1973	Allez France	D. Wildenstein	A. Klimscha	Y. Saint-Martin
1974	Highclere	H.H. The Queen	W.R. Hern	J. Mercer
1975	No race.			
1976	Pawneese	D. Wildenstein	A. Penna	Y. Saint-Martin
1977	Madelia	D. Wildenstein	A. Penna	Y. Saint-Martin
1978	Reine de Saba	J. Wertheimer	A. Head	F. Head
1979	Dunette	Mrs. H. Love	E. Chevalier du Fau	G. Doleuze
1980	Mrs. Penny	E. Kronfeld	I.A. Balding	L. Piggott
1981	Madam Gay	G. Kaye	P. Kelleway	L. Piggott
1982	Harbour	Ecurie Aland	Mme. C. Head	F. Head
1983	Escaline	Mme. J. Fellows	J. Fellows	G.W. Moore
1984	Northern Trick	S. Niarchos	F. Boutin	C. Asmussen
1985	Lypharita	L-T. Al Swaidi	A. Fabre	L. Piggott
1986	Lacovia	G.A. Oldham	F. Boutin	F. Head
1987	Indian Skimmer	Sheikh Mohammed	H. Cecil	S. Cauthen
1988	Resless Kara	J.L. Lagardee	F. Boutin	G. Mosse
1989	Lady in Silver	M.A. Karim	R. Wojtowiez	A.S. Cruz

Gary Moore and Bering win the 1986 Prix du Jockey Club, completing a rare double for the Moores. Father George was on the winner in 1960.

Deauville steps into the limelight for one month each year, when the town welcomes the whole French racing world and turns over its beaches, stables and hotels to visiting horses and trainers. Created in 1864 by the Duc de Morny, to humour the Parisian smart set who had taken to holidaying in Normandy, Deauville was the Duc's idea of improving on the strand races which have been held on the neighbouring Trouville beach in previous years.

That first day justified his plans. The sun shone brilliantly, the women looked perfect in their best Parisian outfits, the orchestra of the Casino serenaded the spectators and the racing was an enjoyable afterthought. But the concept caught on and gradually more and more of the best Parisian horses came up to the coast as the prize money and the prestige of the meeting grew.

The Prix de Morny and the Grand Prix de Deauville were as valuable as many of the Longchamp or Chantilly races and by the

DEAUVILLE

turn of the century, Deauville had become an established part of France's racing calendar. Come August, the whole of Chantilly, Maisons-Laffitte and even the Société Sportive d'Encouragement pack their bags and move up to the small but chic resort on the Normandy coast.

Holiday town

As holidays go, it proves costly, as one might expect with more than 500 horses making the journey as well as their owners and trainers. There have been persistent cries in the French racing world to abandon the whole affair and lengthen the Chantilly summer season – a much more practical idea. But those pleas have been repeatedly turned down for several reasons.

Firstly, Deauville relies on the influx of Parisians to fill its hotels and Casino and so maintain its reputation as the place to be.

The loss of its racing clients would be disastrous to the town's finances. Secondly, Deauville, because it is situated in the middle of the French stud country, hosts the premier yearling sales which everyone has to attend. If they are there anyway, they might as well have some racing to pass the time. Thirdly, the town has become established as the broking house of the French turf, the place where all the deals are worked out. In the relaxed atmosphere and ozone-rich air, the important questions of who is working for whom, and which horses will go to which trainer, are settled. They say it could never be done in Paris.

The track itself, shaped like a small letter

With the stands in the background the field race round the back straight in the brilliant Normandy sunshine.

'd' with a straight mile joined by a right-handed round course, is a testing course to ride and one on which knowledge is invaluable. Hardly any of the races are won from the front and, despite the fact that the straight is only two and a half furlongs long, it is often the jockey who waits longest who wins the day.

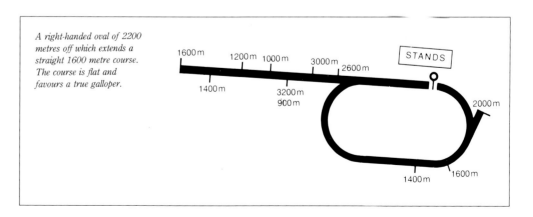

A right-handed oval of 2200 metres off which extends a straight 1600 metre course. The course is flat and favours a true galloper.

STANDS

1600m 1200m 1000m 3000m 2600m 2000m
1400m 3200m 1400m 1600m
900m

Right: *Horses on holiday. This quartet are having a break from the usual training routine by paddling on the beach.*

Below: *One of the numerous great winners of the Jacques-le-Marois, Kenmare, whose '78 victory marked him out as one of the best of his generation.*

PRIX DU HARAS DE FRESNAY-LE-BUFFARD JACQUES LE MAROIS

1,600m. Three-year-olds and up, colts and fillies.

Year	Winner	Owner	Trainer	Jockey
1971	Dictus	J.M. Soriano	R. de Mony-Pajol	Y. Saint-Martin
1972	Lyphard	Mrs. P. Wertheimer	A. Head	F. Head
1973	Kalamoun	H.H. Aga Khan	F. Mathet	H. Samani
1974	Nonoalco	Mrs. M. Berger	F. Boutin	L. Piggott
1975	Lianga	D. Wildenstein	A. Penna	Y. Saint-Martin
1976	Gravelines	D. Wildenstein	A. Penna	G. W. Moore
1977	Flying Water	D. Wildenstein	A. Penna	Y. Saint-Martin
1978	Kenmare	Baron G. de Rothschild	F. Mathet	A. Badel
1979	Irish River	Mrs. R. Adés	J. Cunnington Jr.	M. Philipperon
1980	Nadjar	Capt. A.D.D. Rogers	A. Paus	A. Lequeux
1981	Northjet	S. Fradkoff	O. Douieb	F. Head
1982	The Wonder	Marquise de Moratalla	J. de Chevigny	P. Eddery
1983	Luth Enchantee	P. de Moussac	J. Cunnington	M. Philipperon
1984	Lear Fan	A. Salman	G. Harwood	P. Eddery
1985	Vin de France	D. Wildenstein	P.L. Biancone	E. Legrix
1986	Lirung	Gestüt Fahrhof	H. Jentzsch	S. Cauthen
1987	Miesque	S. Niarchos	F. Boutin	F. Head
1988	Miesque	S. Niarchos	F. Boutin	F. Head
1989	Polish Precedent	Sheikh Mohammed	A. Fabre	C. Asmussen

Jacques le Marois

The 16 or 17 days racing are of a quality that is the equal of any other course in the world and the two highlights, the Prix Morny for the two-year-olds and that top-class mile race, the Prix Jacques Le Marois, draw horses from all over Europe. But the horses do more than race at Deauville. Galloping on the beach in the morning, it is a break from their normal routine, and many horses thrive on their four weeks' holiday. Triptych, who made her name on the course as a two-year-old, is one in particular who used to benefit no end from her break by the sea.

Deauville itself has plenty of recreational amenities outside the the races. The polo fields draw large crowds for evening games after the racing has finished and on those afternoons when the thoroughbreds take a break; the golf courses are another popular diversion and as soon as the strings of horses leave the beaches in the morning, less athletic figures take their places. By night, the Casino replaces the Pari-Mutuel booths as the place to try to lose one's money, but because it is all done with such style, no one complains.

Deauville and its racecourse, its beaches and its high life epitomize the French attitude. Stylish, classy, fun and full of horses that go very fast, it is all there for those whose palates have been jaded by an early season excess of racing and who need to recuperate.

SAINT-CLOUD

Village Star on the inside starts to respond to Cash Asmussen's vigorous driving to pass Saint Andrews and Frankly Perfect to win 1988's Grand Prix de Saint-Cloud.

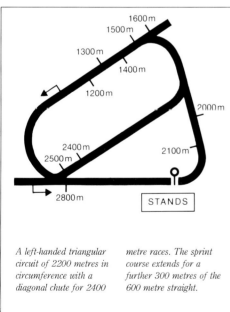

A left-handed triangular circuit of 2200 metres in circumference with a diagonal chute for 2400 metre races. The sprint course extends for a further 300 metres of the 600 metre straight.

Saint-Cloud was born in 1901 when the old Société du Demi-Sang was thrown out of Vincennes by the army. They retreated to a strip of land owned by Edmond Blanc and carried on with their trotting. After the end of the First World War, the course was handed over to the Société Sportive d'Encouragement, who handled the thoroughbred racing at Maisons-Laffitte, and who have subsequently steered the Saint-Cloud to the top of the Parisian circuit.

With over 60 days racing in the year, Saint-Cloud is the most heavily used of the Paris tracks, but the grass always seems to be in fine condition and the course can withstand its heavy workload. With a season that starts in late February and continues, with a two-month break in August and September, through to December, the classy Saint-Cloud welcomes in and sees out the French Flat season.

The major event at the course is the Grand Prix de Saint-Cloud, which has been run under its current title and conditions since the end of the last war, but under its former title, Prix du Président de la République it has a history that goes back to 1904.

It has thrown up numerous great winners including the Epsom Derby heroes Relko and Teenoso, the immortal Sea Bird and other Arc winners of the quality of Rheingold and Sagace, but it was also the scene of Vaguely Noble's one defeat.

A triangular course with a very short straight, Saint-Cloud is a good galloping track, but one on which all the sprints are run with a bend. Despite that drawback, the course is a popular one with both trainers and spectators and the overall standard of racing is second only to Longchamp.

AMERICAS

Whilst the character of racing in the Americas differs vastly from that of Europe, the past twenty years has seen ever closer links growing between the two continents.

The main reason for this is the strength of the North American bloodstock industry. For over the last forty years, owners in the United States have been buying up the best of the European bloodlines and operating a hugely successful breeding industry in Kentucky.

Now the Europeans have to come to the US to purchase the talent needed to keep its racing at its prestigious level. But the bulk of the raw material bred in America stays there and races on the continent's dirt tracks in a style that is totally un-European.

The riches are there aplenty. Given the predominance of the Mutuel pool system, American courses can stage million dollar contests that can attract horses from all over the world to their shores, and it is in North America that an unofficial World Championship, the Breeders' Cup, has sprung up.

The breathtaking backdrop of the San Gabriel mountains make a wonderful sight as the runners turn into Santa Anita's back straight.

CHURCHILL
DOWNS

The outer dirt track is one mile in circumference with a chute for mile races. The newly completed inner turf course is seven furlongs long.

T he Kentucky Derby, or the Run for the Roses, is without doubt America's most famous race. On the first Saturday of each May the hopefuls line up at Churchill Downs for a ten-furlong race on dirt that transforms the winner into a hero. In its relatively short history the race has acquired as much kudos as its more venerable Epsom equivalent and the twin spires of the Churchill Downs clubhouse are invariably packed with cheering crowds enjoying the annual treat that Kentucky lays on for the racing world.

Yet, as so often is the case with great sporting events, the birth of the race was almost an accident. It was only through the wonderful publicity skills of Colonel Matt Winn that the Kentucky Derby reached international prominence. Churchill Downs racecourse was founded in 1874 not to stage a thoroughbred spectacular but to halt the

Crowds throng to Churchill Downs for Derby Day and watch the action from the paddock and the parade to the post-race celebrations.

decline of the local stock farming industry, which was still in a bad depression following the strictures of the Civil War.

Colonel Clark

A Colonel Lewis Clark set up the Louisville Jockey Club and leased 32,375 sq m (80 acres) of land from the Churchill brothers to found a racecourse on which he would improve the reputation of the horses of the district. The Colonel had crossed the Atlantic to study the methods of the English Jockey Club and the conditions of the great English races. He returned fired with enthusiasm to create a modern track and a series of rich stakes races named the Clark Handicap, after himself, the Kentucky Oaks and the Kentucky Derby after the two great Epsom Classics.

Raising $32,000 from the local business community, he built a one-mile, oval, left-handed track complete with stabling for 400 horses, a 2,000-seater grandstand and a clubhouse for members of the Jockey Club and their guests. He had visions of an exclusive racecourse which would compare to the best in America and pretentiously named the circuit Churchill Downs, after the owners of the land and the downland areas in England on which racing was held.

His efforts were rewarded by a crowd of 10,000 people turning up on 17 May 1875 to watch the running of a 12-furlong race round the new circuit for a 43cm (17in) silver cup and the honour of winning the first Kentucky Derby. Aristides, owned by H.P. McGrath and ridden by Oliver Lewis, won that first running.

As the operation had proved to be a popular success, though a financial disaster, Clark persevered with the experiment.

Above: *For once it is a filly in the winner's enclosure. Winning Colours, her trainer Wayne Lutas and jockey Gary Stevens have beaten the colts to take the '88 Derby.*

Right: *As the field break from the stalls only ten furlongs separates one of them from the Roses and a place in history.*

The early runnings threw up a hero in the black jockey Isaac Murphy who won the race three times in 1884, 1891 and 1892, and became the only jockey to win all three big races in the same meeting when he added the Clark Handicap and the Oaks in 1891.

All the meetings continued to lose money and Clark's attempt to gain some income through the introduction of Pari-Mutuel machines, whose profits would go to the course, failed to get off the ground since the local bookmakers complained that they were taking away their profits. Finally Clark, demoralized by the lack of financial

success of his plan, cut his losses and sold the control of the course to a syndicate headed by William Schulte in 1894.

First roses

Schulte oversaw the moving of the club-house to the other side of the course so that the spectators were not troubled by the glare of the late afternoon sun. That new clubhouse still stands and first brought the twin spires to Churchill Downs. The other major change by the new board was the reduction of the race to a ten-furlong

contest, since they thought that a mile and a half was too far for a three-year-old to handle so early in the spring.

On a lesser note, they awarded Ben Brush a garland of roses after he had won the 1896 running. That small gesture was the start of a tradition that has lasted ever since.

But none of these innovations succeeded in improving the course's finances and Churchill Downs changed hands once again in 1902 when a syndicate headed by Charlie Price and a local tailor, Matt Winn, bought the track. They made several improve-

ments and the first meeting under their control in 1903 was also the first to show a profit.

By then the race's reputation had risen and it was not only the locals who flocked to see the Kentucky Derby but racing enthusiasts from all over the East Coast. This was the result of Winn's work in persuading the top New York connections that something worthwhile was happening out in Kentucky. With the arrival of their better horses the race began to justify its Championship pretensions.

Lean years

In 1908 bookmaking was abolished in the town, which allowed Winn to reintroduce the Pari-Mutuel machines on which the course was so dependent for its finances. However, the moral crusaders who had succeeded in having bookmaking outlawed were also pressing for the outright banning of gambling and the course, like so many American courses at the time, came under heavy pressure to close.

Racing in California, Tennessee, Arkansas and Louisiana was halted and only Kentucky, Maryland and New York managed to escape the zealous fervour of the moral crusaders. But the ever shrewd Matt Winn turned even this to his advantage and encouraged horses that then had nowhere else to race to join him in Kentucky for the ever richer prizes.

The three races between 1913 and 1915 all produced stories which helped to push the race into the national consciousness. Donerail in the first of those years came home as the complete outsider at over 90-1 and hit the headlines as the longest-priced winner of the race. His unlikely triumph was followed by that of Old Rosebud, of Citizen Kane fame. The colt smashed the course record to enter the hall of fame where he was joined the following year by Regret, who became the first filly to win the race.

By then racegoers had come to look forward to the first Saturday in May, the established date for the race, and Winn had succeeded in dragging the Kentucky Derby from provincial obscurity to international renown. In 1918 he and his partners sold the course, which they had bought for $40,000,

for $650,000 to a syndicate headed by James Brown, though Winn himself retained his stock and stayed on as vice-president and manager.

Sir Barton and the Triple Crown

The following year Sir Barton became the first winner of the Triple Crown. That was the name now given to the treble of Kentucky Derby, Pimlico's Preakness Stakes and Belmont's Stakes, the three top races on

the East Coast. Sir Barton came to Kentucky as a maiden to make the pace for his more fancied stable companion Billy Kelly, but slipped his field and beat Billy Kelly by five lengths. Four days later he added the Preakness to his tally before coming home alone in the Belmont by a record 11 lengths.

It is interesting to note that New York's champion of the following season, Man O'War, was not even entered in the Derby by his owner Sam Riddle as he did not believe in racing three-year-olds over such a trip so early in the season. It goes without

Left: *The twin spires dominate the background as a Derby field turn out towards the backstretch in the States' biggest race.*

Right: *The winning smile that says it all. Gary Stevens with his roses aboard Winning Colours.*

saying that Man O'War would have become the second winner of the Triple Crown had he been allowed to compete as he won every start that year with the greatest of ease.

Despite his absence the race had become a major Championship and had attracted all the brou-ha-ha that goes with such events, some of it forgettable, but some magically memorable.

It was on the 50th running of the race in 1925 that the phrase 'Run For The Roses' was coined by Bill Corum, the famous New York Times sports columnist, and as the moniker stuck, the track commissioned Mrs Kingsley Walker, a local florist, to make a special garland for the winner every year, a practice that continued up to 1984 when the florist's business was sold.

Great winners

By the 1930s the race was firmly established as the race of the year in America, and as the demand to see the event grew, Churchill Downs opened up the infield for the first time in 1938 to accommodate crowds that had increased to almost 100,000 on Derby Day itself. Omaha in 1934, War Admiral in 1937 and Whirlaway all won the Triple Crown before the war, which almost halted the running of the race. The 1945 running had been cancelled, but was reprieved at the last moment and run a month late in June.

Below: *The blinkered Alysheba is driven out by Chris McCarron to win the Roses in the 1987 Derby.*

A very particular Derby Day combination. The finery and the hats can be seen on any racecourse, but the mint julep is a Kentucky special.

The course has gone from strength to strength since the war and can now attract runners from abroad for its great day. The crowds still flock into Louisville in their thousands for the event and pack the grandstand and the infield, hoping to see duels such as the one between Affirmed and Alydar, who fought it out down the home straight, or heroes of the quality of Secretariat, the first horse to break the two-minute barrier for the race, and Spectacular Bid, who lived up to his reputation with a blistering display to win in 1979.

Picnics and mint juleps

Some come solely for the spectacle and bask in the heat with their picnics and their mint juleps, the local drink that tastes innocuous but kicks like the Derby winner in the home straight.

For others this is the fulfilment of a lifetime's dream as they see their silks led down to the start by pony and pray that fortune favours their horse. With 150,000 in attendance Churchill Downs is always rich in characters wanting to give you the winner of the big race, offer you another mint julep, tell you about the great Derbys of the past or just welcome you to Kentucky in true Southern style.

Outside the big day, Churchill Downs is usually a much quieter place with the rest of the Season's racing not much better than run-of-the-mill. But in 1988 the course was given the honour of staging the Breeders' Cup, that now famous world championship series. For that Churchill Downs had to build a turf track on the inside of the mile-long left-handed dirt track, which is the standard course for all racing in the States.

For unlike Europe, uniformity of courses is *de rigueur* Stateside. The circuits may be smaller or larger, but they are all left-handed ovals and if you asked an American horse to go round right-handed, he would probably stop dead in his tracks with surprise. The turf circuit was completed in 1987 and raced over several times before the arrival of the European turf stars. But despite torrential rain on the day of the Festival, both turf and dirt courses took

KENTUCKY DERBY
1¼ miles. First run 1875.

Year	Winner	Owner	Trainer	Jockey
1970	Dust Commander	R. Lehmann	D. Combs	M. Mangarello
1971	Canonero II	E. Caibett	J. Arias	G. Avila
1972	Riva Ridge	Meadow Stable	L. Laurin	R. Turcotte
1973	Secretariat	Meadow Stable	L. Laurin	R. Turcotte
1974	Cannonade	J. Olin	W. Stephens	A. Cordero, Jr.
1975	Foolish Pleasure	J. Greer	L. Jolley	J. Vasquez
1976	Bold Forbes	E. Tizol	L. Barrera	A. Cordero, Jr.
1977	Seattle Slew	K. Taylor	W. Turner, Jr.	J. Cruguet
1978	Affirmed	Harbor View Farm	L. Barrera	S. Cauthen
1979	Spectacular Bid	Hawksworth Farm	G. Delp	R. Franklin
1980	Genuine Risk	Mrs. B. Firestone	L. Jolley	J. Vasquez
1981	Pleasant Colony	Buckland Farm	J.P. Campo	J. Velasquez
1982	Gato del Sol	A.B. Hancock III & L.J. Peters	J. Edwin	E. Delahoussaye
1983	Sunny's Halo	D.J. Foster Stable	D.C. Cross	E. Delahoussaye
1984	Swale	Claiborne Farm	W. Stephens	L. Pincay, Jr.
1985	Spend a Buck	Hunter Farm	C. Gambolati	A. Cordero, Jr.
1986	Ferdinand	Mrs. H.B. Keck	C. Whittingham	W. Shoemaker
1987	Alysheba	D. & P. Scharbauer	J.C. Van Berg	C. McCarron
1988	Winning Colors	E.V. Klein	D.W. Lukas	G. Stevens
1989	Sunday Silence	Hancock, Gaillard & Whittingham	C. Whittingham	P. Valenzuela

their racing well and threw up the wonderful wins of Miesque over the turf and Alysheba on the dirt.

The other major difference between American and European racing is that the stables are attached to the tracks. In both Newmarket and Chantilly large training centres are located next to the racecourses, but the two continue to function independently. Newmarket racecourse is for racing, and the Newmarket gallops are for training; although trainers are given permission to work a horse on the racecourse, that is only allowed after racing has finished.

Training on the course

In the States and throughout the Americas and predominantly the rest of the world, the training and the racing of horses is much more closely linked. Every course has its own training gallops which are open to those horses stabled at the course either permanently or who are just there for a particular race.

Naturally the leading trainers in a country as large as the States have separate operations at different courses. D. Wayne Lukas, who has become the star trainer of the American circuit, is primarily based in Arcadia, California, next to the Santa Anita track, but he also has horses stabled and racing at Belmont for the big New York prizes, in Florida for the winter racing and of course at Churchill Downs for the Derby meeting.

Churchill Downs has continued to thrive around its centrepiece throughout this last

The flying French filly Miesque becomes the first horse to win two Breeders' Cup races by taking the '88 Mile at a wet Churchill Downs.

decade. With the profits from the track being reinvested in improvements to the facilities, the course has kept pace with all modern developments, over $22 million having been spent on the course between 1984 and 1988.

With evening racing, a spectacular paddock balcony, a private Turf Club and good viewing facilities, Churchill Downs offers its patrons one hell of a day's racing as is proved by a regular attendance figure of almost 20,000.

A left-handed oval circuit of one mile with an inner turf course of seven furlongs. Chutes off the main course hold the six and ten furlong starts.

Main Course

6 f Chute

Turf Course

5 f

1 ml

1 ml 2 f Chute

STANDS

PIMLICO

Pimlico is the home of the Maryland Jockey Club which proudly boasts that it is older than the Republic of the United States itself. Having been founded in 1870, Pimlico is also the second oldest course in the States and its attractive Maryland setting has seen some titanic struggles.

It is best known for the Preakness Stakes, the second leg of the American Triple Crown, in which speed is of the essence. At nine and a half furlongs, the Preakness is the shortest of the three races, but one which has long been accorded the honours of a major championship race.

When the Maryland Jockey Club decided to hold their spring meeting at Pimlico for the first time in 1873, they wanted to start a major stakes race which could draw the best horses to the State. They decided on a 12-furlong contest named after the course's first equine hero, Preakness, who had triumphed twice at Pimlico's inaugural meeting in 1870. Twelve thousand came to see seven horses fight it out for the $2,000 prize,

but the race proved no contest as Survivor ran away from his field in the final two furlongs to win by ten lengths.

Changing circuits

All seemed set fair at Pimlico after that first triumph, and for 17 years both the race and the course prospered, but in 1890 for various political reasons the Maryland Jockey Club suspended all racing at Pimlico, so the Preakness fell into abeyance. In 1894 the Brooklyn Jockey Club decided to renew the race and run it at their Gravesend course over a new distance of a mile and half a furlong, but the race never seemed to be at home at the course and failed to live up to its former stature.

Therefore, when racing was resumed at Pimlico in 1908, the race returned to its original home to be received with renewed enthusiasm and a richer purse. Those are two important ingredients for consistent success of any race and ones that the Baltimore public have continued to provide

throughout the remainder of this century, so the race has subsequently thrived after its early difficulties.

The Woodlawn Vase

Since 1917 the winner has taken home the Woodlawn Vase, which has been assessed as the most valuable trophy in American sport. It was originally made in 1860 by Tiffany and Co for the Woodlawn Racing Association. After the Civil War had interrupted racing in the South, the trophy went from course to course until it was won in perpetuity by Thomas Clyde's champion colt Shorthouse in 1904. Clyde, a director of the Maryland Jockey Club presented the trophy to that board in 1917 when it was added to the spoils for the Preakness.

Kalitan won the race that year to give his owner Edward Bradley the honour of taking the Vase home for the first time after the Preakness. The vase was subsequently offered to the winning owner every year until 1953 when Native Dancer's owner Alfred Vanderbilt refused to take on the responsibility for looking after the trophy. Since then a half-sized reproduction has been offered in perpetuity to every winning owner, whilst the original trophy is now kept in Baltimore Museum of Art. But the Woodlawn Vase is brought out and displayed in the winner's enclosure immediately after the race itself.

The female counterpart of the Preakness Stakes is the Black-Eyed Susan Stakes which is no longer reckoned to be part of the fillies' Triple Crown.

But the race, run as the Pimlico Oaks up until 1951, used to be a part of the old Crown, which included the Kentucky Oaks and Belmont's Coaching Club American Oaks, a triple that has been completed by only three fillies: Wistful in 1949, Real Delight in 1952 and most recently the fine Davona Dale in 1979.

Other major events staged at Pimlico include the Dixie Handicap, which is the eighth oldest stakes race in the States and the John B. Campbell Handicap.

Three seasons

Pimlico, unusually for an American track, has three separate seasons. The first which starts in February, continues until the third Saturday in May, the now traditional date for the running of the Preakness. Then follows a high summer meeting that runs through July and August and after a short interval an autumn meeting which continues until the beginning of October.

So it is surprising that Pimlico has stabling for only 1,000 odd horses and does not hold down a large regular team.

Pimlico attracts horses trained at nearby Laurel Park and Bowie, but cannot produce enough rich purses to rival the big New York courses like Belmont and Aqueduct or New Jersey's Monmouth. Despite that, the facilities offered by the track are of the high standard that is virtually universal throughout the American circuit.

Both the main grandstand and the clubhouse are glass-enclosed and air-conditioned, offering the patrons respite from the cold winters and stifling summers that are habitual in the region. The course regularly attracts 80,000 for Preakness Day, when the infield of the course is opened up to accommodate the crowds but general attendance is usually about 11,000.

The weather-vane

The great feature of the course is the weather-vane on top of the old cupola. In 1909 the Jockey Club commissioned a new weather-vane to replace one that had been struck by lightning. Depicting a horse with mounted rider, it was christened by painting it in the colours of that year's Preakness winner, Effendi.

Left: *Two up and only Belmont to go. Affirmed is the centre of attention after his Preakness Stakes victory over Alydar. The colt went on to complete the Triple Crown, the last horse to do so.*

Above right: *There's little between Affirmed and Steve Cauthen (nearside) and Alydar but that's the way they finished in all three Triple Crown races in 1978.*

That practice soon became a tradition and now minutes after the race has been won, Tommy Ennis climbs up to decorate the weather-vane in the new colours of the winning silks. Although the original building was destroyed in a fire in 1966, a replica cupola with an aluminium vane was built in the winner's enclosure so Tommy's job, which he has been doing for almost 30 years, is not so difficult or dangerous.

Given its close proximity to Washington, both the Maryland Jockey Club and Pimlico itself have often been graced with the presence of Presidents. George Washington was a frequent visitor to the old Annapolis course, whilst Andrew Jackson was a member of the Jockey Club when it first moved to Baltimore. More recent visitors include Lyndon Johnson and Richard Nixon, who have taken time out from the burdens of state to enjoy a day at Pimlico's races.

Right: *The Woodlawn Vase, a miniature of which is awarded to the winner of the Preakness Stakes, is America's most valuable sporting trophy.*

PREAKNESS STAKES

1 miles. Three-year-olds. First run 1873.

Year	Winner	Owner	Trainer	Jockey
1970	Personality	E. Jacobs	J. Jacobs	E. Belmonte
1971	Canonero II	F. Caibett	J. Arias	G. Avila
1972	Bee Bee Bee	W. Farish III	D. Carroll	E. Nelson
1973	Secretariat	Meadow Stable	L. Laurin	R. Turcotte
1974	Little Current	Darby Dan Farm	T. Rondinello	M. Rivera
1975	Master Derby	Golden Chance Farm	W. Adams	D. McHargue
1976	Elocutionist	E. Cashman	P. Adwell	J. Lively
1977	Seattle Slew	K. Taylor	W. Turner, Jr.	J. Cruguet
1978	Affirmed	Harbor View Farm	L. Barrera	S. Cauthen
1979	Spectacular Bid	Hawksworth Farm	G. Delp	R. Franklin
1980	Codex	Tartan Farms	D.W. Lukas	A. Cordero, Jr.
1981	Pleasant Colony	Buckland Farm	J.P. Campo	J. Velasquez
1982	Aloma's Ruler	N. Scherr	J.J. Lenzini, Jr.	J. Kaenel
1983	Deputed Testamony	F.P. Sears	J.W. Boniface	D. Miller
1984	Gate Dancer	K. Opstein	J.C. van Berg	A. Cordero, Jr.
1985	Tank's Prospect	Mr. and Mrs. E.V. Klein	D.W. Lukas	P. Day
1986	Snow Chief	C. Grinstead & B. Rochelle	M.F. Stute	A. Solis
1987	Alysheba	D. & P. Scharbauer	J.C. Van Berg	C. McCarron
1988	Risen Star	L.J. Roussel III & R. Lamarque	L.J. Roussel III	E. Delahoussaye
1989	Sunday Silence	Hancock, Gaillard & Whittingham	C. Whittingham	P. Valenzuela

BELMONT

Belmont is home to the third and final race of the Triple Crown, the Belmont Stakes, the longest of the three races and one which has so often dashed the hopes of those seeking the prized Crown. But Belmont, to a greater extent than the other two courses, is more than just the home for that one race: it is one of the oldest centres for thoroughbred racing in the States and the scene of a large number of the great American races.

Situated some 20 miles from the centre of New York in the city's Jamaica district, Belmont has established itself over the past 120 years as the most famous racetrack in the States and the one where inevitably all the best horses and jockeys have to compete.

Although the current track has only been in existence since 1905, there has been racing in and around the area for much longer. Indeed, of the grand old tracks of the great city, Coney Island, Long Island, Morris Park and Jerome Park, only Belmont and Aqueduct have survived to carry the banner of the New York Racing Association into the present day.

Man O'War

The names of the great horses who have galloped their way to superstardom on this mile and a half left-handed oval of American history reads like a Who's Who of the American thoroughbred. Man O'War, who was unbeaten at the course and won the old American Triple Crown of the Withers, the Belmont and the Lawrence Realization Stakes; Zev, War Admiral, Citation, Kelso Forego, Spectacular Bid . . . the list is as open-ended as history.

Given that New Yorkers have a notoriously limited interest in the other 49 states, it is not surprising that the first Triple Crown in American racing was competed for solely in the city. Even today Belmont stages all three races in the Fillies Triple Crown and in the handicap Triple Crown, but it is still the Belmont Stakes that means the most to the course.

The race did not even start at the course, but began life at the old Bronx racetrack Jerome Park, where it was run over a mile and five furlongs, where that first running was won by Ruthless. In 1870 the race was moved to the old Belmont Park and run over its now standard trip of a mile and a half. Despite undergoing many changes through its lifetime, the Belmont Stakes has a longer history than any other of the American Triple Crown races and has been the scene of just as many dramatic incidents.

Man O'War won the 1920 Belmont Stakes running round right-handed, for it was not until the following year that Belmont accepted that it would have to fall into line with all the other American tracks and change the direction of their races. 'Big Red', as Man O'War was nicknamed, was one of the outstanding champions of American racing. He started at odds-on for every one of his 21 races and won all bar one of them, and that failure was blamed on the jockey rather than the horse.

Kentucky v. Epsom

His place as the darling of the New York crowds was taken over by Zev, who in 1923 supplemented his victories in the Kentucky Derby and the Belmont Stakes by winning a match with that year's Epsom Derby winner Papyrus. The English colt had been rushed across the Atlantic after being beaten in the St Leger, but there were plenty of people interested in betting on him.

A crowd of 45,000 turned out to watch the two fight it out for a $110,500 purse. Wall Street virtually came to a standstill that afternoon as brokers wagered over $3 million on the outcome. But on the dirt track that had become a muddy quagmire, the American champion, who was sent off the

Man O'War, or Big Red, as he was popularly known, scores yet another triumph at Belmont, this time in the 1920 Jockey Club Gold Cup.

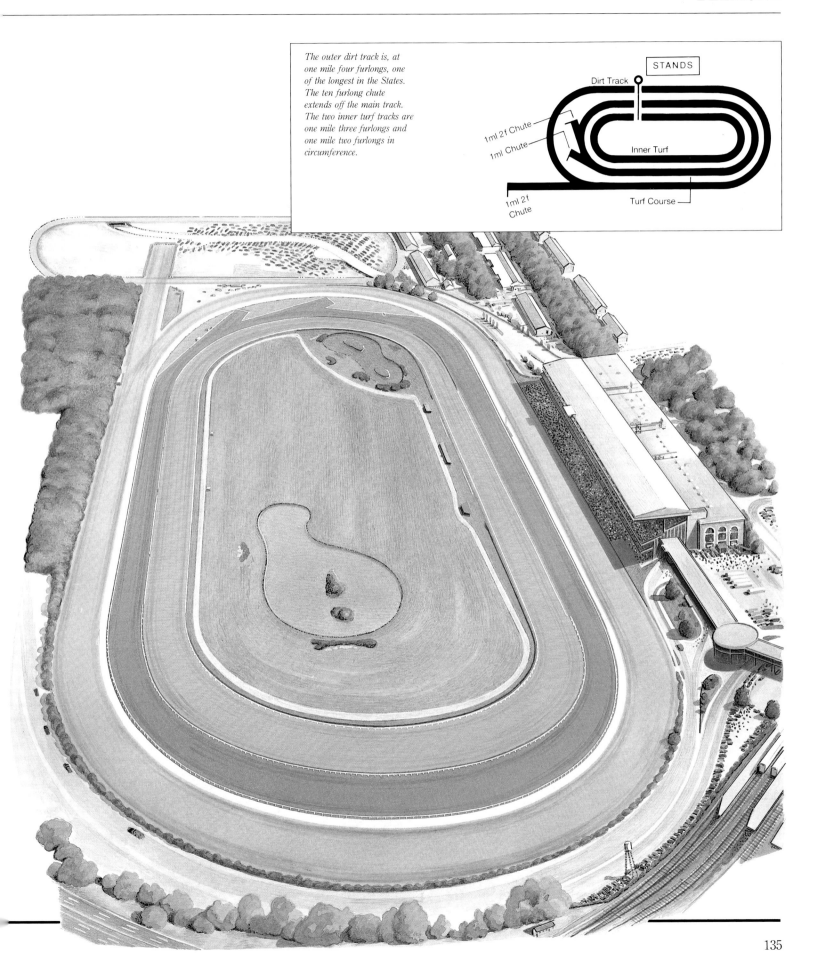

The outer dirt track is, at one mile four furlongs, one of the longest in the States. The ten furlong chute extends off the main track. The two inner turf tracks are one mile three furlongs and one mile two furlongs in circumference.

STANDS

Dirt Track

1ml 2f Chute

1ml Chute

Inner Turf

1ml 2f Chute

Turf Course

The wet weather that had reduced the dirt track to a mud-patch fails to stop Conquistador Cielo galloping away with the 1982 Belmont Stakes and start a sequence of five consecutive wins for his trainer Woody Stephens.

5-4 on favourite, was always going the better and came home alone over ten lengths in front of Papyrus, who looked completely out of place in what to him must have been bizarre conditions.

The next hero of New York, Citation, who raced on the course throughout the 1947 and 1948 seasons, achieved something that not even Man O'War or Zev managed: the Triple Crown. Winner of an incredible 28 races from 30 starts in those two years, Citation was never beaten at Belmont. Apart from the Belmont Stakes in his Triple Crown year, he won in the space of two weeks the Syonsby Mile, the Jockey Club Gold Cup, which was then run over two miles, and the Belmont Gold Cup.

Citation was replaced by Kelso, whose reign was the longest yet. As a gelding, Kelso was kept in training for that much longer and even as he aged, he retained his speed. His specialities were the handicaps and he remains one of the few horses to have captured Belmont's Handicappers Triple Crown.

His three successes in those races in 1961 assured Mrs duPont's gelding a second Eclipse Award, the prize which is given by the racing journalists to the horse they vote as the most outstanding of the year. Kelso's greatness can be judged by his unique feat of winning the Eclipse Award for five successive years.

But not a single win at Belmont was notched up during the last two of those years. For little beknown to the crowd witnessing their hero astonishingly get beaten in the 1962 Man O'War Handicap by the complete outsider Beau Purple, they were watching what was to be the last day's racing at Belmont for five years. Serious structural defects had been found in the grandstand, which made the course a potential deathtrap. The whole stand had to

JOCKEY CLUB GOLD CUP STAKES

1½ miles (2 miles until 1976). First run 1919.

Year	Winner	Owner	Trainer	Jockey
1971	Shuvee	Mrs. W. Stone	W. Freeman	J. Velasquez
1972	Autobiography	S. Sommer	F. Martin	A. Cordero, Jr.
1973	Prove Out	Hobeau Farm	H. Jerkens	J. Velasquez
1974	Forego	Lazy F. Ranch	S. Ward	H. Gustines
1975	Group Plan	Hobeau Farm	H. Jerkens	J. Velasquez
1976	Great Contractor	H. Wilson	R. Laurin	P. Day
1977	On the Sly	Balmak Stable	M. Gross	C. McCarron
1978	Exceller	Dr. H. Schnapka & N.B. Hunt	C. Whittingham	W. Shoemaker
1979	Affirmed	Harbor View Farm	L. Barrera	L. Pincay, Jr.
1980	Temperence Hill	Loblolly Stable	J. Cantey	E. Maple
1981	John Henry	Dotsam Stable	R. McAnally	W. Shoemaker
1982	Lemhi Gold	A.U. Jones	L. Barrera	C. McCarron
1983	Slew o' Gold	Equusequity Stable	S. Watters	A. Cordero, Jr.
1984	Slew o' Gold	Equusequity Stable	J. Hertler	A. Cordero, Jr.
1985	Vanlandingham	Loblolly Stable	C.R. McGaughey III	P. Day
1986	Creme Fraiche	Brushwood Stable	W.C. Stephens	R. Romero
1987	Creme Fraiche	Brushwood Stable	W.C. Stephens	L. Pincay, Jr.
1988	Waquoit	J. Federico	G. Federico	J. Santos
1989	Easy Goer	O. Phipps	C. McGaughey	P. Day

be taken down and completely rebuilt before crowds could be allowed back in the course.

In the intervening years all Belmont's racing was shared between the fellow NYRA tracks of Aqueduct and Saratoga, whilst the repairs which eventually cost over $30 million were carried out.

Belmont came back with a bang in 1968, the centennial year of the Belmont Stakes. All the world wanted to be there to enjoy the course's greatest hour and share in the rebirth. Stage Door Johnny somewhat ruined the day by winning the race and preventing Forward Pass from completing a Triple Crown which would have been cheered to the echo.

Belmont, however, continued to give its patrons something to cheer about through the next few decades. The largest crowd in the course's history turned out in 1971 to see Canonero's bid for a Triple Crown fail through lack of stamina. But they were left gasping two years later when Secretariat demolished his four opponents to go and win by an astonishing 31 lengths.

Ruffian

The filly Ruffian brought both pleasure and tragedy to the track. Having won the 1975 fillies' Triple Crown of Belmont's Acorn Stakes, Mother Goose Stakes and the Coaching Club American Oaks, she was

BELMONT STAKES
1½ miles. First run 1867.

Year	Winner	Owner	Trainer	Jockey
1971	Pass Catcher	October House Farm	E. Yowell	W. Blum
1972	Riva Ridge	Meadow Stable	L. Laurin	R. Turcotte
1973	Secretariat	Meadow Stable	L. Laurin	B. Turcotte
1974	Little Current	Darby Dan Farm	T. Rondinello	M. Rivera
1975	Avatar	A. Seeligson, Jr.	A. Doyle	W. Shoemaker
1976	Bold Forbes	E. Tizol	L. Barrera	A. Cordero, Jr.
1977	Seattle Slew	K. Taylor	W. Turner, Jr.	J. Cruguet
1978	Affirmed	Harbor View Farm	L. Barrera	S. Cauthen
1979	Coastal	W. Perry	A. Whiteley	R. Hernandez
1980	Temperence Hill	Loblolly Stable	J. Cantey	E. Maple
1981	Summing	C.T. Wilson, Jr.	L. Barrera	G. Martens
1982	Conquistador Cielo	H. de Kwiatkowski	W.C. Stephens	L. Pincay, Jr.
1983	Caveat	A. Belmont III	W.C. Stephens	L. Pincay, Jr.
1984	Swale	Claiborne Farm	W.C. Stephens	L. Pincay, Jr.
1985	Creme Fraiche	Brushwood Stables	W.C. Stephens	E. Maple
1986	Danzig Connection	H. de Kwiatkowski	W.C. Stephens	C. McCarron
1987	Bet Twice	Cisley Stable & B.P. Levy	W.A. Croll, Jr.	C. Perret
1988	Risen Star	L. Roussel III & R. Lamarque	L. Rousell III	E. Delahoussaye
1989	Easy Goer	O. Phipps	C. McGaughey	P. Day

matched against that year's Kentucky Derby winner Foolish Pleasure, but broke down when in front and had to be destroyed.

Trainer Woody Stephens then entered the scene with a record five Belmont Stakes wins between 1982 and 1986, whilst in 1987, his Alysheba came to Belmont poised to take the Triple Crown. He failed, but later went on to surpass John Henry's record of prize money by winning the 1988 Breeders' Cup, although that chapter of the story, unlike so many others in the history of the American turf, was not written at Belmont.

Above: *Belmont, which is just a subway ride from the centre of New York, draws a large and enthusiastic crowd to every day's racing the course stages.*

Right: *Risen Star, the eventual winner, heads the field in the 1988 Belmont Stakes, as the Kentucky Derby heroine Winning Colours drops back on the rails.*

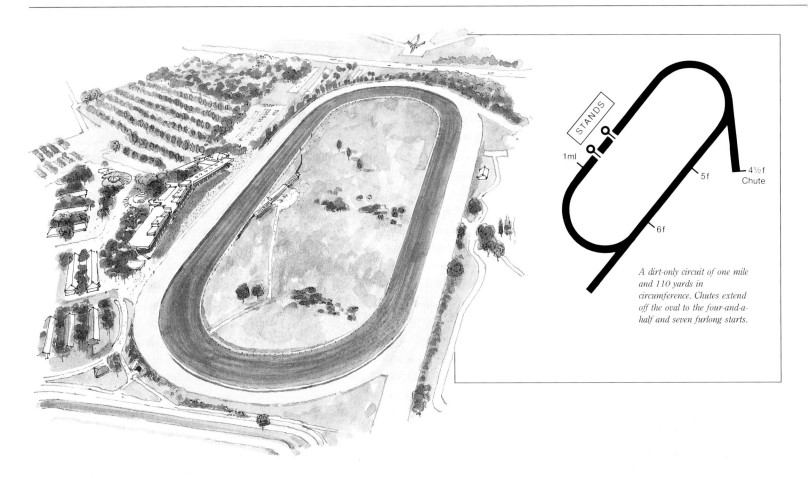

A dirt-only circuit of one mile and 110 yards in circumference. Chutes extend off the oval to the four-and-a-half and seven furlong starts.

KEENELAND

Keeneland, on the outskirts of Lexington, Kentucky, probably sees more champions than any other place in the world. It is not only the home of a beautiful racecourse, but also the world's most important thoroughbred sales.

Although the course's spring and fall meetings stage important races, notably that most significant of Derby trials, the Bluegrass Stakes, and the top fillies' race, the Spinster Stakes, Keeneland has earned its particular place on the racing map for the hundreds of choicely bred yearlings that pass through its sale ring.

Each year the sales attract the leading trainers from America and Europe who battle it out for the best lots which have fetched up to $14 million dollars. Yearly totals from the five sales can reach $400 million as top owners like Gene Klein, the

Maktoum brothers and Robert Sangster, invest in what they hope to be their champions of the future.

Outside the sales, the town lives and breathes the sport of racing. Deep in the Kentucky bluegrass country, surrounded by the famous studs like Calumet, Claiborne, Spendthrift and Greentree, Keeneland is the centre of what can be regarded as a horses' Utopia.

The course itself, which has been in use since 1936, holds a spring meeting amidst the flaming dogwood blossoms that is run on strictly traditional lines. Not for them the course commentary and multiple race cards of other American tracks, for Keeneland prides itself on staging horse racing as it used to be.

The Bluegrass Stakes continues to throw up Derby winner after Derby winner, some 12 odd in the last 30 years, and will always

The bidding stops at $13.1 million. The colt, to be named Seattle Dancer, has just become the most expensive yearling in history.

hold a special significance because of its proximity in both time and distance to the major event. With stabling for over 1,500 horses, Keeneland offers enough attractions to hold down a good local team, although not nearly equal to the quality of the yearlings that are sold in the neighbouring ring.

SARATOGA

In upstate New York, palatial Saratoga Springs is the oldest course in the States. Every summer when racing at Belmont finishes at the beginning of August, New York's racing set moves to the lovely old Spa town for a luxurious and relaxing holiday.

Although the old ways are somewhat over emphasized, the homely touch of the rural setting does add an air of familiarity to the proceedings that a European will not find on the other racetracks in the States. But make no mistake: when the gates open, the racing that is seen is strictly American and very much of the highest quality.

Saratoga's feature event is the Travers Stakes, a top quality three-year-old race that once again pits the best of the Classic generation against one another with smart late developing types thrown in. Run since the opening meeting in 1864, the race has a rich history and was for many years the high summer goal of all the top horses.

Perhaps the most dramatic of all runnings was in 1978 when Alydar, three times narrowly beaten by Affirmed in the Triple Crown, gained his revenge on his great rival, although it was only through the disqualification of Affirmed that Alydar stole the honours in yet another breathtaking race.

An equivalent race for fillies, the Alabama Stakes is but eight years younger and it too has enjoyed its fair share of drama. Since Saratoga's season is held at a time when the best juveniles are coming to the fore, contests like the Spinaway Stakes, the Saratoga Special and the Hopeful Stakes are normally highly competitive and are always won by a two-year-old on his way to the top.

Friendly but competitive, Saratoga is always a popular track with the professionals and will draw all the major faces to its gates, if not for the racing then for the prestigious yearling sales that are held during the meeting.

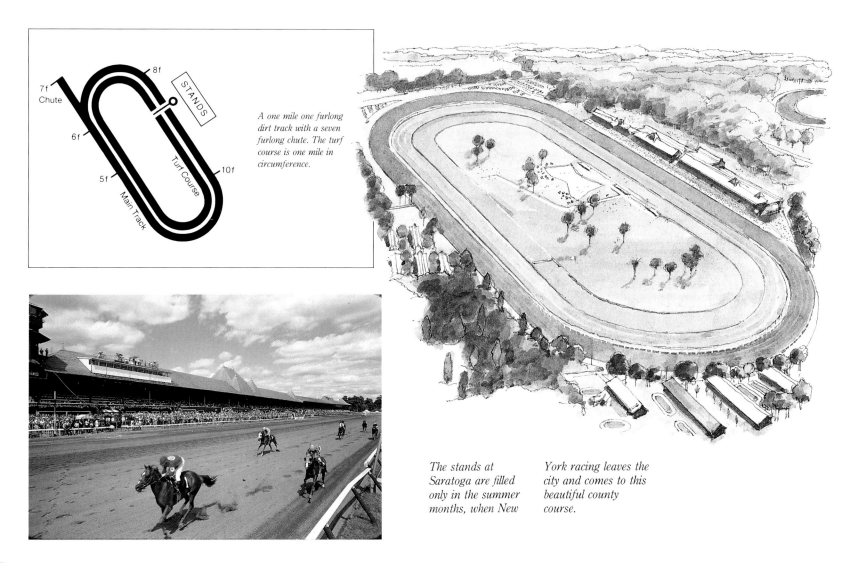

A one mile one furlong dirt track with a seven furlong chute. The turf course is one mile in circumference.

The stands at Saratoga are filled only in the summer months, when New York racing leaves the city and comes to this beautiful county course.

ARLINGTON

Arlington had just reached international prominence through the success of the Arlington Million, the world's first million dollar race, when a disastrous fire destroyed the entire grandstand in 1985. The fire broke out only days before the fifth running of an event that had hit the headlines almost immediately after the course announced the inaugural race back in 1981.

As it turned out, that 1985 running was held under the forbidding shadow of the burnt-out stands and has come to be known as the Miracle Million. Canvas-covered shelter was all that the course could offer, but the race itself proved the spectacle it has always been, as one of the most famous colours in the history of racing – the black with white cap of Lord Derby, carried by Tony Ives on the great strapping gelding Teleprompter – passed the post three-quarters of a length in front of the favourite Greinton for a historic victory.

That running apart, races have been few and far between at Arlington over the succeeding years. After the devastation the owners had little alternative but to go right back to the drawing board and rebuild the whole course over again. That has proved a lengthy process and the course only re-opened for the 1989 summer season after taking four years of hard work. The end product now offers the Chicago racegoer facilities the like of which have only been dreamed about by other courses.

But Arlington has also enjoyed its good times. The course was opened in October 1927 when the 1920s had reached their dazzling zenith. America was on the up and up, and heroes abounded especially in Chicago.

Curly Brown, who had planned and built more than a few racecourses in his time, conceived and built Arlington as his 'super-track', the showcase of his race-promoting abilities. He picked a 404,690 sq m. (1,000-acre) site of rich farmland to the north-west of Chicago. There a nine-furlong track with a sandy loam surface was laid out with an inner turf course of a mile. Both were of the highest quality as were the stands and clubhouse. Stabling for up to 2,000 horses was built in the surrounds.

The depression years

That dizzy era of prosperity came to an abrupt halt with the Great Depression of 1929. Brown had overstretched himself and had to sell his 'baby' to relieve his financial difficulties. Arlington was bought by the local bigwig John Hertz, who guaranteed its future and ensured the continuation of the major races namely the Arlington Classic and the Arlington Handicap. Hertz was astute enough to position the course's summer meeting between the end of Belmont's and the start of Sartaoga's sum-

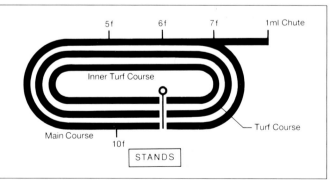

The one mile one furlong dirt track contains two inner turf courses of one mile and seven furlongs. A one furlong chute off the dirt track holds the seven furlong and one mile starts.

5f   6f   7f   1ml Chute

Inner Turf Course

Main Course

10f

Turf Course

STANDS

Races at Arlington have been few and far between since the '85 fire, but the course reopened in 1989 for its regular summer season.

Arlington prides itself on the quality of its turf racing and from 1989 has extended the Million into a two-day turf festival which will attract the best in Europe to the Chicago course.

mer seasons and managed to attract the best of the New York horses to Chicago.

With stars like Triple Crown winner Gallant Fox, Derby winner Cavalcade and other top-class performers like Granville Equipoise and Top Flight amongst the early stakes winners at the track, the success of Hertz's policy was clear. Hertz surrendered control of the course to Ben Lindheimer in 1940 who built on the former owner's policy by exploiting the wartime weakness of racing on both the East and West coasts.

Throughout the 1950s the racing at Arlington's summer meeting and the subsequent meeting at neighbouring Washington Park was some of the finest in the country. But Lindheimer's death in 1960 led to a decline in the fortunes of the course.

Involvement in politics, the amazing growth of the sport in California and the increased popularity of harness racing amongst the denizens of Chicago meant a decline in both attendance figures and the amount of money gambled. As a result the course was no longer able to offer the large purses necessary to attract the stars away from either the East or the West coasts.

The Arlington Million

Two further changes in ownership failed to halt the decline and it took the arrival of firstly the Arlington Million, a race which could really stand out and grab the world's headlines, and secondly a man of the promotional flair of the current owner, Dick Duchossois, to halt the decline.

The Arlington Million quickly reached the popular consciousness with the two successes of America's champion of the early 1980s, John Henry, a gelding who was unusual in so far as that he proved to be equally at home on grass or turf.

John Henry got up on the line to beat The Bart in the first running in 1981, missed the second through injury, and was only narrowly beaten in the third by the English raider Tolomeo before regaining his crown in 1984. His second success ensured that John Henry retired with a record sum of prize money to his name and a place in the Hall Of Fame.

Successive years have continued to keep the race's prestige at that high point.

Teleprompter's victory in 1985 was as popular as any, whilst the filly Estrapade the following year became the first distaffer to scoop the jackpot.

In 1988, as the Arlington rebuilding neared completion, the race was held at the grand course at Woodbine in Canada, where France scored their first success as Cash Asmussen brought the grey Mill Native through with a beautifully timed run to take the honours.

Now that racing has returned to the course, the success of the Million can once again be capitalized on and as the new look Arlington is second to none, the course should soon be able to return to the prosperity it enjoyed in the 1950s.

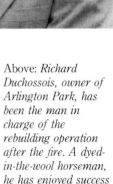

ARLINGTON MILLION STAKES

1¼ miles (turf). First run 1981. Run at Woodbine in 1988.

Year	Winner	Owner	Trainer	Jockey
1981	John Henry	Dotsam Stable	R. McAnally	W. Shoemaker
1982	Perrault	Baron T. van Zuylen	C. Whittingham	L. Pincay, Jr.
1983	Tolomeo	C. d'Alessio	L. Cumani	P. Eddery
1984	John Henry	Dotsam Stable	R. McAnally	C. McCarron
1985	Teleprompter	Lord Derby	J.W. Watts	T. Ives
1986	Estrapade	A.E. Paulson	C. Whittingham	F. Toro
1987	Manila	B.M. Shannon	LeRoy Jolley	A. Cordero, Jr.
1988	Mill Native	Evergreen Farm	A. Fabre	C. Asmussen
1989	Steinlen	Wildenstein Stables	D.W. Lukas	J.A. Santos

Above: *Richard Duchossois, owner of Arlington Park, has been the man in charge of the rebuilding operation after the fire. A dyed-in-the-wool horseman, he has enjoyed success on both sides of the Atlantic.*

Left: *The great John Henry gets up in the last strides of the first Arlington Million in 1981 to beat The Bart. The gelding went on to set a new record winnings, with his second success in the race in 1984.*

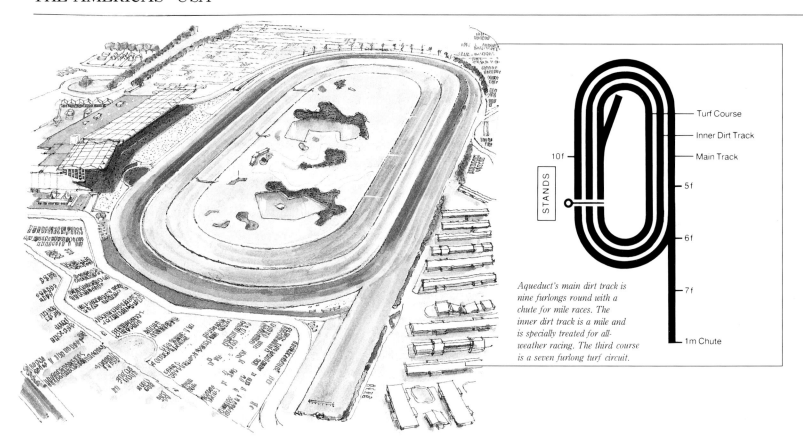

Aqueduct's main dirt track is
nine furlongs round with a
chute for mile races. The
inner dirt track is a mile and
is specially treated for all-
weather racing. The third course
is a seven furlong turf circuit.

AQUEDUCT

Though Aqueduct plays a second-
ary role to Belmont in servicing
the New York racing public, the
course is still one of the more
important East coast tracks and one that
can attract a huge crowd to its bigger days.
It is racing at Aqueduct's specially treated
course that keeps New York's racing going
during the winter. The innermost of the
three tracks is salted to lower the freezing
point of the dirt track, a trick which has
worked well enough to enable horse racing
to take place on all but the most severe of
winter's days.

Since 1977, the Aqueduct season has
begun at the end of Belmont's autumn
meeting in October and continued right
through to the beginning of May, during
which time some 160 days' racing is held.

Given the honour of being the first East
coast track to stage the Breeders' Cup Series

*Not even heavy snow
can stop Aqueduct
from staging meetings.
The specially treated*

*dirt track remains
raceable in all but the
most freezing
conditions.*

in 1985, Aqueduct staged a wonderful
afternoon's racing of which the highlight
was the British-trained filly Pebbles' win in
the Turf.

The original track was opened in 1894,
but when the New York Racing Association
took over the course in 1955, they decided to
demolish all the old stands and rebuild the
whole track. The new look Aqueduct was
reopened in 1959 and the now enormous
plant rivals Belmont in facilities if not in the
quality of racing. The main dirt course is
30.48m (100 ft) wide and nine furlongs in
circumference, whilst there is seating for up
to 37,000 punters.

Aqueduct, like many courses, now opens
its gates even on non-racing days to show
live simulcasts of the racing at the other
New York tracks, an arrangement which is
reciprocated by the authorities at Belmont
and Saratoga.

With one of the longer histories behind it, Monmouth is a grand old seaside course which has all the elegance of the old New Jersey. Though it is not the course that it once used to be, its recent purchase by Robert Mulcahy should ensure that Monmouth continues to host racing of an entertaining nature.

The 70-day season is stretched out over high summer and contains several valuable prizes that will draw some of the superstars south from Belmont to compete at the track. Races like the Haskell Invitational for the top three-year-olds, the Monmouth Oaks and the Iselin Handicap are all good Grade I races which will continue to attract the crowds.

Two-year-old races are also very much to the fore during the latter half of the meeting. Both the Sapling for the colts and the Sorority for the fillies are races that have thrown up more than their fair share of decent animals and look certain to carry on doing so.

There is a relaxed air at Monmouth similiar to that of Saratoga. Whether that is because of the summer holiday flavour of the racing or just the old charm of the place matters not, for both the horses and the spectators allow each other to get on with the sport.

They even stage hurdle racing on the turf course which is nearly unheard of in the States outside the Deep South. In what has become a very serious and undoubtedly multi-million dollar industry in the States, it is a welcome change to enjoy a slight relaxation in attitude.

Monmouth Park was moved to its current Oceanport setting in 1946 and although it is not the largest of courses, the stands are usually packed on Haskell day with an enthusiastic crowd of holiday-makers as well as the course regulars.

MONMOUTH

Although the prestige of Monmouth has dipped in recent years, the grand old seaside course still stages some big races, notably the Haskell Invitational.

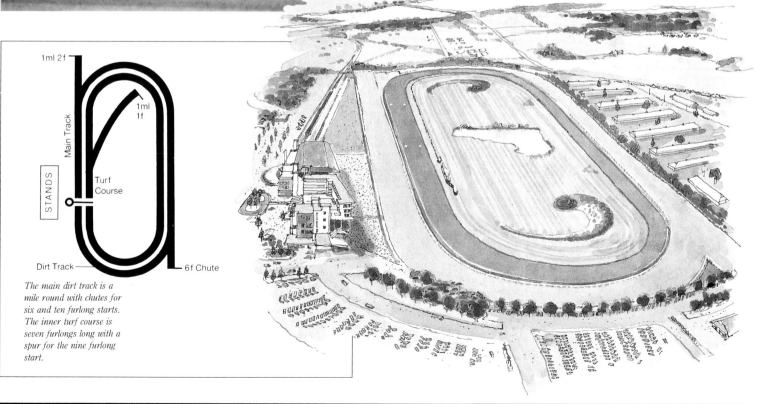

1ml 2f
1ml 1f
Main Track
STANDS
Turf Course
Dirt Track
6f Chute

The main dirt track is a mile round with chutes for six and ten furlong starts. The inner turf course is seven furlongs long with a spur for the nine furlong start.

Laurel, home of the
Budweiser
International, is one of
the world's most
international courses.
The wide galloping
track is overlooked by
a modern stand giving
the customer every
possible amenity.

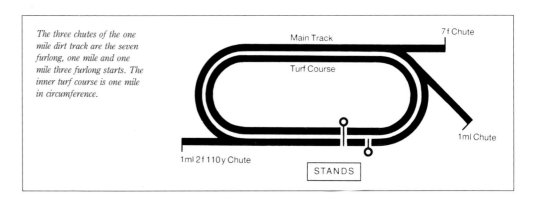

The three chutes of the one
mile dirt track are the seven
furlong, one mile and one
mile three furlong starts. The
inner turf course is one mile
in circumference.

Main Track

7 f Chute

Turf Course

1 ml Chute

1 ml 2 f 110 y Chute

STANDS

LAUREL

As the world grows ever smaller, the travelling horse becomes an ever greater facet of the racing industry. In 1987 a French-trained colt called Le Glorieux had a disappointing start to his three-year-old career, failing to win in his native land. However, his trainer Robert Collet then pursued an intriguingly international campaign with his charge.

Le Glorieux was placed to win a Group 2 event in Munich before again running badly in the Prix du Jockey Club, the French Derby. Then in rapid succession came victory in the Grosser Preis Von Berlin, one of Germany's top races, two more places in top-class German races, success in the Washington International and the Japan Cup, before a below-par run, when injured, in the Tancred Stakes in Australia.

All this amounted to a haul of over £1 million in prize money, only a few francs of which had been gained in his native land. Le Glorieux is perhaps the most extreme example of the travelling horse, but his record is sure to be surpassed in the near future by another hardy traveller.

Horses have travelled for prize money and glory for a long time, but it was only recently that races designed for international competition have come into being. The first of these was the Washington International, which was one of the cups picked up by Le Glorieux.

Laurel Park came to international prominence by staging the inaugural running of the Washington DC International Stakes in 1952, but the course has a history that stretches back much further. Starting life as part of the Laurel Four County Fair in 1911, the course was little more than a country point-to-point course half-way between Washington and Baltimore. But the purchase of the course in 1914 by James Butler started Laurel moving in the right direction.

Butler employed Colonel Matt Winn, who had successfully established the Kentucky Derby as the country's premier race, as general manager and gave him the task of attracting both horses and crowds to the course. Winn's method was to set up matches between top horses and three in particular caught the public's attention.

Matches

In 1917 he persuaded the owners of the Kentucky Derby winner Omar Khayyam and the Belmont winner Hourless to restage their battle in the Brooklyn Derby when Omar Khayyam had won by a nose. With two great champions engaged in a grudge match, Winn could not lose. The race was headline material and there looked to be little between the two over the ten-furlong trip. And so it proved with the race being head to head until the strong late run of Hourless took him a length clear at the post.

The following year the two top two-year-

Though Laurel is principally known for its turf racing, the course, like every US track, stages the majority of its events on the dirt track.

olds were pitted against each other for a prize of $20,000. Eternal got a head verdict over Billy Kelly in a six-furlong race. Eternal's owner John McClelland donated his prize to the Red Cross, so pleased was he with the colt's victory.

The third of the great matches took place in 1923 and was again between two two-year-olds, Sarazen and Happy Thoughts. However, unlike the first two which had proved to be as evenly balanced as the pre-race betting had suggested, this was no race

as Sarazen waltzed away from Happy Thoughts.

When Winn retired there was no immediate successor to rival him and Laurel Park drifted back into the mediocrity of anonymity. The course lacked a race which would give it an identity, and although the autumn season staged some interesting races, there was nothing that would grab the country's or even the state's attention.

So following the Second World War, the course was sold to the Maryland Jockey Club, which already owned Pimlico and Timonium, and hoped to be able to transfer the Laurel meeting to Pimlico. However, that move was blocked by the Maryland Legislature, so the Jockey Club, disenchanted with the dead duck that it then had on its hands, looked for a buyer on whom it could dump the course.

John Schapiro

In 1950 the Maryland Jockey Club sold the course to Morris Schapiro, a local industrialist, who handed over the running of the course to his son, John. Along with improving all the facilities, he introduced the first-ever race specifically designed to attract an international field.

BUDWEISER INTERNATIONAL

1¼ miles (1½ miles until 1985). First run 1952.

Year	Winner	Owner	Trainer	Jockey
1971	Run the Gantlet	Rokeby Stable	E. Burch	R. Woodhouse
1972	Droll Role	J. Schiff	T. Kelly	B. Baeza
1973	Dahlia	N.B. Hunt	M. Zilber	W. Pyers
1974	Admetus	M. Sobell	J. Cunnington	M. Philipperon
1975	Nobiliary	N.B. Hunt	M. Zilber	S. Hawley
1976	Youth	N.B. Hunt	M. Zilber	S. Hawley
1977	Johnny D	H. Wilson	M. Kay	S. Cauthen
1978	Mac Diarmida	Dr. J. Torsney	F. Schulhofer	J. Cruguet
1979	Bowl Game	Greentree Stable	J. Gaver, Jr.	J. Velasquez
1980	Argument	Summer Stable and B. Gordy	M. Zilber	L. Piggott
1981	Providential	S. Fradkoff	C. Whittingham	A. Lequeux
1982	April Run	Mrs. B.R. Firestone	F. Boutin	C. Asmussen
1983	All Along	D. Wildenstein	P.L. Biancone	W.R. Swinburn
1984	Seattle Song	S. Niarchos	F. Boutin	C. Asmussen
1985	Vanlandingham	Loblolly Stable	C.R. McGaughey III	D. MacBeth
1986	Lieutenant's Lark	L.T. Stevens, Jr.	H.M. Tesher	R. Davis
1987	Le Glorieux	W. & Mrs. Wolf	R. Collet	L. Pincay Jr.
1988	Sunshine Forever	Darby Dan Farm	J.M. Veitch	A. Cordero
1989	Caltech	D.S. Romanik	E. Azpurua, Jr.	R. Douglas

The first running achieved everything that Schapiro could have hoped for. Runners from five countries contested the event, and England's Wilwyn, who was a multiple winner in his home country, although not of the bigger prizes, found an extra gear in the home straight to pass all the rest and win for Manny Mercer, George Colling and England.

Successive runnings went to France, the home country, Venezuela and France again. By 1958, when the Australian horse Sailor's Guide won, the race had become firmly established as part of an international calendar and an October prize that drew runners from around the globe. The French, who have long mastered the art of sending a horse around the world and getting the animal ready to win there, have won the race more times than any nation other than the home country, whose horses do undoubtedly have an advantage.

Piggott at Laurel

However, Lester Piggott has as good a record as any other jockey. His three wins were gained on horses from Ireland, the mighty Sir Ivor in 1968, England, Karabas in 1969, and France, Argument in 1980. Although his idiosyncratic style was never appreciated by the Americans, he proved himself to be as effective a jockey there as he had done in Europe.

The race entered a decline in the early 1980s, which has only recently been halted. In 1984 the course was sold by John Schapiro to Frank de Francis, who has overseen a reversal of that decline. The tracks, both dirt and turf, have been relaid to wide acclaim from those who have to use them, the clubhouse and grandstand have been refurbished and a new Sports Palace has been built to bring the course's facilities into line with the modern era.

Concurrently, the race itself has been revamped. Cut in distance from twelve to ten furlongs, the Budweiser International, as it is now known, is supported by four other top-class events which have boosted the status of the card and again made it a Festival worthy of the best turf horses in the world.

For the first running of this festival in 1988, Ravinella, the dual Guineas heroine from France, won the mile race, whilst a top British two-year-old Luge won one of the juvenile events. But the big race itself saw a thrilling finish in which the American turf champion Sunshine Forever came back from the dead to beat off two French challengers and steal the glory for America.

The crowds came in larger numbers than had been seen for some time and the course again looked the international flagship it had once been. Given the difficult history Laurel has had, it is to be hoped that this current upswing in its fortunes is one that will last and that the International will again be a race for Champions.

In a dramatic final furlong flourish, Sunshine Forever gets up to win the 1988 Budweiser International from the French pair Frankly Perfect (on the far side) and Squill.

Hialeah is a racecourse that handily doubles up as a major tourist attraction. Situated just 12 miles from the downtown Miami, the course has become a centre for the East Coast's winter racing and has indirectly led to the growth of Miami as a resort. Although the racing at Hialeah has recently been overtaken by another Florida racecourse, Gulfstream Park, it continues to be a major feature of a thoroughbred's winter and Kentucky Derby runners are still prepared at the track.

The Flamingo Stakes is the most important of the Derby trials to be run there and past winners include the Triple Crown victors Citation, whose statue stands at one end of the walking ring, and Seattle Slew.

Come the summer, the tourists are a different breed, attracted primarily by Hialeah's landscaped grounds and its now famous flock of flamingos and the other wildlife that is allowed to flourish in the course's infield lake. Created out of the swamps of the Everglades in 1925, it took the energy of Joseph Widener to make the track a proper racing circuit. In 1931 he entirely reconstructed the course and landscaped the gardens, placing great emphasis on the Turf course, as he was a fervent admirer of European-style racing.

Until then most of racing in the States had been conducted on dirt tracks, and the innovation took some time to catch on. Widener's decision to build a complete infield grass circuit was regarded with some scepticism, and it was some six years before any stakes races were awarded to the turf course.

However, it has now become fully established and races of the quality of the Hialeah Turf Cup and the Widener Handicap draw the best of the American turf horses and the occasional European challenger.

HIALEAH

Dirt racing at Hialeah. The Florida track's winter racing is often the start of the Derby trail, but it also stages a major turf race in the Widener Handicap.

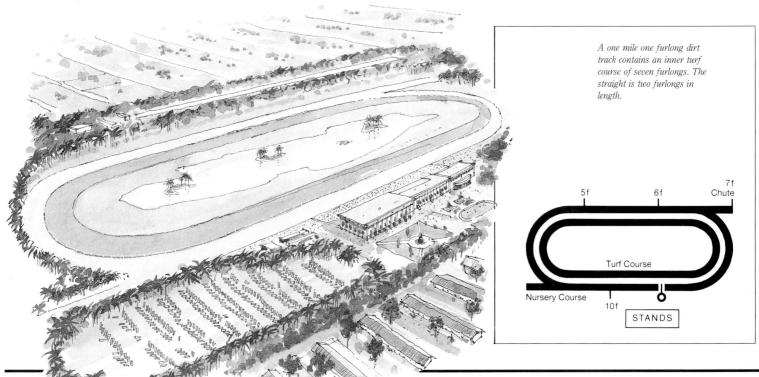

A one mile one furlong dirt track contains an inner turf course of seven furlongs. The straight is two furlongs in length.

5f 6f 7f Chute

Turf Course

Nursery Course

10f

STANDS

GULFSTREAM

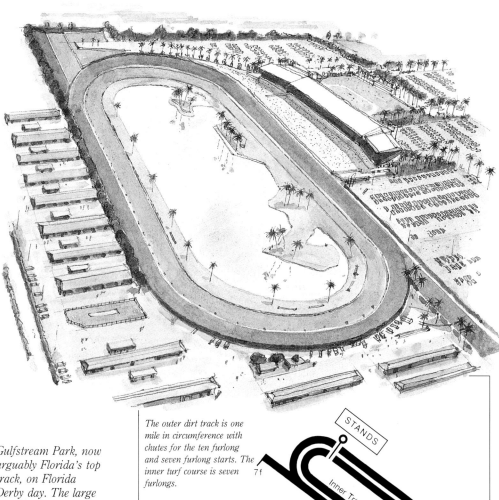

Gulfstream Park, now arguably Florida's top track, on Florida Derby day. The large crowd of winter holiday-makers can instantly check on their bets thanks to the state of art Tote board.

The outer dirt track is one mile in circumference with chutes for the ten furlong and seven furlong starts. The inner turf course is seven furlongs.

STANDS

Inner Track

Dirt Track

7f

10f

The rise of Gulfstream Park through the ranks of America's racecourse hierarchy was confirmed when it was announced in 1988 that it would host the following year's Breeders' Cup Series. Three generations of the Donn family have supervised this rise from the course's inception in 1944. The site that they chose, just outside Fort Lauderdale in southern Florida, did not seem to be a natural place for a racecourse, notwithstanding the growth of Florida as a holiday resort.

The first few years were not particularly auspicious, but the high prize money offered by the course began to attract the better horses and a greater audience. By the mid 1950s, the course had introduced the two major events that have guaranteed its success: the Florida Derby and the Gulfstream Park Handicap.

Since that time, the racecourse has been continually developed, with successive executives stressing the need for comfort. And that is obvious from the moment one sets eyes on the course. There is the huge cantilevered roof capping the vast grandstand, which can seat up to 14,500 people; the new Gulfdome dining terrace beside the winning post, whose covered gardens and quality restaurant belie the fact that the field is galloping past just outside the window; the infield lake and gardens; the roof-top garden viewing area, which provides one of the most dazzling panoramas of any racecourse...all of these have helped to draw in a wide audience, all of whom appreciates the lengths Gulfstream Park go to keep their punters happy.

But these facilities would be as nought without some pretty hot racing to back them up. Gulfstream now boasts the most competitive winter card in Florida, and the Run for the Orchids, as the Florida Derby is called, is one of the top Kentucky Derby trials. Recent winners include Alydar, second to Affirmed in all three Triple Crown races, Spectacular Bid, winner of two of the three, and Swale.

With the promise of racing the Breeders' Cup, Gulfstream Park can only improve on its record and looks to be assured of continuing its dominance of the Florida winters.

HOLLYWOOD PARK

Hollywood goes to the races, as Walter Matthau explains to Bill Shoemaker what he will do if 'The Shoe' fails to boot home the next winner.

Anything that Hollywood puts on will have its fair share of glitz and glamour, and their racing is no exception. Hollywood Park, which celebrated its 50th anniversary in 1988, is one of the outstanding centres of thoroughbred racing on the West Coast.

The stars troop down from nearby Beverly Hills and Hollywood for the important race days and outshine even the big names of the racing world. The media is always out in force snapping and questioning with the directness that is the hallmark of the States, whilst the everyday horse enthusiast can bask in the comfort that is called the Cary Grant Pavilion.

The brainchild of Jack L. Warner, of Warner Brothers fame, Hollywood Park opened its gates for the first time in June 1938. Its 600 shareholders included Walt Disney, Al Johnson, Sam Goldwyn, Bing Crosby and many others of Hollywood's children. With support like that, it was not surprising that the course quickly became known as the place to be seen.

The Hollywood Gold Cup soon became the most prestigious race in California and over the intervening years, the number of rich Grade I prizes that are on offer at the track have increased. Despite its successful opening, Hollywood Park had to endure a few problems in the 1940s. First, the course was closed for most of the war, and then just as it had got back into its stride, a fire devoured the whole of the grandstand and clubhouse, both of which had just been enlarged at the cost of $1 million.

Citation and Swaps

That catastrophe happened on the eve of the spring/summer meeting, which had to be switched to nearby Santa Anita, but the repairs were made in time for Hollywood to ascend to the throne of greatness in the 1950s. Throughout that decade Hollywood Park attracted more people than any other American course and it was easy to see why. Citation's victory in the 1951 Hollywood Gold Cup made the Triple Crown winner the first equine millionaire. A Gleam, Swaps, after whom the Grade I Swaps Stakes is named, and Round Table all dominated racing at the course, the three of them winning five Stakes races at Hollywood Park in one meeting.

Concurrent with these equine feats, there was also the rise to prominence of the great jockey Bill Shoemaker, who has ridden more winners than any man alive, and whose record of six victories at the course on 20 June 1953 still has not been beaten. Any champion will draw an admiring crowd and Hollywood was providing more than its fair share of such men.

John Henry

In 1967 Hollywood opened its turf course which soon became the home of the Hollywood Invitational Turf Handicap. Constructed round the infield lakes, the course is unusual by American standards in that it has a chute bisecting the obligatory oval. The turf course rapidly proved to be as successful as the dirt track, and winners of the Invitational include John Henry, who was cheered into the winners' enclosure three times by his doting Californian fans.

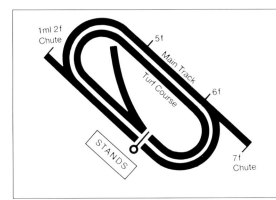

The one mile dirt track has two separate chutes for the seven furlong and one mile two furlong starts. The inner turf course is seven furlongs in length with a diagonal spur into the middle of the course for the nine furlong start.

His victories in 1980 and 1981 were followed by, for him, one lean year at Hollywood. His 1983 victory in Hollywood's other great turf race, the Turf Cup, took his winnings over $4 million, and his third and final success in 1984's Invitational allied to a second success in the Arlington Million, ensured that he retired from racing with a then record total of over $6 million. Other great winners of the Invitational include the ex-European champion Dahlia and her son Rivlia.

Concurrent with these events on the turf, the main track was also throwing up its own heroes – in particular Native Dancer. Mrs Shapiro's horse wrote his way into history by winning the Hollywood Gold Cup for three successive years in the mid-1960s, the last as an eight-year-old.

Home of the big bets

Hollywood has led the field in innovative bets. The size of the money gambled at the course, some $5 million a day on average, is made up mainly by various combination bets that lead the way as far as Americans are concerned. The idea of picking six successive winners may be regarded on the other side of the Atlantic as reducing the art of gambling to the level of the pools.

In 1971 Hollywood introduced the exacta – that is picking the first two home in the correct order – to American racing. That proved to be so popular that nine years later the Pick Six was invented. However, there turned out to be a few wrinkles in that system. Finding six winners was not always the easiest of jobs and the jackpot was not always won. So in 1983 in came the Perfect Six. A carry-over of 50 per cent of an unwon pool ensured that after a few unsuccessful days, there was a monster jackpot to be won. Naturally this could also be bigger, so the Pick Nine was introduced.

The size of money on offer is staggering. A carry-over pool for the Pick Nine, in 1987 of over $2 million was augmented by almost another $3 million in bets on the day. So with a total pool of nigh on $5 million there was always going to be a big pay-out. It was a day for the unfancied horses and few had picked them. The winning dividend to those lucky few was a record $2,168,338.60, which must have paid a few bills.

Back in the 1970s when the humble exacta was the draw, betting pools only averaged $3 million. The innovations of the pool have brought that figure up to its current level, and the course's share enables Hollywood to continue to offer the big purses that draw the good horses.

Hollywood's distinctive stalls in action yet again as another race gets under way at the top Californian track.

HOLLYWOOD GOLD CUP HANDICAP

1¼ miles. Three-year-olds and up. First run 1938.

Year	Winner	Owner	Trainer	Jockey
1971	Ack Ack	Forked Lightning Ranch	C. Whittingham	W. Shoemaker
1972	Quack	Bwamazon Farm	C. Whittingham	D. Pierce
1973	Kennedy Road	A. Stollery	C. Whittingham	W. Shoemaker
1974	Tree of Knowledge	Pin Oak Stable	C. Whittingham	W. Shoemaker
1975	Ancient Title	E. Kirkland	K. Stucki	L. Pincay, Jr.
1976	Pay Tribute	Elmendorf	R. McAnally	M. Castaneda
1977	Crystal Water	Mrs. C. Ring	R. Clapp	L. Pincay, Jr.
1978	Exceller	Dr. H. Schnapka and N.B. Hunt	C. Whittingham	W. Shoemaker
1979	Affirmed	Harbor View Farm	L. Barrera	L. Pincay, Jr.
1980	Go West Young Man	Wild Plum Farm	M. Tack	E. Delahoussaye
1981	Eleven Stitches	C. & M. Mirkin	G. Jones	S. Hawley
1982	Perrault	Baron Zuylen & S. Fradkoff	C. Whittingham	L. Pincay, Jr.
1983	Island Whirl	Elcee-H-Stable	D.W. Lukas	E. Delahoussaye
1984	Desert Wine	Cardiff Stud Farm	J. Fanning	E. Delahoussaye
1985	Greinton	M.J. Bradley, C. Whittingham & H. Wynne	C. Whittingham	L. Pincay, Jr.
1986	Super Diamond	R. & R. Sahm	E. Gregson	L. Pincay, Jr.
1987	Ferdinand	Mrs. H.B. Keck	C. Whittingham	W. Shoemaker
1988	Cutlass Reality	H. Crash & J. Hankoff	C.A. Lewis	G. Stevens
1989	Blushing John	A.E. Paulson	R. Lundy	P. Day

The Breeders' Cup

When the Breeders' Cup series was started, Hollywood Park was given the honour of staging the first running. A great day's racing attracted over 60,000 people, and saw both top-class racing and controversy. A local horse Wild Again won the big race, the Classic, but the second horse home, Gate Dancer, was disqualified and placed third.

Earlier in the day, Fran's Valentine had been disqualified from first place in the Juvenile Fillies, and the afternoon was capped by a long-running disqualification case concerning the one European winner Lashkari, who was first disqualified for drugs, but later reinstated following the protests of trainer Alain de Royer Dupre.

Despite those small hiccups, Hollywood Park was asked to stage the fourth running of the Series in 1987. This produced an outstanding race in the Classic when Ferdinand, who had won the Hollywood Gold Cup earlier in the year, just beat Kentucky Derby winner Alysheba in a thrilling race.

Improvements continue apace at Hollywood with the construction of a new course in 1984 that, unusually for America, allows for a mile race to be run round one bend, with an extended chute off the oval. The Cary Grant Pavilion a massive stand on five levels which provides some fantastic viewing was unveiled in the same year. In keeping a level of sophistication off course to match the great names racing, Hollywood Park should continue to be the standard-bearer of the Californian racing scene.

As the field turns for home in the '88 Hollywood Gold Cup, Cutlass Reality, the eventual winner, has the call over the two champs Ferdinand (on the inner) and Alysheba (on the outside).

OAK TREE

Although the Oak Tree Racing Association does not have a course to call its own and has to rely on Santa Anita to provide the facilities, the meeting which is staged under its authority every autumn is considered to be one of the foremost events on the West Coast.

The Association was only started in 1968 when Del Mar racecourse decided, in a fit of pique, to relinquish its autumn meeting after being handed a split meeting by the Californian racing authorities.

Rather than see good racing days go to waste, Clement Hirsch assembled a group of local notables who agreed to guarantee a meeting out of their own pockets to replace Del Mar. That must have seemed a mighty big risk when a strike by the Mutuel clerks prevented the meeting opening on schedule, but racing under the Oak Tree aegis finally became a reality on 7 October 1969.

Since that first meeting, Oak Tree has built itself up into one of racing's foremost international courses. It has links with Goodwood racecourse in England, which stages an annual Oak Tree Stakes at its August meeting, and hosts a two-day international turf festival centred round the Oak Tree Invitational and its fillies' counterpart, the Yellow Ribbon Stakes, both of which draw strong fields and number great champions amongst their winners.

It was that international outlook which brought the Breeders' Cup to Oak Tree in 1986 when the great European champions Dancing Brave and Sonic Lady tasted defeat in the searing heat of the Californian autumn, whilst the little fancied Last Tycoon surprised all but trainer Robert Collet by scooping the mile prize.

As a non-profit making body which has built up a large income through the huge success of the meeting, Oak Tree is one of the big donors to equine research and breeding in the State, as well as generously sponsoring other worthy courses in southern California.

The '86 Breeders' Cup day at the Oak Tree meeting. In an afternoon of thrilling finishes, none was closer than the duel between Manilla (far side) and Theatrical (near) in the Breeders' Cup Turf.

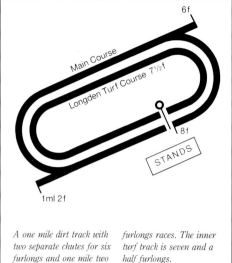

A one mile dirt track with two separate chutes for six furlongs and one mile two furlongs races. The inner turf track is seven and a half furlongs.

To see men and women walking round in toppers and tails and elegant formal dresses and picture hats is not common in southern California. But once a year Bay Meadows hosts an Annual Ascot day when traditional clothes are to be seen in carriages, and Pimms and Champagne are the only drinks drunk. A strange sight, maybe, but not a dull one.

Indeed racing at Bay Meadows has rarely been dull. Founded in 1934 by William Kyne, who is known as 'the man who brought racing back to California', the opening day's racing attracted a crowd of over 15,000. That success proved to be no flash in the pan as the crowds grew throughout that first season with an attendance of almost 30,000 for the course's big race, the Bay Meadows Handicap.

Almost immediately after the war, the course's most famous and favourite son began his career. In 1948 Bill Shoemaker, then aged 17, started riding out at the course. The following year, he had both his first ride and his first winner, both at Bay Meadows, and now 40 years later, 'the Shoe', as he is affectionately known, nears retirement with almost 8,800 winners to his credit, a record that will never be surpassed.

Situated just south of San Francisco, Bay Meadows is reponsible for introducing both the photo-finish camera and the electric starting stalls to American racing. More

Above: *Bay Meadows: racing round clubhouse turn.*

Right: *The stalls explode open and another race is under way at the San Francisco course.*

BAY MEADOWS

One of the course's major features is its annual international jockeys' race when European jockeys take on their Stateside counterparts.

recently the course staged an annual International Jockeys Competition between teams of local and European rivals.

With a season that starts in late August or early September and lasts throughout the winter into February, Bay Meadows stages important late and early season races. The Bay Meadows Handicap is still the major race in December, but the El Camino Real Derby in February has become one of the most significant Kentucky Derby trials to be held on the West Coast.

SANTA ANITA

'Lucky' Baldwin, the former prospector who struck it rich in the Californian Gold Rush and then devoted the rest of his life to nurturing the growth of horse-racing on the West Coast and in particular at Santa Anita.

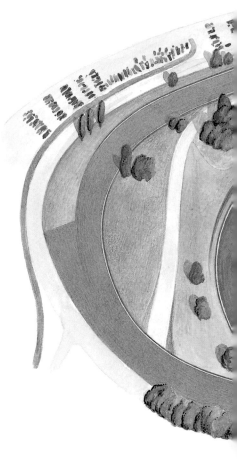

Santa Anita, under the watchful guidance of Jimmy Kilroe, has become the most popular track in the States, with attendances averaging over 30,000 people, who will daily wager over $6 million.

This success has been built on three factors: a course set in the beautiful surroundings of the San Gabriel mountains just outside Los Angeles, the wonderful Californian climate that offers sun on just about every one of the 125 days racing that Santa Anita manages to cram into its racing year and some of the best horses in the land.

Santa Anita, though barely 50 years old, has a long association with the thoroughbred. The Spanish Dons used to race their horses on this site, and following the adoption of California into the United States, 'Lucky' Baldwin, an old-style prospector who had struck it rich in the Californian gold rush, took over their role, holding rough and ready events on the Spaniards' former playground.

In 1907 Baldwin built the first proper racecourse on a 100-acre site that is within

spitting distance of the current site. This mile long track only lasted two years. For the death of Baldwin, who had been associated with Californian breeds for over 40 years and had proved to be one of the top owners in the States, led to the closure of the course.

However, when legislation permitting the reintroduction of Pari-Mutuel betting in the state was passed in 1933, the old Rancho Santa Anita was bought by the Los Angeles Turf Club. It built a new racecourse on the current site, which opened its gates to the public for the very first time on Christmas Day 1934.

Strub and Roach

The course was the brainchild of a local dentist, Charles H. Strub, and a Hollywood entrepreneur, Hal Roach. Strub had been granted a permit to build and run a racecourse by the Californian Jockey Club, but had been unable to find a site, whilst Hal Roach had bought 809,380 sq m (200 acres) of old 'Lucky' Baldwin's land, but

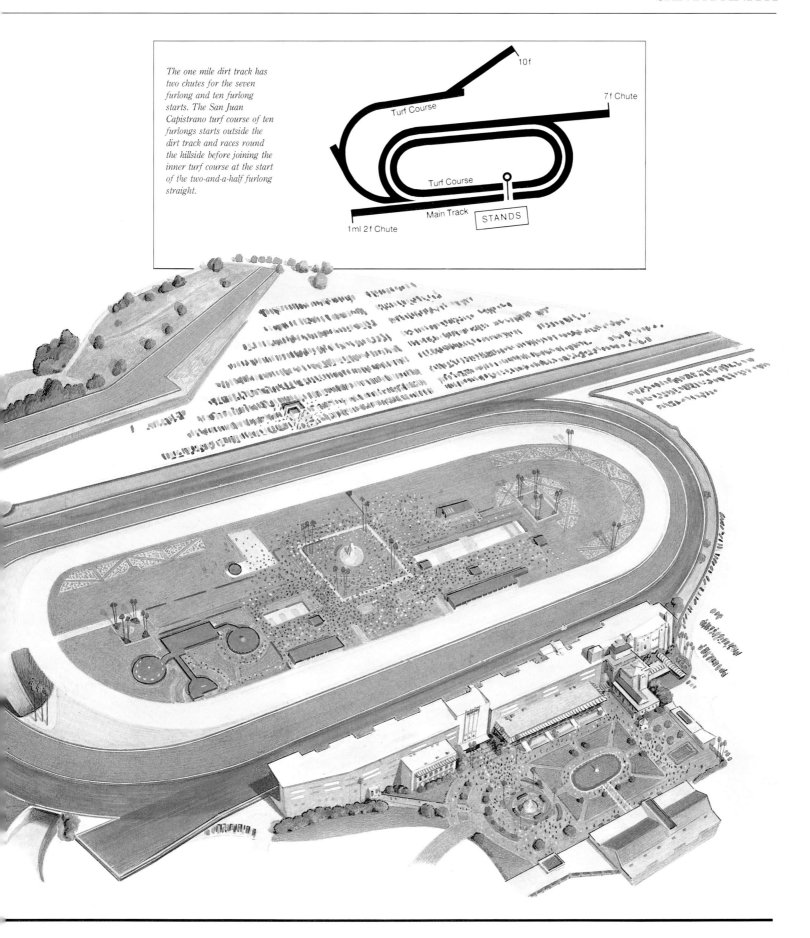

The one mile dirt track has two chutes for the seven furlong and ten furlong starts. The San Juan Capistrano turf course of ten furlongs starts outside the dirt track and races round the hillside before joining the inner turf course at the start of the two-and-a-half furlong straight.

10f

7f Chute

Turf Course

Turf Course

Main Track

STANDS

1ml 2f Chute

Dawn breaks over Santa Anita's stands. All is quiet at the moment, but soon the horses will be out exercising.

had been refused a licence by a Jockey Club which was leary of the honesty of Roach, the movie man.

The two men were made for each other and within a year of their first meeting, Santa Anita was ready for racing. Both men had big ideas for the course and decided that for a race track to be successful, it had to offer the big prizes to draw the best horses. If the best horses came to the course, then the crowds would naturally follow.

For that first day's racing, there was no race worth less than $800, which was a considerable prize in those days, and the feature race was worth $5,000. The horses came and so did the spectators, some 30,000 of them, and the betting turnover of $250,000 ensured the success of the afternoon.

Considering that this was all happening in the aftermath of the Great Depression and other courses were tempting the public in with free entry, the approach of Strub and Roach was astonishing in its boldness. But it worked and ever since Santa Anita has been leading the way in big stakes.

The Big 'Cap

The first major prize was the Santa Anita Handicap, the first-ever $100,000 race in California. A field of 20 runners was drawn to Santa Anita for the race, including such notables as Kentucky Derby winner Twenty Grand, Equipoise, both of whom had been tempted out of retirement, and Mate, but none of those three could match a seven-year-old ex-English steeplechaser Azucar who stunned the field by winning in a record time.

At the end of that decade it was Seabiscuit who dominated the Santa Anita headlines. A great champion, undoubtedly, but he had the unhealthy knack of getting beaten by a lightly weighted horse in the 'Big Cap'. Second in 1937 and 1938, he broke down in training before the 1939 race, but he too was tempted out of retirement for a crack at the 1940 running. It turned out that his name was indeed written on the cup and Seabiscuit ran out the winner to take his earnings to over $400,000, the first time such a sum had ever been achieved.

Great horses have continued to win the 'Big Cap' throughout its history and recent winners of the class, Affirmed, Spectacular Bid, the incomparable John Henry and Cougar II, show that the race is still a big draw.

The Santa Anita Derby started in the same year as the Handicap and that too has thrown up its fair share of champions. It was almost 20 years before the race provided its first winner of the Kentucky Derby in Hill Gail, but since then Determine, Lucky Debonair, Affirmed and most recently, the courageous grey filly Winning Colours have added Kentucky's roses to their Santa Anita Derby honours.

Other leading prizes include the San Juan Capistrano Handicap, the first $100,000 race on turf, the Charles H. Strub Stakes, the Santa Margarita Invitational Handicap, the Yellow Ribbon Stakes for fillies and the Oak Tree Invitational Stakes, which is run under the auspices of the Oak Tree Association.

The course stables are now equipped to house over 2,000 thoroughbreds in 55

The field rounds the only right-hand turn in the USA on the San Juan Capistrano turf course at Santa Anita.

barns. One can guarantee that many of the best horses in the States will spend part of either spring or autumn at the course going for one of the numerous big stakes races.

The course and crowds

The marvellous facilities, which have been constantly updated since the inauguration, but still retain the flavour of that era, will accommodate over 80,000 people, a crowd that is often drawn for the Santa Anita Handicap, traditionally the biggest day of the year. A crowd of that size was also present when Santa Anita hosted the 1986 Breeders' Cup under the aegis of the Oak Tree Racing Association.

The course itself is the traditional American left-handed oval of a mile in length with spurs for the seven- and ten-furlong starts. The Camino Real Turf course is unusual for the States since it is modelled on European tracks. The full length of that course is 14 furlongs, winding its way down from a start to the north of the course for almost a mile and then joining on to the main body of the course for a circuit of the oval track before reaching the winning post.

The Strub family legacy is still present: Robert Strub, son of the founder, currently holds the reins at the course as he has done since 1960. During that time he has overseen the growth of the racing prowess, something that he has encouraged with the riches on offer at his course, and by his association with the Oak Tree which has taken over Santa Anita every autumn since 1969 and run its own meeting at the course.

SANTA ANITA HANDICAP

1¼ miles. First run 1935.

Year	Winner	Owner	Trainer	Jockey
1971	Ack Ack	Forked Lightning Ranch	C. Whittingham	W. Shoemaker
1972	Triple Bend	F. McMahon	V. Longden	D. Pierce
1973	Cougar II	M. Jones	C. Whittingham	L. Pincay, Jr.
1974	Prince Dantan	S. Sommer	F. Martin	R. Turcotte
1975	Stardust Mel	M. Everett	C. Whittingham	W. Shoemaker
1976	Royal Glint	D. Lasater	G. Potter	J. Tejeira
1977	Crystal Water	Mrs. C. Ring	R. Clapp	L. Pincay, Jr.
1978	Vigors	W. Hawn	L. Sterling	D. McHargue
1979	Affirmed	Harbor View Farm	L. Barrera	L. Pincay, Jr.
1980	Spectacular Bid	Hawksworth Farm	G. Delp	W. Shoemaker
1981	John Henry	Dotsam Stable	R. McAnally	L. Pincay, Jr.
1982	John Henry	Dotsam Stable	R. McAnally	W. Shoemaker
1983	Bates Motel	J.G. Phillips & M. Riordan	J. Gosden	T. Lipham
1984	Interco	D. Sofro	T. West	P. Valenzuela
1985	Lord at War	P. Perkins	C. Whittingham	W. Shoemaker
1986	Greinton	Bradley, Whittingham & Wynne	C. Whittingham	L. Pincay, Jr.
1987	Broad Brush	R.E. Meyerhoff	R.W. Small	A. Cordero, Jr.
1988	Alysheba	D. & P. Scharbauer	J.C. Van Berg	C. McCarron
1989	Martial Law	Clover Racing Stables	J. Canani	M. Pedroza

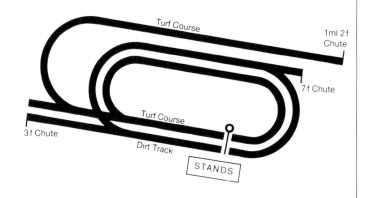

The outer dirt track is one mile in circumference with chutes for three furlong and seven furlong starts. The Marshall turf course runs back one mile two furlongs and joins the six furlong inner turf course at the start of the straight.

Turf Course

1 ml 2 f Chute

7 f Chute

3 f Chute

Turf Course

Dirt Track

STANDS

The typically low position of the jockey tells us that this race is being run in North America and the hoardings confirm that this is racing at Woodbine.

WOODBINE

Compared to the neighbouring United States, Canadian racing has a much more European feel to it, a fact which is totally borne out by a visit to Woodbine, the country's leading course. But there are really two Woodbines.

The original Woodbine, which for many years was the standard-bearer of the Ontario Jockey Club. Racing began at the original Woodbine back in 1874. But it was only following the creation of the Ontario Jockey Club in 1881 that the course became the home of Canada's flat racing.

But situated in what is now downtown Toronto, Woodbine was becoming too cramped in the 1950s for any real improvements to be made possible on the course, so the genius of Canadian racing, Eddie Taylor decided that a new course should be built outside the city to take over the donkey work of the older course. That racetrack too was called Woodbine, and the new course which was opened in 1956 has swiftly become a major North American and international course.

Old Woodbine, as the original track was renamed, carried on with the common or garden everyday racing, until in 1963 the confusion became too much for the locals to bear and its name was changed to Greenwood.

Queen's Plate

The original track was only three-quarters of a mile in circumference and specialized in trotting or harness racing. But Queen Victoria requested that the Queen's Plate, a race named in honour of her, should never be run outside Toronto. Faced with the dilemma of a big race and no course to run it on, the Ontario Jockey Club moved into Woodbine in a big way and relegated harness racing to a supporting level. The Queen's Plate was held there for over 70 years before being moved to the new course.

Other major prizes joined the Queen's Plate at the Old Woodbine: firstly, the Breeders' Stakes in 1889 and more recently the Canadian International Championship, which was started in 1938 in the hope of attracting more of the States' stars north of the border. In recent years, that contest has been sponsored by Rothmans and as the Rothmans International has succeeded in attracting not only horses from the States, but also top European challengers, it is now the centrepiece of the new course's autumn season.

Greenwood is one of the busiest courses in the world, since it holds racing throughout the year. The spring, summer and autumn meetings are evenly divided between Flat and harness racing, to which the tight course is much more suited, whilst even the rigours of a Canadian winter fail to deter some winter harness racing which is truly a sight to see.

Although Greenwood still packs in the crowds, who take full advantage of having a track in the city centre, favouring the summer evening meetings especially, all the serious racing now takes place at the new Woodbine, which is some ten miles to the north-west of Toronto's city centre.

E.P. Taylor and Northern Dancer

Eddie Taylor's importance to racing both in Canada and the world over cannot be exaggerated. On a national level, he led the Ontario Jockey Club into a complete revitalization of its Flat racing, to which he also contributed through the quality of the horses he was breeding from his Windfields Farm, which he founded in 1949 in nearby Oshawa.

On an international level he will be always remembered as the man who bred and raced Northern Dancer, who now dominates the world's bloodlines, and is set to continue to do so well into the next century through his progeny. As a yearling, the late-foaled Northern Dancer, from the first crop of Nearctic, failed to attract any bids when he was auctioned, so Taylor kept the colt and raced him himself.

As a two-year-old, Northern Dancer soon established himself as the best in Canada before going south to New York, where he gained two valuable victories. At three he picked up the Kentucky Derby in a then record time and the Preakness before failing to see out the trip in the Belmont Stakes. On his return to his native Canada, he again proved much too good for the locals in the Queen's Plate, but unfortunately bowed a tendon in that race and never raced again.

Retired to stud at the Windfields Farm where he was foaled, he proved an instant success; so much so that after four years he was forced to leave Canada for Maryland whither it was easier for the top-class brood mares clamouring for his service to reach him. His stud fee which had started at $10,000 in 1965, rose to almost $1 million at its peak in the early 1980s and the list of champions he has bred contains many of the champions of those intervening years.

Northern Dancer's success in the Queen's Plate is just one of the many triumphs that Eddie Taylor has chalked up in Canada's top races. But even he has to take a back seat in the Rothmans International race, whose greatly increased prize money has meant that the race has become that much harder for the locals to win what has become Canada's most important international contest.

ROTHMANS INTERNATIONAL STAKES
1½ miles. First run 1938.

Year	Winner	Owner	Trainer	Jockey
1971	One for All	J. Bell, III	H. Luro	T. Turcotte
1972	Droll Role	J. Schiff	T. Kelly	B. Baeza
1973	Secretariat	Meadow Stable	L. Laurin	E. Maple
1974	Dahlia	N.B. Hunt	M. Zilber	L. Piggott
1975	Snow Knight	Windfields Farm	M. Miller	J. Velasquez
1976	Youth	N.B. Hunt	M. Zilber	S. Hawley
1977	Exceller	N.B. Hunt	M. Zilber	A. Cordero, Jr.
1978	Mac Diarmida	Dr. J. Torsney	F. Schulhofer	J. Cruguet
1979	Golden Act	Marino Beach Stable	L. Rettele	S. Hawley
1980	Great Neck	Tartan Stable	S. Nerud	M. Venezia
1981	Open Call	Greentree Stable	J. Gaver, Jr.	J. Velasquez
1982	Majesty's Prince	J. de Witt Marsh	J.B. Cantey	E. Maple
1983	All Along	D. Wildenstein	P.L. Biancone	W.R. Swinburn
1984	Majesty's Prince	J. de Witt Marsh	J.B. Cantey	L. Pincay, Jr.
1985	Nassipour	Dogwood Stable	S. di Mauro	J.L. Samyn
1986	Southjet	Dogwood Stable	A. Penna	J. Santos
1987	River Memories	A. Clore	R. Collet	C. McCarron
1988	Infamy	G. Leigh	L. Cumani	R. Cochrane
1989	Hodges Bay	G.E. Robb	W.C. Freeman	D. Seymour

International Woodbine

Secretariat's victory in 1973 heralded in an era when foreign horses swept the board. One man in particular seemed to be most attached to the prize and that was the canny French trainer Maurice Zilber. He won the race three times in four years in the middle of the 1970s with the great Dahlia, Youth and Exceller - a run that was only interrupted by Taylor's Snow Knight, winner of Epsom's Derby prior to his Canadian triumph and the only Derby winner to have gone on to great things in North America.

Such is the honour in which Taylor is

Left: *Northern Dancer, the horse that has dominated the stud world since his retirement, is led into the winner's enclosure by top-hatted Edward Taylor after his triumph in the 1964 Queen's Plate.*

Right: *There is still a long way to go in the 1988 Rothmans International as the field rounds the Clubhouse turn.*

held at his local track that the supporting race on Rothmans International day is the E.P Taylor Stakes, which has in its short history become a valuable and prestigious prize in itself.

Since Woodbine was only built in 1956, the planning of both course and facilities could incorporate all the pluses of different courses around the world. It contains the good points of both European and Stateside tracks and offers a great day out.

Though the oval circuit is of the same size as most American tracks, Woodbine has been built with various chutes to give that much more variation to the racing. The inner turf course has spurs that cross over the dirt track to offer much longer distances to the competitors.

The paddock's weeping willow trees, the elegant terraces and stands and the overall greenness of the course make it a much more attractive track to visit than many in North America. Woodbine pulls in the crowds for the big days of the Queen's Plate in summer and the Rothmans in October.

The willows and the greenery give Woodbine's paddock a European feel, which is born out by the course itself. But the crowds and the racing are decidedly North American.

QUEEN'S PLATE STAKES
$1\frac{1}{4}$ miles. Three-year-olds. First run 1860.

Year	Winner	Owner	Trainer	Jockey
1971	Kennedy Road	Mrs. W. Stollery	J. Bentley	S. Hawley
1972	Victoria Song	E.P. Taylor	L. Grant	R. Platts
1973	Royal Chocolate	Stafford Farm	G. Rowntree	T. Colangelo
1974	Amber Herod	Stafford Farm	G. Rowntree	R. Platts
1975	L'Enjoleur	J. Levesque	J. Starr	S. Hawley
1976	Norcliffe	Norcliffe Stable	R. Attfield	J. Fell
1977	Sound Reason	Stafford Farm	G. Rowntree	R. Platts
1978	Regal Embrace	Windfields Farm	M. Benson	S. Hawley
1979	Steady Growth	Kinghaven Farm	J. Tammaro	B. Swatuk
1980	Driving Home	C.F.C.W. Racing Stable	G. Magnusson	W. Parsons
1981	Fiddle Dancer Boy	J. Carmichael	J. Bentley	D. Clark
1982	Son of Briartic	Paddockhurst Stable	J.G. Lavigne	P. Souter
1983	Bompago	C. Cardella	J. Cardella	L. Attard
1984	Key to the Moon	BKY Stable	G. Rowntree	R. Platts
1985	La Lorgnette	Windfields Farm	M. Benson	D. Clark
1986	Golden Choice	R. Sanderson	M. Tammaro	V. Bracciale
1987	Market Control	Kinghaven Farms	R. Attfield	K. Skinner
1988	Regal Intention	Sam-Son Farms	J.E. Day	
1989	With Approval	Kinghaven Farms	R. Attwood	D. Seymour

MEXICO CITY

Mexico City's Hippodromo de las Americas is one of the highest racecourses in the world, and has taken over as the country's premier course following the demise of the old Calienti track by the Californian border.

Racing at the course is conducted along the lines of North America, with claiming and condition races forming the bulk of a day's or evening's racing. The occasional Stakes or Graded race gives the card some extra quality.

Racing is held on four days a week throughout the year with a ten-race card often starting in the late afternoon and going on deep into the night. The huge grandstand is divided into three separate areas: the Jockey Club and Club Derby enclosures, which are members only, and the Grand Stand, which is nearly always packed with the general race-going public.

Though the racing is not the equal of that over the border, the races are competitive and attract a huge volume of betting.

The field begin the turn out of the back straight at the Hipodromo de las Americas high up in Mexico City.

SAN ISIDRO

Top Argentine sprinter Mali scorches up the track clear of his rivals to win the Felix de Alzaga Unzue at San Isidro on Carlos Pellegrini day, 1986.

O f all the faraway places around the world, Argentina's Pampas country seems the most fitting for horses. Acre after acre of thick lush grass invite horsemen to race and train their charges across the grasslands. Ever since the Conquistadores brought the horse with them to South America, prompting the locals to mistake the animal as a god, horse breeding and rearing has flourished in Argentina and the country has become renowned for its excellent polo ponies.

The racing there is of a pretty high standard too. The Argentine blood has been exported widely to the States where Forli in particular became a sire of great repute and even greater demand. Many brood mares wing their way northwards to join their more illustrious sisters in the bluegrass paddocks of Kentucky.

The centre of racing in Argentina is at

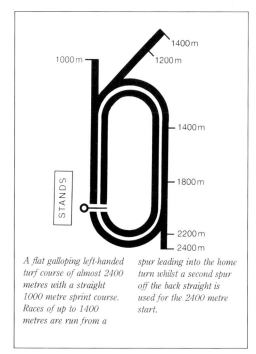

A flat galloping left-handed turf course of almost 2400 metres with a straight 1000 metre sprint course. Races of up to 1400 metres are run from a spur leading into the home turn whilst a second spur off the back straight is used for the 2400 metre start.

San Isidro, 14 miles north of the country's capital deep in the heart of the Pampas. Founded in 1935 by the Argentine Jockey Club, the course hosts the Gran Premio Internacional Carlos Pellegrini, the country's most important race and one which will attract the attention of all the racing world, and indeed on occasions even challengers from the outside world, which is not surprising given the amount of pesos on offer to the winner.

The Quadruple Crown

The race is also the fourth and final leg of the country's Quadruple Crown, an institution unique to Argentina. The Classic generation of three-year-olds begin by competing amongst themselves in Argentina's equivalent to the European Classics. Firstly there are the Polla de Potrillos and

Polla de Potrancas, the Guineas, both of which are run on dirt at the Argentino racecourse at Palermo in the heart of Buenos Aires. Then the action is switched to San Isidro's grass for the 12-furlong Gran Premio Club, their equivalent of the Derby.

Having proved their versatility once, they then have to do it all over again. The next race and the final one to be confined to three-year-olds is the Gran Premio Nacional, back on Palermo's dirt, before the generations are pitched against each other in the Carlos Pellegrini.

For a horse to be able to win top Stakes races on both dirt and grass and against other age groups, he or she really has to be top-class and winners of the Quadruple Crown are few and far between. Forli made himself a national hero in 1966 when he accomplished the feat but it has only once been achieved subsequently by Telescopico in 1978.

The value of the Quadruple Crown is exemplified by the purchase of Forli. He was recognized as a true champion and taken to the States to stand at stud there. That rare honour for a horse from outside the big racing nations proved to be an instant success as Forli sired great winners like Thatch, who has in turn become a useful sire. The owners of Telescopico also believed that their Quadruple Crown winner was worthy of international status and decided to send him over to Europe for a crack at the Arc, where although he did not win or even get placed, neither did he disgrace himself.

Argentina has one of the world's largest thoroughbred populations but because they have so few tracks, only the best make

GRAN PREMIO CARLOS PELLEGRINI

Year	Winner	Owner	Trainer	Jockey
1980	Regidor	R.A. Escariz	Degregorio	A. Pla
1981	I'm Glad	J.A. Bosano	D.E. Pascual	J. Valdivieso
1982	Sir Gold	J.C. Fronnbellia	C. Giani	L.A. Alzamora
1983	Inmensity	Fahd Jamil	A. Cabreira	A. Bolino
1984	Reverente	J.D. Ftorino	C.A. Ferro	N. De Mezzotero
1985	Salvate Tel	F. Lococo	D.A. Gomez	J.A. Maciel
1986	Fain	J.A. Bosano	D. Pascual	J. Valdivieso
1987	Larabee	J.A. De All	C.A. Bianchi	R.E. Laitán
1988	Montubio	J.E. Santamarina	A. Gaitán Dassie	O.L. Zapata
1989	Snow Figure	R.J. Estrugamou	A. Larrandart	V. Centeno

Above: *A packed crowd is assembled in the modern-looking stand for a day's racing.*

Left: *After work at San Isidro a horse and lad who have come through the cavalcade unscathed enjoy a cooling break.*

it on to the racing circuit. One would find that difficult to believe on seeing morning exercise at the San Isidro course. For as in the States, all the horses are trained on the tracks where they are stabled, and to see the 4,000 odd horses at work is a quite terrifying experience.

Training at San Isidro

Line after line canter and gallop on the work gallops and seem to miss each other by the

The afternoon has long gone, but the show goes on deep into the night at San Isidro. The diners at the course restaurant can enjoy their food and the finishes at the same time.

smallest of margins. There is hardly room to see the turf for horses, all bareback with apparently mad or 'loco' lads up on board turning them every which way without a care in the world. One would think that the full-time presence of an ambulance by the side of the gallops is there to save a constant stream of telephone calls yet surprisingly it is rarely required. What is also surprising is that the trainers, from their favourite view-point, are able to work out which is their string amongst the crazy cavalcade.

Yet it all seems to work, and the horses do produce the results on the course, although it is almost impossible to assess the quality of the Argentine thoroughbreds against those of North America or Europe.

Firstly, because Argentina is in the Southern Hemisphere, the foaling date will be in August or September and the official equine birth date is 1 July rather the 1 January date used in the North. Secondly, the impossibility of racing the two Classic crops against each other is compounded by the distances that would have to be trav-elled to do so.

Telescopico's lack of success in the Arc can be equated with a similar lack of

success by the French, German and North American horses who have tried to win the Carlos Pellegrini, but nevertheless the horses in and around Buenos Aires seem to be able to go plenty fast enough.

The favourable climate allows the course to race throughout the year – 120 days in all – and the grass track is always kept in immaculate condition despite the hard use to which it is subjected.

There are two or three days racing each week at San Isidro with the dark days being filled with racing at either Palermo or La Plata, the country's third main course.

Fourteen racecards

The daily card includes up to 14 races and the programme, which usually begins in mid-afternoon, stretches out into the night with the later races being run under flood-lights. There is a delightfully unhurried air to the proceedings, and all the starters amble rather than canter down to the start, which is always delayed until the Tote has taken enough money.

All the main races are run in the Argen-tine spring and early summer, with the

Jockey Club at the end of October and the Carlos Pellegrini in the middle of December, but the autumn and winter racing is still of a high standard with many big races includ-ing the Gran Premio Internacional 25 de Mayo and the Gran Criterium standing out.

San Isidro is a long and wide track. Nearly two miles in circumference, the course can race its major events round one bend, something which is unheard of in the States, and the five- furlong race can be run in a straight line.

The modern-looking grandstand can hold up to 30,000 people, whilst the course itself can officially hold 100,000 but that figure was stretched in 1952 when 102,000 managed to prise their way in to see the Carlos Pellegrini.

San Isidro has had its problems with the government, who took control of the course in 1974. However, they found that they could not run it at a profit and so handed it back to the Jockey Club in 1978. Neverthe-less racing has sat alongside the various administrations fairly happily and the course seems to be assured of retaining its lofty position as the foremost course in South America.

GAVEA

The horses make their way onto the course while the packed Gavea stands rise above them.

Racing in Brazil will never be able to rival that in neighbouring Argentina, for not only is most of the country unsuitable for the racing of thoroughbreds, but also most Brazilians seem to be more concerned with partying than the pursuit of matters equestrian. That said there are 23 racecourses in the country, a large equine population and enough people whose idea of fun is following the horses to make the sport profitable – and, to cap it all, one of the most spectacular racecourses in the world is Gavea.

Situated on the south side of the Ipanema Bay and overlooked by the statue of Christ the Redeemer which is perched on top of the Sugarloaf mountain, Gavea is a wonderful excuse for a racecourse, and one which is well used by the populace of Rio. Though racing is conducted on similar lines to those followed in Argentina, Brazil has more in common with the other South American countries in regard to the quality of the horse racing.

Although the equator runs through the country, the Southern Hemisphere birth date is used for the ageing of horses and consequently the main racing season's are in the spring and autumn. All horses run in a strict grading system unless they are of

The outer turf course is one mile two furlongs in circumference and contains an inner dirt track of one mile one furlong, which has two separate turns out of the home straight.

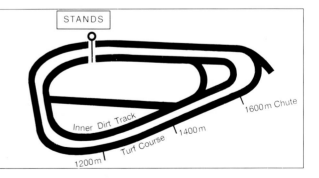

STANDS

Inner Dirt Track
Turf Course
1200m
1400m
1600m Chute

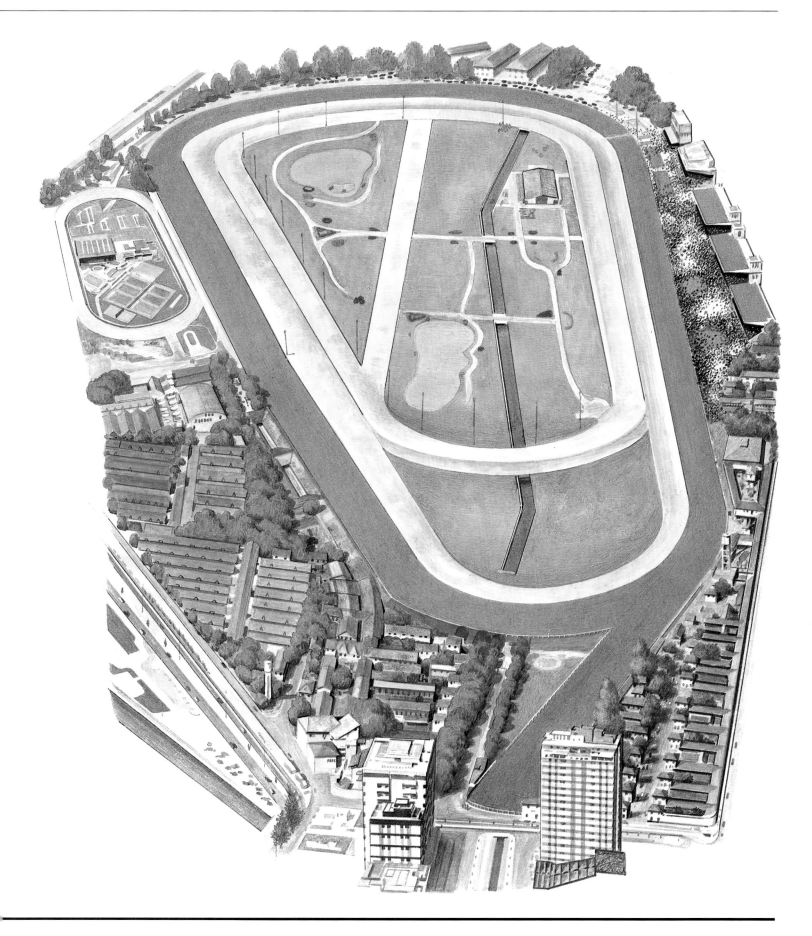

Graded race status. A maiden will compete only amongst his peers, and having won a race, he will progress to races for the winners of only one race, then on upwards through the scale, receiving or giving weight depending on how much prize money he has amassed.

This leads to competitive, if slightly repetitive racing. Few horses will race outside the circuit on which they are trained, and then only for the big prizes which are shared between Gavea, San Paulo, the country's major track, and Cuidade Jardim.

The Season

Gavea's spring racing season is its most important, with good races like the Gran Premio Frederico Lundgren, the Gran Premio Lineu de Paula Machado and the Gran Premio Joaquim Marques de Lisboa amongst the better races conducted during October and November.

Since the level of prize money is so poor in a country where inflation necessitates changes in prices almost every day, the top Brazilian horses tend to run for the richer prizes on offer in Sao Paulo and elsewhere abroad.

Peru and Uruguay figure on the list of countries that are raidable, but Argentina with prize money being over double what is available in Brazil is a more difficult nut to crack. The reason is simply because their horses are a grade or two above those the Brazilians would meet elsewhere on the continent.

The South American International Championship perennially falls to the Argentines and only top-quality Brazilian horses like Duplex at the beginning of the 1980s have made an impression on the Argentinian circuit.

Gavea has a charming atmosphere and the old stands are in sharp contrast to the flashier apartment buildings that stand beneath the Sugarloaf mountain.

The tight course has both a turf and a grass track. Whilst the facilities may leave something to be desired, an evening spent watching the racing under the floodlights in the comfort of the most exclusive enclosure can be most enjoyable.

Above: *There are excellent stabling facilities at Gavea; here a horse is being hosed down after a race.*

Left: *The backdrop of the Sugarloaf Mountain in Rio de Janeiro makes Gavea one of the most spectacular courses in the world.*

REST OF THE WORLD

If Europe is where the sport was born and America is where it has flourished, Australasia and the Far East is where it is growing fastest.

For they have combined the best of the Old World and shaped it into an increasingly rich and powerful industry, and are beginning to breed horses that can take on and beat all but the best.

Australia has a long and rich heritage in the sport, but it is only in recent years that the domination of the old Cup races has been shrugged off and the breeding of horses to win over Classic distances become paramount.

The prizes in that country are matched by those on offer in Japan, a country that has only recently entered the world stage, but one which is growing in importance year by year.

Gambling may still be the major factor in racing in Hong Kong, Malaysia and India, but it is the revenue from gambling that is the life blood of racing wherever it takes place.

Spectacular view of Hong Kong's Happy Valley track at night.

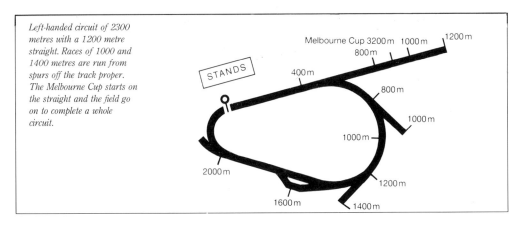

Left-handed circuit of 2300
metres with a 1200 metre
straight. Races of 1000 and
1400 metres are run from
spurs off the track proper.
The Melbourne Cup starts on
the straight and the field go
on to complete a whole
circuit.

Melbourne Cup 3200 m   1000 m   1200 m
800 m
400 m
STANDS
800 m
1000 m
1000 m
2000 m   1200 m
1600 m   1400 m

FLEMINGTON

I f any country's great races, the Melbourne Cup is the one most widely celebrated by its people. The whole of Australia literally grinds to a standstill on the first Tuesday of each November to watch, party, gamble on and celebrate the biggest moment in Australia's racing year.

At around 2.40 pm on that day, the field sets out on a two-mile trip into the record books. One of them will bring home the bacon - and it is some bacon with the prize money now standing at over Aus $1.8 million - and become the most feted horse of the year. That the race is just a two-mile handicap of no particular merit to the racing purists is unimportant. In Australia, racing means the Melbourne Cup and the Melbourne Cup means Flemington Park on the first Tuesday of November.

For days before the race Melbourne readies itself for the annual celebrations that accompany Melbourne Cup day. The spring weather does not always help the street parties, picnics and barbecues that begin on the Friday night, but it is not allowed to threaten or curtail activities. On the Tuesday, the state of Victoria awards itself a day's holiday and prepares for the big event. The rest of Australia either grudgingly goes to work or takes a "sickie",

the popular name for a day off ill.

The media join in the shenanigans with interview after interview of owners, trainers, jockeys and indeed anyone who can muster up a few words on the subject. Tips fly about like bullets as everyone prepares to have a bet at TAB, the legal off course Tote, offices around the country.

Run-up to the race

Melbourne has its own way of doing things. A bizarre service is held at St Francis' Church in the town centre: the Racing Fraternity Mass, where prayers are offered up for the physical and mental prosperity of the racing community in the year to come.

Bourke Street, the city's central

At times it looks like the whole of Melbourne has descended upon Flemington to celebrate 'Cup day.

The grey Ideal Centreman loses out to Buckerol in the battle for minor placings in the 1988 Melbourne Cup won by the mare Empire Rose.

thoroughfare, is taken over by a carnival and a procession of previous winners who are paraded to those out savouring the atmosphere.

All around the place since cocktail parties have been on the go since mid-morning, where – depending on the host's lifestyle, either morning suits and designer dresses or wild and crazy fancy dress are sported by the guests. And the racecourse itself begins to fill up. Up to 100,000 people will make their way to Flemington for the day's racing. Some will have been invited to smart lunches in private boxes and some will come with the whole family and will picnic by their cars or in the cheaper enclosures.

The carnival atmosphere is closer to Epsom on Derby Day than to Kentucky's big race, but with one difference: the size of the bets. The Australians do like a gamble and if they have the money, they like to play for high stakes.

Those Australian tycoons who like to play, play big and bets of up to Aus $1 million have been reported. The willingness of bookmakers to stand such wagers does them great credit, for they would be refused in most other countries.

The crowd as a whole chip in with their own sixpennyworth. On average the bookmakers will take Aus $4 million plus a sum matched by the on-course Tote operation. Add to that the Aus $45 million wagered at the off-course TABs around the country and one can work out that every man,

woman and child of Australia's 16 million population will have had three or four dollars on the Cup.

The race dates back a long way: the first running was in 1861, some 20 years after a pair of Ayrshire brothers had taken to riding against each other on a site near the Saltwater river.

Their contests brought some local renown to the place, especially when gold was found in the locality in 1851. Melbourne became a boom town and of course it had to have a racetrack to entertain the prospectors who had hit it big.

The Melbourne Cup

Flemington racecourse was officially set up in 1855. It did not take much longer for the Melbourne Cup to come along. In 1861 the Victoria Turf Club decided to add an extra race to its spring meeting, a two-mile handicap for three-year-olds and upwards for which the prize was to be 220 sovereigns and a gold watch.

A Cup was substituted for the gold watch immediately after the first running of the race, but a permanent trophy was not established until 1919. Then a 5cm (12in) high trophy on a plinth of Australian blackwood was awarded to Artilleryman, that year's winner.

Ever since, with the exception of the war years, a new Cup has been commissioned each year to be kept in perpetuity by the winning owner.

The huge modern stand is packed with crowds yelling themselves hoarse as the runners in the Cup run down the straight.

Outside the entrance to the Members' Enclosure at Flemington stands a bronze of Phar Lap, the horse who epitomises racing to Australians.

Archer

The race became a national event after the first running, for as is so often the case, the story of that first race quickly became a legend. In a hurly-burly affair, in which two horses fell, one failed to start and a fourth ran away, Archer beat the top-weight Mormon in a thrilling finish. When it was learnt that Archer had walked the 550 miles from his New South Wales stable to take part in the race, the Australian public took both him and the race he had won to their hearts and turned it into the race of the year.

That Archer under the top-weight of 10 stone 2lb should go on and win the second running of the race, again with the luckless Mormon beaten into second place, only further consolidated his greatness in the eyes of his public. The horse had become the new country's first sporting hero and symbol of the hopes and aspirations of its people. They have looked to the Melbourne Cup for that kind of inspiration since.

The great champions are so heavily burdened with weight that the underdogs have a chance of getting their revenge on their more illustrious brothers and seeing their names up in lights. Yet the really memorable winners - the ones that are mentioned in the same breath as the race itself - are not those underdogs who sprang a surprise victory, but true champions who managed to rise above the average and, like Archer, forge themselves into national heroes.

Racing enthusiasts still talk of winners such as Carbine, whose victory in 1890 was achieved carrying a staggering 10 stone 5 lb, a record which will never be matched; Peter Pan, the first horse since Archer to win two Cups, Rain Lover, another dual winner and probably the best of the modern age who brought glory to Bart Cummings, the King of the Cup; and Phar Lap, the greatest of them all.

Phar Lap

Phar Lap was and still is more than just a horse to the Australians. He was a national hero who brightened the lives of the whole population as the Depression hit Australia. Bought for £168 as a yearling in New Zealand, Phar Lap was trained by Harry Telford, who leased him from his owner David Davies. A big ugly gelding, he failed to make any impression as a juvenile and was unfancied when he ran in the 1929 AJC Derby, his first major race.

But he had grown into himself and won first that Classic and then a whole string of other races, including the AJC St Leger, the VRC St Leger, which is also held at Flemington, and the W.S. Cox Plate before the Melbourne Cup.

Phar Lap, however, had to survive drama even before he reached the starting post. His connections had gone for a touch on his victory in the Melbourne Cup and book-makers facing a large pay-out tried to shoot him after exercise at Flemington one morning. He was rushed into hiding and returned to the course only minutes before the off. In the race, he made light of his top-weight of 9 stone 12 lb to win the Cup in a canter. Given

ever more and more weight, he continued his winning ways until he had to carry an unprecedented 10 stone 10 lb in his defence of the Melbourne Cup in 1931. As always he came to take up the running as the field entered the straight, but this time the burden proved to be too great and the people's champ faded away in the final furlong.

Realizing that from then on Phar Lap would be weighted out of contention in his native land, owner Davies and trainer Telford sent the five-year-old over to Calienti, Mexico, for what was to be the world's richest ever race, the Agua Calienti, in March 1932. Despite having to adjust to the foreign conditions and suffering from a split hoof, Phar Lap put in his greatest ever performance on the alien dirt surface to beat the finest of the locals.

Tragedy

But tragedy was not far away. For the second time, Phar Lap's life was threatened and when he died under mysterious circumstances just 17 days later, the whole of Australia believed that the great horse had been poisoned. His carcass has been preserved and stuffed, and to this day is still kept in Melbourne's National Museum. But, come Cup day, old Phar Lap is taken out of his mothballs and paraded before the countrymen who doted on him.

Now the prize money on offer in Melbourne has started to get horses to travel the opposite way to Phar Lap, and top Northern Hemisphere stayers trek down to Australia for a shot at the Cup. Although Comedy King, the winner in 1910, was a northern-bred horse as was Backwood in 1924, it was not until the tail end of the 1970s that the migration began in earnest.

Robert Sangster, whose farsightedness has been proved right in so many spheres of racing, started the ball rolling when his Beldale Ball won the 1980 running. Since then each race has seen a fancied runner from either Europe or the States who has been shipped over to Australia and put into training with a leading local handler. But only one more – Sheikh Hamdan Al-Maktoum's At Talaq in 1986 – has so far taken the prized three-handled Cup.

Four-day meeting

There is more to Flemington than just the Melbourne Cup. It is also the home of the Victoria Derby, the oldest established race in Australia. This has been competed for ever since 1854 and is run on the first day of the four day Melbourne Cup meeting, as is the L.K.S. McKinnon Stakes.

The first day is traditionally the Saturday and after the Cup on the Tuesday, racing resumes on the Thursday when the showpiece is the VRC Oaks, whilst the final Saturday of the meeting boasts the Ampol Stakes and the Queen Elizabeth Stakes as its feature races. The McKinnon Stakes has often been used as the final prep race for the Melbourne Cup and the fact that it should be run only three days before the major event would really surprise many racegoers in Europe. But the Australians do not believe in mollycoddling their horses and the average horse in Australia runs twice as often as his counterpart in the North.

The practice appears to work well, with few of the top horses seeming to break down through being over-raced, and to see a champion racing so often endears it to the public. A typical Epsom Derby winner these days has a racing career of ten or so races before being retired at the end of his three-year-old season.

Down under, a horse would have only begun to be accepted as a champion after two seasons on the course; the champions come out for at least three or four seasons of racing before they are regarded as having earned their rest. This is primarily because the stud value of an Australian champion is nothing like as high as the figures earned in the United States or Europe, so there is a much greater incentive to keep a good horse on the go in the hope of winning more of the large prizes on offer. Those include Flemington's big race of the autumn season, the Australian Cup, a top weight-for-age race which pits the three-year-olds who have won the Classics in October and November against their older rivals.

A grand old course that deserves its position as the shop window of Australian racing, Flemington is a good left-handed galloping track of 11 furlongs with a straight six-furlong course, over which the prestigious Newmarket Handicap is run. The four stands are always full on Melbourne Cup day, but a regular crowd of 10,000 can be expected for most Saturdays when racing is held at the course.

MELBOURNE CUP

Year	Winner	Owner	Trainer	Jockey
1971	Silver Knight	Sir Walter Norwood	E. Templeton	R.B. Marsh
1972	Piping Lane	R.W. Trinder	G.M. Hanlon	J. Letts
1973	Gala Supreme	J.P. Curtain	R.J. Hutchins	F. Reys
1974	Think Big	R.J.O'Sullivan & C.N. Tan	J.B. Cummings	H. White
1975	Think Big	R.J. O'Sullivan, C.N. Tan & Tunku Abdul Rahman	J.B. Cummings	H. White
1976	Van Der Hum	L.H. & R.A. Robinson & L.L.G. Abel	L.H. Robinson	R.J. Skelton
1977	Gold and Black	Mr. & Mrs. J. Harris & Mr. & Mrs. H.B. Gage	J.B. Cummings	J. Duggan
1978	Arwon	Doon Bros. Syn (Mgr. E.C. Doon, R.A. Wilson, B. Wakefield & J. Watson)	G.M. Hanlon	H. White
1979	Hyperno	Mr. & Mrs. T.L. North, Mr. & Mrs. G. Herscu & Dr. R. Lake	J.B. Cummings	H. White
1980	Beldale Ball	Swettenham Stud. Syn. (Mgr. R.E. Sangster)	C.S. Hayes	J. Letts
1981	Just A Dash	L.J. Williams, G.N. Frew & T.R. Pettiona	T.J. Smith	P. Cook
1982	Gurner's Lane	William Street Syn. No. 2; (Mgrs. A. Ramsden & T. Borthwick)	G.T. Murphy	L. Dittman
1983	Kiwi	Mr. & Mrs. E.S. Lupton	E.S. Lupton	J. Cassidy
1984	Black Knight	M.R. Holmes a' Court	G.M. Hanlon	P. Cook
1985	What A Nuisance	Mr. & Mrs. L.J. Williams & D. Gowing	J.F. Meagher	P. Hyland
1986	At Talaq	Sheikh Hamdan Bin Rashid Al Maktoum	C.S. Hayes	M. Clarke
1987	Kensei	H. Lawton	L. Bridge	L. Olsen
1988	Empire Rose	Mr. & Mrs. Fr. Bodle	L. Laxon	T. Allan
1989	Tawriffic	Avery, Griffiths & McKeon	L. Freedman	S. Dye

Either you take a picnic or else a picnic takes you. An ambitious diner at Flemington.

Morphettville in Adelaide is South Australia's premier course, and its racing has been dominated for many a year by Colin Hayes.

MORPHETTVILLE

South Australia has never been quite able to match the metropolis of Melbourne and Sydney when it comes to racing, but Adelaide has an honourable tradition in racing and in Morphettville has secured for itself a top-class course.

Run by the South Australian Jockey Club since it was founded in 1860, Morphettville is as good a track as one can find in the Southern Hemisphere. A good galloping track of 12 furlongs in circumference, albeit with a short straight, Morphettville has its fair share of top races and has been boosting its prize money of late to come into line with the rest of Australia.

The principal meetings are held in February when the South Australian Derby and Oaks are run and the major autumn carnival in May when the Adelaide Cup and the Marlboro Plate, formerly the Goodwood Handicap, are the feature events.

Morphettville's racing has recently been dominated by Colin Hayes, whose Lindsay Farm Stud and training centre lies 100 miles north of Adelaide. Hayes has been champion trainer of the state without interruption for the past 26 years and his domination of both Morphettville and indeed the rest of the country shows little sign of diminishing.

In 1976 Morphettville's grandstand was burnt to the ground and the course had to be closed, but a spectacular new stand has risen from the ashes, offering its patrons all the best of modern facilities, comfort and good viewing.

This has helped to increase the course's popularity and crowds now come in their thousands, even if they do seem to place more money on the racing conducted in Melbourne and the races shown at the course live via satellite, than they do on their own races.

The almost round Morphettville circuit is 2300 metres long with a short straight of almost 400 metres. Chutes off the main track house the 1200 and the 1800 metre starts.

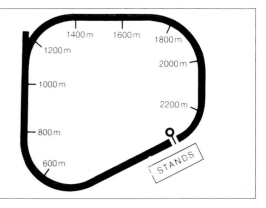

ROSEHILL

Flat right-handed galloping circuit of 2000 metres with a 500 metre straight. The 1200 metre races start from the centre of the course and are run round a long bend into the straight.

O ne of the country's most beautiful racecourses, Rosehill shares with Randwick the distinction of being Sydney's major track. Fifteen miles west of the city centre, Rosehill is known as Sydney's garden course.

Of late the course has become famous as the home for the Golden Slipper Stakes, the country's premier two-year-old race since its inauguration in 1957. Now it vies with the Melbourne Cup for the honour of being Australia's richest race, with the two respective sponsors, the rival breweries Fosters and Tooheys, upping the ante each time a race is run.

The course stages major festivals in both the spring and the autumn, though the August/September meeting can in no way compete with the incredible prize money on offer at the three-Saturday March meeting.

Besides the Golden Slipper, the other important races then include the H.E. Tancred Stakes, a second US $1 million bonanza event, which is being promoted as a major international event and is regularly attracting runners from the Northern Hemisphere.

Though Rosehill does perhaps lack the stature of Randwick or Flemington, it has worked its way into the international limelight through the shrewd promotion of its feature races and is likely to be one of the country's most famous tracks for a long time to come.

A ten-furlong course with a good flat run-in of two furlongs, Rosehill has been almost completely refurbished in the last 20 years, boasting two modern stands in its Paddock and Southern enclosures to hold the throngs that regularly pour out of Sydney for the racing.

The runners parade before the stands for the 1988 Tooheys Golden Slipper, Australia's top two-year-old contest and worth over Aus $1.5 million.

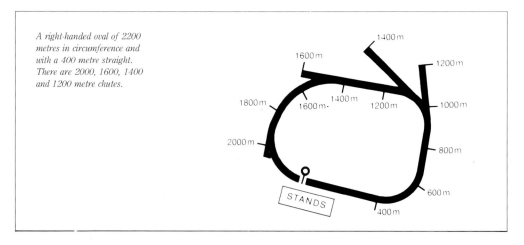

A right-handed oval of 2200 metres in circumference and with a 400 metre straight. There are 2000, 1600, 1400 and 1200 metre chutes.

RANDWICK

Randwick, home of the Australian Jockey Club, which is the oldest racing body in the country, is a delightful combination of the old and the new and is still regarded as Sydney's premier racecourse.

Given that Sydney's racing is reckoned to be the hottest in Australia and the winners of its championships are regarded as the champions of all Australia, that is a prestigious banner to have to carry and one which Randwick is proud to bear in view of the fierce competition that Rosehill is offering.

Racing was first staged at the course in 1860 after the Club's original home, Homebush, was deserted in favour of the current site. That first year at Randwick saw the inaugural running of Sydney's oldest Classic, the AJC St Leger. The AJC Derby joined the Leger the following year, making it the same age as the Melbourne Cup, but it was to be a further 6l years before the fillies were given their chance and the AJC Oaks was first run.

Classics, though important, have always been overshadowed by the Cup races. The Sydney Cup, which was for years the most important race run at Randwick, was introduced into the calendar by the Jockey Club for the first time in April 1865.

The Sydney Cup

To date, only the great Carbine has won both the Sydney and Melbourne Cups in the same year, a double which eluded even the renowned Phar Lap in 1931. But try as it might Sydney, which leads the country in so many fields, has not been able to promote the status of its Cup above that of Melbourne. It is certainly a big event in its own right and will draw a crowd of 50,000 to Randwick, but in no way does it capture the imagination of the country at large in the same way as its big rival.

Randwick is almost unique in Australia by hosting two important racing festivals each year. Either the spring or the autumn meeting is the stronger one at most other courses, but Randwick's spring meeting at the start of October, as Australians gear themselves up for another season's excitement, is just as important as the April festival that follows on from the heady events at Rosehill.

Carbine, though never as dear to the Australian public as Phar Lap, remains the only horse to date to win both the Sydney and Melbourne Cups.

Above: *Australian Oaks day at Randwick. The wealth of Australian racing has drawn owners from all over the world, especially Robert Sangster, whose blue and emerald green colours are sported by the jockey on the blinkered horse.*

Right: *Randwick's imposing stand towers above the infield lake. The course fights it out with Rosehill for the honour of being the premier course in Sydney.*

The pre-eminent races in the spring are the Metropolitan Handicap over 13 furlongs, the first major staying handicap of the new season, the George Main Stakes, and on the first Saturday in October three Group 1 races incredibly on the same card. Two top-class three-year-old races, the Flight Stakes for fillies and the Spring Champion Stakes, usher in the horses that will be in the headlines though the season, but the most valuable race is the Epsom Handicap, the country's top mile handicap.

Recently Beau Zam came to the fore with a stunning victory in the 1987 Spring Champion Stakes before winning Rosehill's Segenhoe Stakes and the first million dollar Tancred Stakes, beating some hot Northern Hemisphere rivals. He then continued on his trail of triumph by adding Randwick's AJC Derby and St Leger, at the incredibly short odds of 16-1 on, to his earlier Champion Stakes triumph, but such is the richness of Australian racing that ideas of sending him over to either the States or Europe were soon scotched for that year.

Neville Voight

On that same day Neville Voigt entered the record books by becoming the first man both to ride and train the winner of the Metropolitan. Voigt had been one of the most popular jockeys on the Sydney circuit over his 20-odd-year riding career, during which he won the Metropolitan twice with Tails in 1969 and Hayai in 1983.

Having retired from the saddle in 1986, Voigt won his first major race as a trainer when Balcaino, a son of the great Balmerino, ran out an easy winner in the following year's Metropolitan and came home to the sort of reception reserved for the winner of the Melbourne Cup.

Autumn comes early to Randwick, with the season starting again in February with a one-day meeting, but it is not until April that the big races are staged. AJC Derby day, at the start of the month, is the most important day of the meeting with the Doncaster Handicap a major supporting race on the same card, but each of the succeeding four days' racing has a top-class race to recommend it.

The Queen Elizabeth Stakes is often a valuable pointer to both the Sydney Cup and the following spring's Melbourne Cup. Recently this race, like so many others on the circuit, has been dominated by the Cup king, Bart Cummings, who trained the most expensive horse ever to have raced in Australia – the Irish import Authaal – to win the 1988 renewal of that race.

The Sydney trainers

Cummings' rivalry with Tommy Smith and the up-and-coming Brian Mayfield-Smith is always one of the highlights of the Sydney racing scene. With such powerful competition and the increasing strength of their stables, even the minor races at the Randwick festivals take a lot of winning.

Although the season does not end until Canterbury's meeting at the end of April, the outcome is nearly always worked out by the finish of the Randwick festival, for which all the trainers save their big guns.

The Australian Jockey Club also run Warwick Farm, Sydney's so-called picnic track some 20 miles from the city centre, where the racing is conducted round a sharp 10-furlong track that seems to be one long bend. The racing there is more laid back and entertaining than that which one sees at the principal track, but even so prize money never drops below Aus $10,000.

RANDWICK AJC DERBY				
Year	Winner	Owner	Trainer	Jockey
1970	Silver Sharp	Mr. & Mrs. McSweeney	T.J. Smith	N. Voigt
1971	Classic Mission	R. Got	S. Brown	G. Moore
1972	Gold Brick	J.H. Ingham	T. Kennedy	B. Selkrig
1973	Imagele	T.J. Smith	T.J. Smith	K. Langby
1974	Taras Bulba	Mr. & Mrs. Marconi	G. Hanlon	J. Slacker
1975	Battle Sign	Mrs. N. Millard	T. Millard	O. Messingham
1976	Great Lover	T.J. & N.C. Smith	T.J. Smith	K. Langby
1977	Belmura Lad	D. Morisson	J.B. Cummings	N. Voigt
1978	Race not run			
1979	Dulcify	A. Malter	C.S. Hayes	B. Thomson
1980	Kingston Town	Mr. & Mrs. D. Hains	T.J. Smith	M. Johnston
1981	Our Paddy Boy	Swettenham Stud	C.S. Hayes	R. Mullyan
1982	Rose of Kingston	Mr. & Mrs. D. Hains	R. Maysted	G. Willetts
1983	Strawberry Road	J. Pantos	D. Bougoure	L. Dittman
1984	Prolific	H. Gaffney	J.B. Cummings	J. Marshall
1985	Tristarc	P. Sheppard	R.S. McDonald	W. Treloar
1986	Bonecrusher	P.J. Mitchell	F. Ritchie	G. Stewart
1987	Myocard	Mr. & Mrs. J.M. Duncan	Dr. G. Chapman	M. de Montfort
1988	Beau Zam	J.B. Cummings	J.B. Cummings	J. Marshall
1989	Research	C. Conners	C. Conners	L. Dittman

Dawn at Randwick and the horses leave their stables for early-morning work on the training course.

In contrast, Randwick's racecourse manages to combine the modern facilities of the Queen Elizabeth and St Leger stands with a traditional atmosphere that is unique on Australia's courses. With a track that would please any trainer, an afternoon's racing at Randwick is as enjoyable as anywhere else in the world. The right-handed course, which is an almost square oval, is a decent 11 furlongs long with a two-furlong straight and offers a true galloping horse a fair race.

The closest of Sydney's courses to the heart of the city, Randwick attracts a healthy crowd, which has been boosted of late with the introduction of the superfecta, a bet open only to those on-course which can build up a jackpot big enough to bring the most avid gambler to the meeting.

MOONEE VALLEY

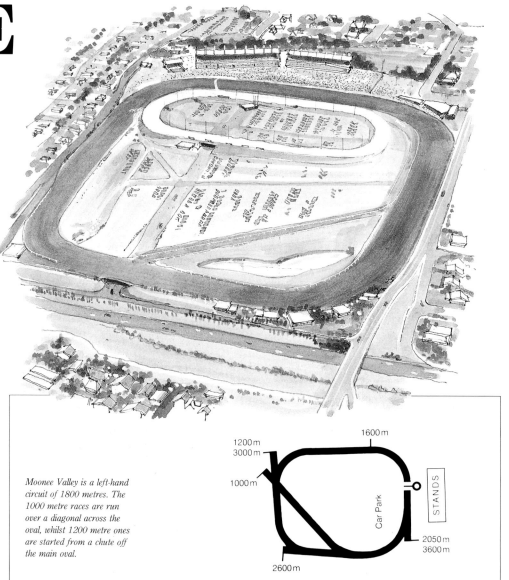

Moonee Valley has to live in the shadow of the more famous Flemington, but Melbourne's second racecourse also stages some hot racing.

Moonee Valley is a left-hand circuit of 1800 metres. The 1000 metre races are run over a diagonal across the oval, whilst 1200 metre ones are started from a chute off the main oval.

1200 m
3000 m
1600 m
1000 m
Car Park
STANDS
2050 m
3600 m
2600 m

Moonee Valley has to take second billing in Melbourne behind Flemington, but the course is never far away from the limelight and it enjoys its greatest moment one week before Flemington's Melbourne Cup. And that is the W.S.Cox Plate, Australia's most important weight-for-age race. Since its inaugural running in 1922, the Plate has continually thrown up champions and, given the rise in stature of the conditions race in Australia, it looks assured of continued prosperity. Nightmarch in 1929 and Phar Lap in 1930 and 1931 put the race on the map. On the first two occasions, the race was used as a

final conditioning outing before the big Cup, but subsequently only one horse.

Perhaps the most talked about race was the 1986 clash between the New Zealand champions Bonecrusher and Our Waverley Star. Both came into the race with strong claims and there was little to separate them in the betting. Both horses went for home four furlongs out, and time after time around the final turn Our Waverley Star repulsed Bonecrusher's challenge.

With both jockeys driving their horses for all they were worth, it looked as if Our Waverley Star had done just enough. But in Moonee Valley's short straight, Bonecrusher was asked for one final effort

by Gary Stewart and the gelding responded by reaching and then passing his great rival to win by a neck.

A sharper track than either of its two Melbourne rivals, Flemington and Caulfield, Moonee Valley is nevertheless as popular a course with the locals. The spring meeting, with the Cox Plate, is without a doubt better attended than the autumn, but crowds of 20,000 will turn up for the big races. As with so many Australian courses, Moonee Valley has an inner hurdles and steeplechasing course to provide an alternative type of entertainment, though one which has never really established itself in the country.

ASCOT

The distance that separates Perth from the rest of Australia has hindered the development of Western Australia's racing. The courses out in Perth cannot attract stables of the same quality as the illustrious Sydney and Melbourne tracks.

However, the Ascot track in the heart of the city does hold a major meeting over the Christmas holiday period, when the Eastern trainers do send some of their better charges across the country to run in races like the Perth Cup, the west coast version of Melbourne's more famous race, the Australian and West Australian Derbies and the Railway Stakes.

The growth of the course in recent years has been helped by the much increased prize money on offer at Ascot and its near neighbour Belmont, which is more frequently used during the winter months. This is a result of the general development of the state and an influx of rich new owners.

The Perth Cup, which is as old as Ascot racecourse itself, was first run in 1879, but has only seen one horse, Blue Spec, complete the double in successive years. As the stock of the old staying handicaps is having difficulty in keeping up with the current vogue for weight-for age races, the Cup is unlikely to start throwing up more top-class winners.

One reason for that lack of success is the hard ground which is so often found at Ascot. This can deter trainers from running their best horses at the course, especially as they would have to cross the whole country and become acclimatised to the much greater heat found in Perth at that time of year.

A left-handed oval of some ten furlongs in circumference set alongside the famous Swan river, Ascot was given a complete overhaul in 1982, which brought its facilities in line with other Australian courses.

The grey mare Saratov keeps going all the way to line in the '89 Perth Cup to win the West Coast's big race in a new record time.

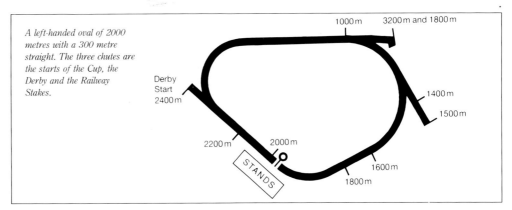

A left-handed oval of 2000 metres with a 300 metre straight. The three chutes are the starts of the Cup, the Derby and the Railway Stakes.

1000m   3200m and 1800m

Derby
Start
2400m

2200m   2000m

1400m

1500m

STANDS

1600m

1800m

BRISBANE

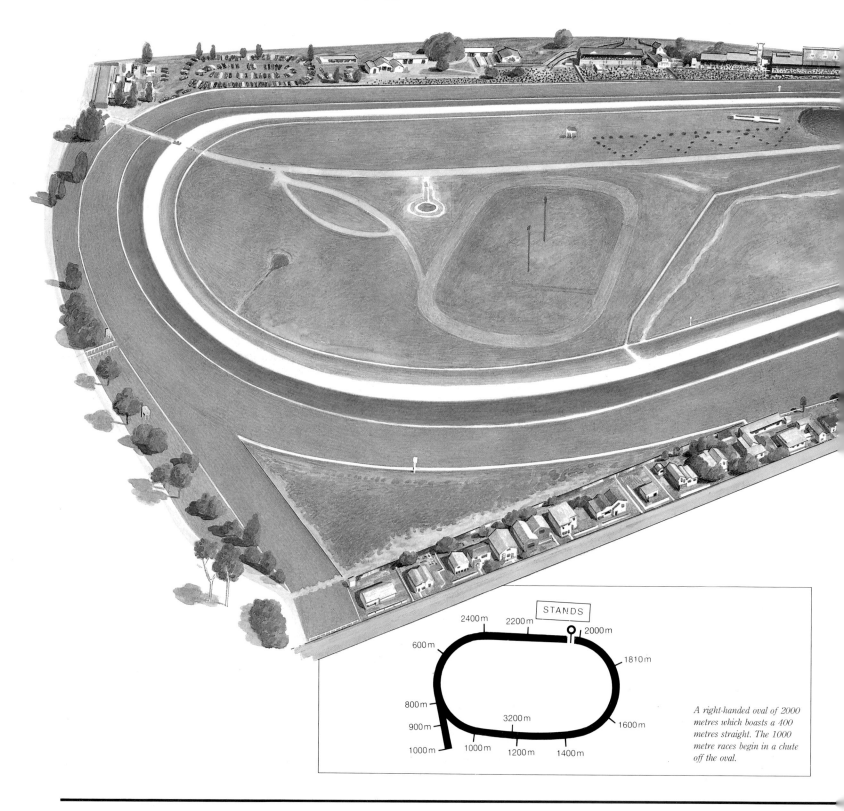

STANDS

2400m 2200m 2000m
600m 1810m
800m 1600m
900m 3200m
1000m 1000m 1200m 1400m

A right-handed oval of 2000 metres which boasts a 400 metres straight. The 1000 metre races begin in a chute off the oval.

If Australian racing is booming, then the most obvious signs of that boom can be seen in Brisbane, capital of the state of Queensland that houses 130 stables. The principal track in the metropolis is Eagle Farm, which lies out in the suburbs, some five miles from the centre of the city. Every winter the top trainers from other parts of Australia and New Zealand bring their animals up to temperate Queensland for the state's rich racing season.

However, the exciting developments are also happening out on the Gold Coast some 50 miles south of Brisbane, which have become the talking point of not only the Australian but the whole racing world. And that is because of the Magic Million Sale. The major Australian sales had always been based in the south of the country before February 1986 when Elders Pastoral introduced the idea of a million dollar race open only to those horses sold at the Gold Coast sale of that year.

Although the book for that opening sale looked none too impressive, the results certainly were. The overall average proved to be the second highest ever paid at a yearling sale, with leading trainers from around the country competing for the lots. That was fine and dandy as a gimmick, but the horses had to prove themselves to be worthy of such offers if the concept was to be a success.

The Million Sale

Luckily the winner of that first Million the following January, Snippets, went on to win the Group 1 AJC Sires Produced Stakes at Randwick in April to end the season as one of the country's top juveniles. The top lot of that first sale, Roman General, who had failed to distinguish himself as a juvenile, then won a valuable stakes race early in his three-year-old career, so the controversy that had immediately raged over the sale died down as the experiment had been vindicated.

In the three subsequent years the prestige enjoyed by the sale both in Australia and throughout the world has increased dramatically. More column inches have been filled with reports about this sale than had ever been considered possible for a bloodstock auction in the Southern Hemisphere. The real proof of the pudding, however, is the number of copy-cat sales that are springing up worldwide.

Jonathan Irwin led the way with his Goffs Million sale in Ireland. Repeated requests for a similar sale at Newmarket, England, have only recently borne fruit, but the English Jockey Club will still not allow a special race to be framed for the sales candidates.

France has gone for the idea and South Africa too have plumped for the pro position, whilst the United States are still undecided though the likelihood of a similar concept now seems likely. There is one vague approximation to the Magic Million Sale in America: a race open only to the offspring of a New Mexico-based stallion, a move that defies not only belief but also any concept of fair play.

Once the idea had taken hold in Australia, it was inevitable that there should be a second race, open only to fillies. The first running was held in January 1989.

Down at the Gold Coast racecourse, Snippets heralds in a new era by winning the first ever sales related race, the 1987 Magic Million.

The Gold Coast

The Gold Coast is proving to be one of Australia's growth centres not only in racing but in many other fields as the potential of the northern half of the country is recognized. Racing has been firmly established in Brisbane for some time. Eagle Farm has been hosting racing since 1866 when the first Queensland Derby and Brisbane Cup were held.

Though long established, it has only been in the recent past that the benefits of a winter campaign at Brisbane have been realized by the trainers from Melbourne and Sydney. Perhaps the deciding factor was the 1959 Melbourne Cup success of Macdougal, who had picked up the Brisbane Cup during his winter at Eagle Farm. That lead was followed and the benefits of

wintering a horse up in the warmer Queensland climate soon became obvious through a spate of spring successes from horses campaigned up there.

The old pattern of racing in Brisbane used to be that Eagle Farm called the opening shots in May and June, staging the Elders Handicap, the country's richest sprint, and the Brisbane Cup in a festival that now rivals the Melbourne and Sydney courses for its prize money, as well as the Queensland Classics.

Doomben

Then in July, Doomben, which is the older of the two courses by some 30 years, took over. The big races at the city's second track are the Rothmans Hundred Thousand

Eagle Farm in 1901 saw a march past by the Highlanders as part of the celebrations of the Declaration of Federation.

and the Fourex Cup, which, unlike the other Cup races, is an 11-furlong affair.

All that changed in the winter of 1988 when the two festivals were switched. Doomben's lesser carnival was used to condition the horses for the richer Eagle Farm racing, a move that was mutually agreed by the Queensland Turf Club, who rule over the racing at Eagle Farm, and Doomben's governing body, the Brisbane Amateur Turf Club.

The growth in the importance of the

course's racing has led to a corresponding upsurge in both the training and viewing facilities at Eagle Farm. With almost all the leading trainers from Melbourne, Sydney and New Zealand being represented at the course, Eagle Farm has made great improvments in its training gallops and stabling areas, which had been somewhat scruffy.

The whole complex can now rival the big southern courses and it has become a most popular course with the locals who have grown in numbers alongside the equine population. Big race days see crowds of up to 30,000.

The course itself is on the sharp side with the right-handed track having a circumference of only ten furlongs and a straight of just over two furlongs, but this apparently only stimulates the excitement of both the actual racing and the crowd's raucous attention.

Empty today, but both the stands and the paddock are always full on a race day at Eagle Farm.

MAGIC MILLION

Year	Winner	Owner	Trainer	Jockey
1987	Snippets	Mr. & Mrs. J. Augustine	S. Rogers	P. Smith
1988	Molokai Prince	Mr. & Mrs. J. Darcy	N. Begg	R. Quinton
1989	Sunblazer	E. Kirwan	E. Kirwan	C. Munce
1990	St Jude	R. Wilton	B. McLachlan	B. York

TE RAPA

Te Rapa takes full advantage of its favourable position to attract many of the country's best horses, and, in its beautiful setting, is an enchanting course to visit.

Opposite: Lester Piggott is led back to the winners' enclosure on Sailing Home after the mare's gallant victory in the 1972 New Zealand International Invitation Stakes.

2400m
2200m
2000m
1000m
STANDS
1200m
1400m
3200m
1600m

Wide galloping left-handed track with a main circuit of 1800 metres and a 420 metre straight. There are a number of starts for both flat and steeplechasing including 1600 and 2400 metre chutes.

Although it is neighbouring Australia that will perennially grab the racing headlines, New Zealand definitely plays a very major role in racing in the Southern Hemisphere since the majority of the top horses in Australasia are bred there. Like Ireland, New Zealand seems to be a country made for horses. Nowhere else in the world is there a higher proportion of equines to humans and their bloodstock exports have won renown throughout the world.

Even though Australia grabs the lion's share of the Flat racers and adopts the most famous ones, such as the legendary Phar Lap, as its own, a fair number of the New Zealand-bred jumping stock have made their way to the UK where they have picked up some major prizes. The English trainer, David Barons has made a name for himself through his handling of the best imports, like Royal Mail, whom he sent out to win the Whitbread Gold Cup in 1980, and Playschool, triumphant in 1987's Hennessy Gold Cup and Welsh Grand National.

Waikato Cup

It is on the grasslands of the North Island surrounding Hamilton that horses are bred, trained and raced. It is, therefore, no surprise that the nearby Te Rapa racecourse, home of the Waikato Cup, is one of the more important racecourses.

Te Rapa - though it is not as famous as Ellerslie racecourse in Auckland, Canterbury's Riccarton in the South Island, or Wellington - has been the scene of some great races. Perhaps the best was Lester Piggott's triumph on Sailing Home in the 1972 New Zealand International Invitation Stakes.

Jockeys from both New Zealand and Australia were overshadowed by the presence of the 'Long Fellow', wintering away from England and taking full advantage of doing so when he was allotted the mare Sailing Home in the draw for the big race. This was one of New Zealand's first attempts to reach an international audience and the authorities could hardly have done better. The result was a promoter's dream.

The top three-year-olds were pitched in against some experienced older horses in what promised to be a tightly fought contest. The massive Sailing Home had already notched up triumphs that season in the Auckland Cup and the Trentham Stakes. Aided by the presence of Piggott on her back, she was made the 5-1 favourite to beat the three-year-old Llananthony, winner of the Wellington Derby, the Melbourne Cup winner Silver Knight and the front-running Game.

Piggott tracked Game for the first half of the 11-furlong race and the pair had stolen four or five lengths on the rest of the field as they turned for home. Sailing Home and Game fought it out head for head throughout the straight before Piggott, riding one of his strongest finishes, galvanized the mare to make one final effort that proved enough to bring her home a neck in front of her courageous opponent.

THE WAIKATO TIMES CUP			
Year	Winner	Trainer	Jockey
1970	Skint Dip	W.C. Winder	R.J. Skelton
1971	Mamselle	P. McEllory	D.A. Peake
1972	Fort Hagen	M.K. Smith	D.H. Harris
1973	Summerosa	G.K. & W. Sanders	W.A. Smith
1974	Kia Maia	T.B. Mathieson Jnr.	J.F. Grylls
1975	Skite	G.K. & W. Sanders	J.P. Riordan
1976	Heidsieck	F.A. Phillips	A.J. Tweedie
1977	Schenley	K. Couper & M.H. Donaghue	J.W. Walker
1978	Bahrain	W. Sanders	C.P. McNab
1979	Sound Wave	G.O. Mudgway	W. Robinson
1980	Drum	D.G. Sellwood	C.P. McNab
1981	Avago	L.R. Douglas & A.L. Jones	P.R. Alderman
1982	Hugel	C.F. Fenwick	T.G. Williams
1983	Avitt	N.D. Landers	R.D. Vance
1984	Mr Duthie	C. McColl	P.D. Johnson
1985	Great Estate	J.J. Steffert	G.J. Grylls
1986	The Filbert	D.N. Couchman	G.L. Cooksley
1987	Precocious Lad	A.L. Jones	C.W. Treymane
1988	Sounds Like Fun	J.A. Gibbs	M.C. Coleman

That race has gone down in the legends of New Zealand racing, but other great horses have succeeded in the New Zealand Invitational, including Battle Heights whom Piggott had schooled and desperately wanted to draw, but had instead to watch when he was allocated Manchero, and a second filly in La Mer, who came from last to first in the straight in 1978.

Poor prize money

The problem with racing in New Zealand is that the prize money is miniscule compared to that on offer on the other side of the Tasman Sea, so it is difficult for the Kiwis to keep the best horses in the country. Even those that do stay and prove successful are often shipped over to Australia for a shot at the rich prizes on offer on the East Coast. Consequently, the prestige of races like the Waikato Cup, the New Zealand Cup and the Auckland Cup – the three big staying handicaps that are run on similar lines to the more famous Melbourne Cup – is minimal outside the country itself.

That said, the breeding of the horses is the basis on which the industry is founded and the racecourse successes of New Zealand-bred horses reflect the high standards of horsemanship evident in the country.

In the 1970s horses either bred or trained in New Zealand ran to success worldwide, headed by the globe-trotting Balmerino. In his three-year-old career in New Zealand, Balmerino picked up both the 1975 New Zealand Guineas and the Derby before going on to score a memorable success in the Brisbane Cup.

In the following season he won races in New Zealand, Australia and the States before being sent to England for a European campaign centred around the 1977

Prix de l'Arc de Triomphe. He won many admirers at Longchamp when he was only beaten a length and a half by the outstanding colt Alleged.

New Zealand breed

Balmerino brought home to a worldwide audience a fact that the Australians had learnt a long time ago: that the New Zealand-bred horses were to be feared. Recent Melbourne Cup winners Kiwi, Kensei and Empire Rose have only reinforced this. Both Kensei, whose Melbourne Cup triumph came in 1987, and the

outstanding Bonecrusher are graduates of the Waikato Sales. These are held adjacent to the Te Rapa course and are run by the same authority, the Waikato Racing Club.

Apart from the Waikato Cup and the Invitational, the course hosts good races like the Lion Brown Stakes, a seven-furlong weight-for-age contest that has been won by some of the leading New Zealand horses. In the best of its recent runnings it witnessed a winning return by the local hero, Bonecrusher, who was coming back to racing after the illness that nearly cost him his life on a trip to the 1986 Japan Cup. Both the Founders Plate over a mile – a race

which Vice Regal made his own at the end of the 1970s – and the Queen Elizabeth II Cup are other top Waikato races.

Steeplechasing is also held at the course and Te Rapa hosts one of the nation's leading jump races in the Waikato Steeplechase, which is held in the course's main winter meeting at the end of May.

The wide expansive galloping track, the large stands and the tree-lined paddock make Te Rapa an enchanting racecourse, but like many of the tracks in New Zealand, it has to fight to draw in the crowds and on some days the lack of spectators makes the place seem almost ghost-like.

Steeplechasing plays an important role in the Waikato calendar. The renown of the New Zealand jumping stock has spread far and wide, and the best come to the course for the Waikato Chase.

TRENTHAM

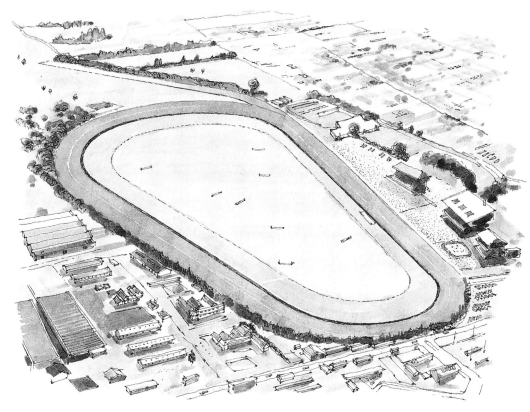

Surrounded by rolling hillsides, Wellington's Trentham racecourse is one of the most beautiful and relaxed places to watch thoroughbreds compete against each other. It was founded in 1870, not long after the city itself was built. Wellington's racing, as befits a capital city, ranks with Canterbury as the best organized in New Zealand and is improving all the time. Yet the course, despite having so much in its favour, has had to endure many troubled years of late and was losing money fast throughout the 1970s, a time when the quality of the horses being produced and raced in New Zealand was on the way up.

It was the general lack of interest by New Zealanders in racing that led to these difficulties. Crowds were dwindling and betting revenue was going the same which led to smaller and smaller purses in com-

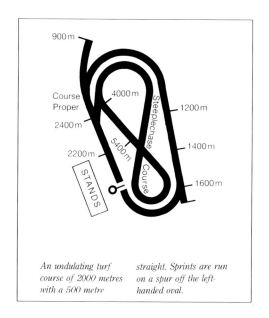

An undulating turf course of 2000 metres with a 500 metre straight. Sprints are run on a spur off the left-handed oval.

parison to the prizes offered by the Australians. This of course meant that the top New Zealand trainers kept as much of an eye on events overseas as at home. The recent successes of Our Waverley Star and Bonecrusher have brought back some of the lost crowds and the situation seems to be

The rolling hills form the perfect backdrop to the finish of the Wellington Cup, one of New Zealand's premier staying races.

healthier now than it has done for some time.

With events like January's Wellington Cup – one of the old-style big races – and the Trentham Stakes, which is run at the same meeting as the Wellington Derby and Oaks, those that do come are treated to some pretty special racing in the spring and summer months.

Like many New Zealand courses, Wellington also doubles up as a National Hunt course during the winter months, but the quality of the winter game does not reach quite the same levels as the course's summer sport.

For many years Trentham was the home of the country's top yearling sales, which were held concurrently with the big January meeting, but in 1987 after an uninterrupted reign of 61 years, the sales were moved north to the major breeding grounds.

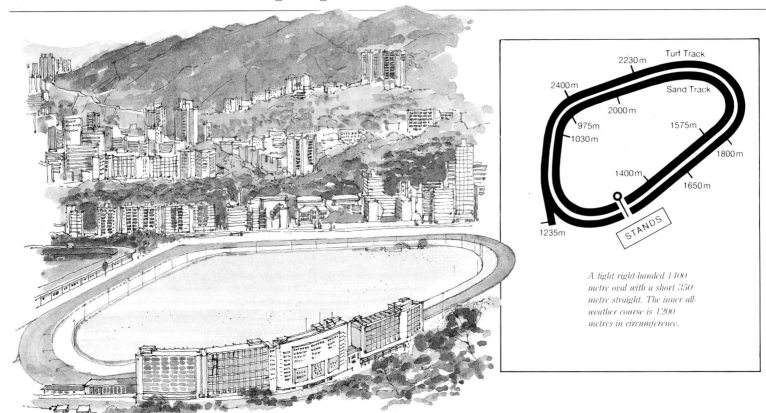

2230m Turf Track
2400m
Sand Track
2000m
975m 1575m
1030m
1800m
1400m
1650m
STANDS
1235m

A tight right-handed 1400 metre oval with a short 350 metre straight. The inner all-weather course is 1200 metres in circumference.

HAPPY VALLEY

Even when the crowds are absent the stands at Happy Valley are an imposing spectacle.

Hong Kong would never strike one as a natural place to race horses. The 7,511 hectares (29 square miles) of Hong Kong Island do not appear to have a single flat acre on them. Yet over the last 20 years, Hong Kong has turned into one of the major gambling centres of the world and one of the most spectacular places to go racing.

Happy Valley is in the middle of the island and has been a home to racing since 1842 when the Colonels used to chase each other on Chinese ponies, which had been handicapped according to their size. The course was known as Yellow Mud Valley, but the passing of more than a century and the advent of public relations have brought about remarkable changes.

It is only since 1971 that racing has turned professional in Hong Kong, but in that brief period, the racing, the prize money and the local interest has grown like an out-of-control beanstalk so that in the short 60-day season every race attracts £1 million's worth of bets and an even larger number of interested parties.

Surrounded by tower blocks on all sides, Happy Valley was the course that made it all possible. It was the success of the racing on this seven-and-a-half-furlong track that allowed the newer Sha Tin course to be built and even now some of the colony's great races are still held at Happy Valley. Both the Queen Elizabeth II Cup and the Centenary Cup are run there and the 'old course' can hold crowds of up to 30,000.

Space being the problem that it is, the horses attached to the course are stabled in the nearby tower blocks and are even exercised around the tops of these buildings, hundreds of feet above the grass and dirt tracks where they race.

Above: *The skyscrapers in the background tower above yet another finish at Hong Kong's older racecourse.*

Left: *Lack of space has forced the thoroughbred to the top of tower-blocks at Happy Valley's training complex. Stabled in the block, horses are walked on the top for morning exercise.*

SHA TIN

Sha Tin is one of the wonders of the modern racing world. Just 20 years ago there was water where now one of the most modern and comfortable racing complexes in the world stands.

In 1969 the idea of reclaiming land from the surrounding water was first broached by Sir John Saunders, the then Chairman of the Royal Hong Kong Jockey Club, to the Governor of the colony. The scale of racing in Hong Kong was becoming too big for Happy Valley to handle on its own and with land space such a limited and highly prized commodity, the possible sites for a new course were obviously restricted.

This was an entirely different approach. No planner would turn down the ambitious project of reclaiming 250 acres from the Sha Tin Bay on which would be built a mile-and-a-quarter course with a five-furlong straight, complete with stable facilities for over 1,000 horses to alleviate the over-crowding at Happy Valley. The problem was not whether permission would be granted, but whether the idea was feasible. Three years of planning were required before the first reclamation work was begun.

A sea wall that stretched for a mile and a half around the site was built before the trucks started dumping the land-fill. Eight hundred men were kept hard at work on this task and trucks were dumping their loads at a rate of one every eight seconds over the two and a quarter years that the reclamation took.

Construction of the course

The 14,000 cubic feet of spoil was taken from the top of one of the local mountains which gave the developers the extra bonus of creating more building land on the hills. The development potential of that new land close to the city centre was more than enough to cover the £60 million that the reclamation cost, so right from the start it

On recently reclaimed land, the superstructure of the new Sha Tin stands rises above the half-completed course. The race to finish the work in time was always tight, but the miracle that is Sha Tin opened on schedule.

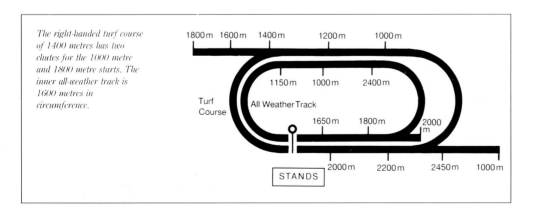

The right-handed turf course of 1400 metres has two chutes for the 1000 metre and 1800 metre starts. The inner all-weather track is 1600 metres in circumference.

One of the racing wonders of the world, Sha Tin is a very successful racecourse and is always packed on race days.

Though racing at Sha Tin may not always be of the highest quality, it is always exciting and it attracts a greater volume of betting money than anywhere else in the world.

was obvious that the Jockey Club had backed a winner.

In March 1975, as the filling-in part neared completion, the Royal Hong Kong Jockey Club announced that the first day's racing would be held on 7 October 1978, a date which must have filled the architects responsible for building on the reclaimed land with a good deal of apprehension.

How would the new land stand up to the sinking of foundations and the construction of grandstands? Would the new turf take on the sea of mud? Would the executives of the new course manage to get the work finished in time?

For the next three years the work continued around the clock and as the vast grandstand took shape, it became clear that not only would Sha Tin open on time, but that it would also be one of the most spectacular courses anywhere in the world.

The grandstand which can, and frequently does, hold 30,000 people, was to be the largest single building in the colony,

spread out over 16½ acres along the home straight. The turf course utilized a spectacularly successful new surface that involved the grass being meshed into a sand and wire basis that allows for easy draining, but which does not jar the horses. It has been widely admired worldwide and could well be a common racing surface in the next century. On the far side of the home straight there is a massive video board that shows both the races and the replays to the watching crowds and which, together with the slickly run Tote operation, gives the punter every convenience.

Opening day

On 7 October 1978 Sha Tin opened its gates to the public for the first time. People poured in on the new road and rail links to ensure that a sell-out crowd was present for the birth of Hong Kong's second racecourse.

Six races later Sha Tin's success was certain. Both the grass and the inner dirt

Above: *The crowds begin to filter into Sha Tin well before the start of the day's racing. As the runners make their way down to the start before the first race, the grandstand is nearly full.*

Left: *Paddock watching is the same throughout the world. The naked eye, allied with the form book, is used to try and spot the fittest and fastest horse in the field.*

atmosphere is as electric as anything that can be found in the world of racing.

The locals are just born punters and they take this occupation very seriously indeed. All possible information is studied in depth before they will commit themselves to a bet, and that includes everything from the gallop reports in the morning paper to last minute tips that are picked up via a radio and headphones on the way to the track.

The Hong Kong Derby

The big races of the Sha Tin season include the Hong Kong Derby for four-year-olds, which is run over nine furlongs in February at the start of the Chinese New Year, the Hong Kong Invitation Cup, a recent innovation that attracts the top Malaysian horses over to compete against Hong Kong's finest, the Centenary Cup, the Remy X O Cup and of course the Sha Tin Trophy.

The stabling and training facilities were built to reap the benefit of the greater space available and allow for serious workouts on the all-weather strip. As the balance of power in the Hong Kong turf world has moved from Happy Valley to Sha Tin, so have the major trainers come to school and stable their best horses at the new course.

Although Sha Tin will never be able to compare itself to the great equine centres of Newmarket and Chantilly, the facilities that are offered to a trainer on the track are of a very high class. Equally, the horses are as well tended in their stables as their more illustrious brothers are in similar on-the-course stables at Belmont or Santa Anita.

Regardless of either the quantity or the quality of the horses performing at the course, one's mind is always drawn back to pictures of what the site was those 20 years ago. It is impossible to believe when one looks at the crowds swarming around the betting points, the horses walking out on to the track, the wonderful Penfold Park in the centre of the course – a veritable Garden of Eden named in honour of Bernard Penfold, the man who saw that the course got built – and the towering grandstand.

But Sha Tin is for real and it is a credit to the Hong Kong Jockey Club that their ingenuity has conjured up one of the great courses of the world.

course had proved true racing surfaces and the longer course gave greater encouragement to the galloping type than did Happy Valley.

The aptly named Money No Object, a 16-1 outsider, won the inaugural race, but the big boys of the Hong Kong scene were soon making their mark at the new course. George Moore, the leading trainer at the time, chalked up a first day double whilst the riding honours fell to Peter Leysham.

The quality of the horses running on the circuit is not as high as elsewhere in the world – for the most part they are either European or Australasian cast-offs who arrive in Hong Kong after an unsuccessful career in their native countries. The horses have their names changed by their new stable and then set about earning their corn in the new surroundings. However, the

KUALA LUMPUR

Malaysian racing is much like that of nearby Hong Kong, except there space is not the problem. Instead it is the heat. Give or take a couple of degrees, Kuala Lumpur is on the equator and it shows. The packed stands at the main Selangor racecourse are full of parasols and fans as the packed spectators try to keep cool as the day progresses.

The typical nine-or-ten-race card will test the stamina of both the performers and the public, but like most people in the Far East, the Malaysians appear to love their racing and flock out from the city centre in crowds of up to 30,000 for a Sunday's racing.

Selangor is the best of the four tracks in Malaysia, the others being at Penang, Singapore and Ipoh, all of which are run by the Malaysia Racing Association. The main racing season is from January to March.

Of all the races held at Selangor, the most prized is perhaps February's Tungku Gold Cup, although there again, like Hong Kong, the quality of the animals performing in such a championship race leaves something

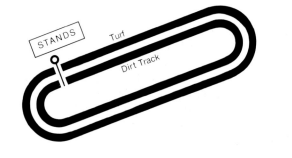

Left-handed turf course which is 2000 metres in circumference and encloses an inner dirt track of 1600 metres.

to be desired.

One of the reasons is undoubtedly the heat. When combined with the dust coming off the dirt track, this can give a horse a condition known as dry coat which prevents it from sweating. Once an animal has developed this condition, it cannot carry on racing until the problem has been cleared up. This requires a spell up in the cooler highlands, so a horse's career can very well

run in fits and starts.

Selangor's sharp grass and dirt tracks are surrounded by the skyscrapers that sprawl out from the heart of the city. Nevertheless, the environs are kept admirably green considering the heat, and this, combined with the thoroughly involved crowd, who demand to see their fancy mounted before backing it, makes for an enjoyable day.

BOMBAY

*The Members'
Enclosure is packed
for Turf Invitation
Cup day at India's
premier racecourse.*

Everywhere the British went in the 18th and 19th centuries, they took their love of racing with them, and India, the Jewel in the Empire's Crown, was no exception. Bombay and Pune are the two major surviving centres of the British Raj and are governed by the Royal Western India Turf Club.

Bombay opened its doors for the first time on 20 February 1883, and has been staging a winter carnival of racing ever since. That meeting includes every single Indian Classic, which are the major events of the country's racing calendar. The races are held between November, when racing returns to Bombay, and April, at which point a ten-week break is taken before Pune starts its summer season in July.

Between the two courses 80 days' racing are staged each year, and the meetings in Bombay are particularly well attended.

Since the racecourse is on the north side of the Bombay peninsula, the opposite side to the fashionable Marine Drive, it is very close to the heart of town and a crowd of 10,000 can regularly be expected and at least double for the big race days.

India is one of the few countries that do not have a Tote monopoly and the on-course bookmakers – for, as in Australia, they are only permitted to operate at the track – provide an unusual sight to eyes which are more accustomed to the garb and habits of the English bookie.

The sport as a whole continues to flourish in India. With an equine population of about 2,000, the competition is good even if the standard, as on so many of the Far Eastern courses, is below that seen in Western Europe.

*A right-handed turf course
of twelve furlongs in
circumference with a three
and a half furlong straight.
Races of up to eight
furlongs are run on a spur
off the main oval.*

8f
9f
8f
7f
7f
6f
6f
11f
STANDS
4f

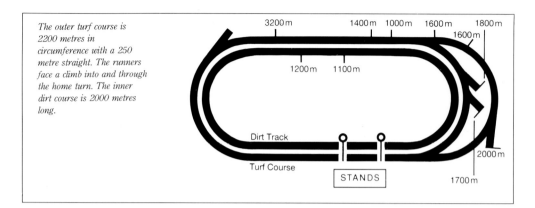

The outer turf course is 2200 metres in circumference with a 250 metre straight. The runners face a climb into and through the home turn. The inner dirt course is 2000 metres long.

3200m 1400m 1000m 1600m 1800m
1600m
1200m 1100m
2000m
Dirt Track
Turf Course
STANDS
1700m

FUCHU

The Japanese are making great strides in the racing world. Their policy of buying interesting stallions to improve the quality of their horses and investing large amounts of money in the sport will surely very soon be paying a massive dividend and the country is rapidly becoming one of the top racing nations in the world.

At the moment, however, the world's eyes turn to Japan solely for the annual running of the Japan Cup, the richest race in the world. For each November the Japan Racing Association invites the best from Europe, Australasia and the States to take on the best of their own in the massive Fuchu racecourse in Tokyo.

Since the first running of this event in 1981, the race has developed into one of the most fascinating international contests of the year and one which has come to intrigue all adventurous trainers, if they have a horse who looks good enough to get an invitation and who will act on the Japanese conditions.

Racing is a recent arrival to the shores of *sushi* and *samurai*. The Japan Racing Association, the governing body of all ten of the country's racecourses, was only founded in 1954, but the methodical approach of the Japanese has been applied to racing as to every other part of their lives. The progress that has been made in the intervening 30 odd years shows what can be achieved if

people make a concerted effort.

As the entire capital of the Association was invested by the government, the industry is regarded as a semi-public entity and the whole operation is overseen by the Minister of Agriculture, Forestry and Fisheries. Quite how the English Jockey Club would react to a similar approach by the same government body in England remains to be seen, but in the land of the Rising Sun, the co-operation has worked the oracle.

Over 8,000 thoroughbreds are foaled annually and the racing population of the country has continued to grow in both size and quality. Once the yearlings reach a trainable age, they are taken by those who will now guide their careers to one of the two massive training centres in which all the country's racehorses are schooled.

From there they will go, when they are ready, to one or other of the courses around the islands for their races. Although all this centralization may again seem something of an anathema to the more free-living nations elsewhere in the world, one can but say that it works and it works well.

South of Tokyo itself, Fuchu regularly attracts crowds of over 100,000 to its luxurious course.

Although none too beautiful, Fuchu is one of the most efficient and best-run courses in the world.

Below: *The grey Tamamo Cross stamps himself as one of Japan's greatest horses by completing the Emperor's Cup double at Fuchu in 1988.*

Above: *The Miho Training Centre houses the bulk of Japan's thoroughbreds in training and the early morning gallops are always a crowded affair.*

Betting shops

With the entire betting operation, including the huge, football-pitch-sized betting shops, also run by the state, the control of the ruling body is evident everywhere as the last thing the government would want is a state-run industry that is suspected of being corrupt.

This control even extends down to the jockeys, who are required to report to the racecourse one hour after declaration time. Once at a racecourse, they are locked away in their own room and not allowed to come into contact with the outside world until the races themselves start at ten o'clock on the Saturday morning.

Racing in Japan is limited to two days a week: Saturdays and Sundays. With 288 racing days each year, there are two or three meetings around the islands every weekend, but the principal races are all held at Tokyo's course. Of those races, the most important national events are the two Emperor's Cups which are held each spring and autumn. For a horse to win both those is to enter the Hall of Fame of Japanese racing.

Tenpointo

At the top of that list is Tenpointo, the first Japanese horse to win over seven billion yen in a career which dominated the middle 1970s and was brought to a premature end when he broke a leg in a training accident as he was preparing to embark on a European campaign in 1978.

His exploits at Tokyo's course were rivalled in 1988 by Tamamo Cross, who also won both the spring and autumn Emperor's Cups and was made a short-priced favourite to win the Japan Cup that year and become the first home-trained winner since Symboli Rudolf beat another Japanese horse Rocky Tiger in the fifth running of the race in 1985. But Tamamo Cross could not complete what would have been an historic hat trick and was beaten by half a length by the American challenger Pay The Butler in what was a thrilling final furlong battle.

That gave the United States a third victory in the race. Having won the first two runnings with Mairzy Doates in 1981 and Half Iced in the following year when the wonder horse John Henry failed to spark, American horses then failed to get in a blow until Southjet ran the French-trained Le Glorieux to three-quarters of a length in 1987.

JAPAN CUP				
Year	Winner	Owner	Trainer	Jockey
1981	*Mairzy Doates*	*A.D. Schefler*	*J.W. Fulton*	*C. Assmussen*
1982	*Half Iced*	*B. Firestone*	*S. Hough*	*D. Macbeth*
1983	*Stanerra*	*F. Dunne*	*F. Dunne*	*B. Rouse*
1984	*Katsuragi Ace*	*Ichiro Node*	*Kazumi Domon*	*K. Nishiura*
1985	*Symboli Rudolf*	*Symboli Farms*	*Y. Nohira*	*Y. Okabe*
1986	*Jupiter Island*	*Marquis of Tavistock*	*C. Brittain*	*Pat Eddery*
1987	*Le Glorieux*	*Frau S. Wolf*	*R. Collet*	*A. Lequeux*
1988	*Pay the Butler*	*E.A. Gann*	*R. Frankel*	*C. McCarron*
1989	*Horlicks*	*G. de Gruchy*	*D. O'Sullivan*	*L. O'Sullivan*

Jupiter Island

With the other runnings of the race falling to the home country in the shape of Katsuragi Ace in 1984 as well as Symboli Rudolf's victory the following year, to Ireland in 1983 with that great filly Stanerra and to England's Jupiter Island in 1986, the spoils have been evenly divided between the major racing nations.

As befits a race of this stature, the arena in which it is staged is a magnificent one. Home of the Tokyo Yuushun or the Japanese Derby, the Yuushun Hinba, the Japanese Oaks, as well as the Emperor's Cup, Tokyo racecourse can expect a crowd of 100,000 for almost every Sunday on which it stages racing.

The 11-furlong outer turf course is in-variably firm and the grass none too luscious thanks to the smog of the city, but it provides a fair test for horses that can act on the going. Although for the main part a level course, there is a steep uphill climb throughout the penultimate furlong that brings stamina to the fore in 12-furlong races. A regular left-handed oval with a run-in of three furlongs, the bends are not sharp, with the bonus of a wide track.

The massive grandstand dominates the home straight. Three-quarters of a mile long itself, it climbs 29 m (95 ft) up into the air and provides five storeys of seats, balconies and restaurants. With over 2,000 Pari-Mutuel windows handling the bets of crowds that can number up to 160,000 people on big race days, the course tries to make everything as easy as possible for its patrons.

An English 1–2 in the 1986 Japan Cup when Jupiter Island (nearest) in the colours of Lord Tavistock, got up close home to beat Allez Milord.

TURFFONTEIN

Just eight miles from the centre of Johannesburg, Turffontein is South Africa's leading racecourse. Home to some of the most prestigious prizes in the country including the South African Derby and Oaks, Turffontein attracts more than its fair share of champions.

Any horse that wins over the Transvaal track knows that he has been in a race, for Turffontein is one of the more demanding courses. The long straight is the final test of a horse's stamina that has already been tried to the limit by a 3-furlong climb round the last bend.

Any horse that tries to make all the running can find that climb into the straight just too testing and the course's riding tactics are to wait, wait and wait and then use the full length of the straight to get up into the lead at the post. Those tactics are very often employed in the runnings of the big staying handicaps that are the major prizes in the South African calendar.

The country's racing resembles that of Australia. The pre-eminence placed on the struggles of the Classic generation that the Europeans and Americans hold dear, is again absent. Rather it is the evenly balanced handicaps over a two-mile trip that excite the most interest. Although the country's major race and its equivalent of the Melbourne Cup is Durban's Rothmans July Handicap, Turffontein's staying handicap, the OK Gold Bowl, is a very close second in both prize money and prestige.

OK Gold Bowl

It is fitting, as Turffontein celebrated its centenary year in 1987, that the future of South African racing looked much brighter than at any time in the recent past. Throughout the country, prize money, attendances and on-course betting were all reported to growing appreciably. In that same year Turffontein announced the first 500,000 rand race: the OK Gold Bowl.

Turffontein shares with nearby Gosforth Park the crowds that flock out of South Africa's major city. Although Gosforth Park gets the larger crowds, its sharp track favours the sprinter and the bigger races

Unlike most of South Africa, blacks and white can intermingle in Turffontein's stands.

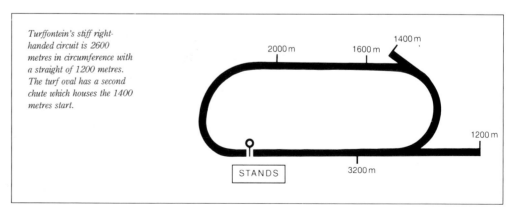

Turffontein's stiff right-handed circuit is 2600 metres in circumference with a straight of 1200 metres. The turf oval has a second chute which houses the 1400 metres start.

2000 m   1600 m   1400 m
1200 m
STANDS   3200 m

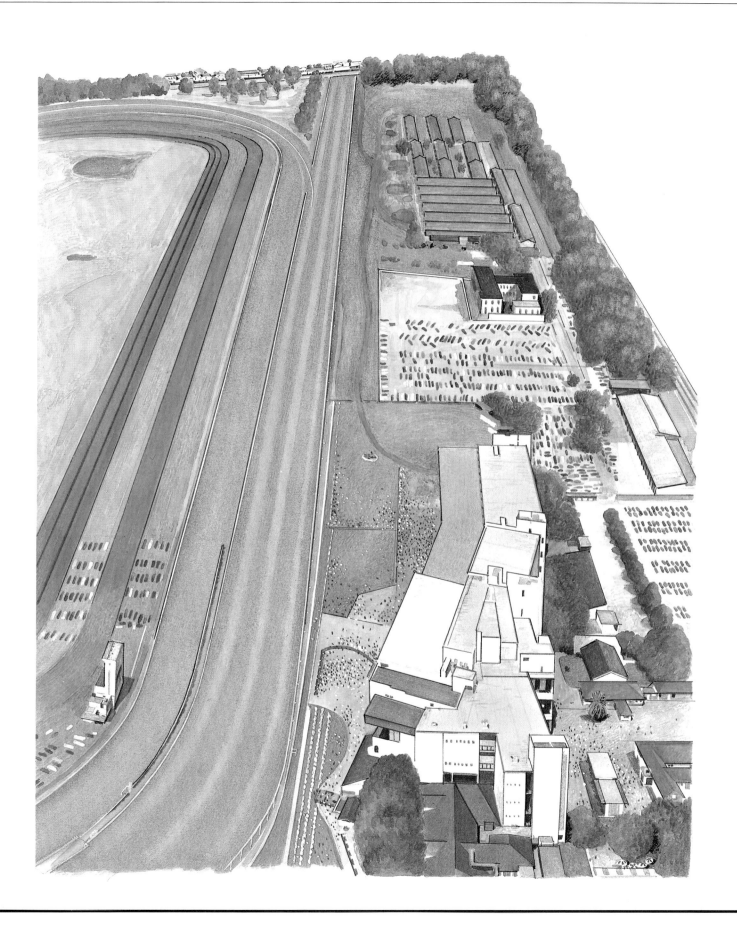

are held at Turffontein.

The 30-odd racing days a year at the course are mainly staged on Saturdays, though occasional Tuesday and Bank Holiday meetings are held. Whereas the summer meetings are run on a beautiful thick cushion of grass, the winter frosts leave the turf brittle and sparse, though the cooler climate is more favourable for racing.

Both the South African Derby and Oaks are staged in the autumn. As the status of the locally bred horses improves, these Classics gain in importance and although they cannot yet rival the all-aged handicaps for prize money, they carry increasingly more stud value for the winner.

For a long time the quality of the South African horses seemed to slip further and further behind that of the rest of the world. Both New Zealand- and Australian-bred horses were imported for their racing careers, whilst many a stallion was brought down from the Northern Hemisphere to boost the quality of the studs.

Now the combined measures of slapping an import surcharge on any foreign-bred horse and a massive improvement in the studs have led to something of a renaissance of the locally bred.

The powerful Main Chance Farm, which was built up by Godfrey Gird, and the new Oakfields Stud, which was floated on the Johannesburg Stock Exchange after the old Oaklands and Coromandel Studs were amalgamated in 1988, have stallions of the quality of Roland Gardens, a Classic winner in England, Jungle Cove and Northfields, a success in Ireland and from the all-important Northern Dancer line, which should ensure future improvement.

Hawaii

South Africa has produced its fair share of champions, most of whom have made their mark on the Turffontein course. Hawaii is perhaps the most distinguished horse to have come out of the country.

Having taken most of the two- and three-year-old prizes the country had to offer including the 1967 South African Guineas,

The finish of the OK Gold Bowl at Turffontein. The stands are packed for the course's biggest race, whilst behind the course lie disused goldmines and the city of Johannesburg.

Hawaii crossed the Atlantic to race with even greater success in the United States, winning the United Nations Handicap and the Man O'War Stakes. He then sired the Epsom Derby winer Henbit at stud.

He has been honoured by Turffontein with the course's introduction of the Hawaii Stakes, but this has since been renamed the First National Stakes. Even dearer to the course than that great champion was Caradoc, who dominated Turffontein's racing in the early 1960s. He won 15 races during his career, the majority of them at Turffontein. After finishing his racing career, he was given to the course by his owners and for many years he was the lead horse at the course.

Muis Roberts

Yet if South African racing is famous for anything, it is not really the quality of the horses that race in the country, but rather the calibre of the jockeys. The most notable example in recently has been Michael Muis Roberts, who for many years was renowned in the South African racing world, winning 11 jockey's championships in the 13 years he had been riding.

Having conquered every peak open to him in his native land, Roberts moved to Europe, where he has proved to be equally successful, especially in his association with Alec Stewart and that champion Mtoto, on whom the jockey was able to show his brilliance and win two Eclipses and the King George VI and Queen Elizabeth Stakes.

The nearby Highveld is also a big breeding area and the country's leading thoroughbred sales are held at nearby Germiston. These sales are the source of what will be the richest thoroughbred race in the country. Like many countries, South Africa is following Australia's lead and creating a sale race. The Million Futurity, worth a million rands, will first be run at Turffontein in 1990 for two-year-olds who have been sold at Germiston. It promises to be yet another cornerstone in the success of the course.

With the skyscrapers of Johannesburg as the backdrop and the pithead of the now disused Robertson Deep goldmine - a reminder of the source of both the city's and the country's prosperity - just 100 yards away from the course, Turffontein offers some fascinating contrasts.

Crowds of 20,000 are commonplace and the combined Tote and bookmaking turnover at a meeting can reach as much as 5 million Rand at the big winter meetings.

KENILWORTH

Fighting out the finish of the J & B Met, Kenilworth's major staying race, and one of the richest in the country.

Kenilworth is the home of the South African Turf Club and the oldest racecourse in the country. Though the Turf Club was established in 1802, it did not move to Kenilworth until 1882, but has been overseeing the sport from the course since then.

Recently the course has been substantially redeveloped with a new track brought into operation in 1976 and a new grandstand opened in 1988, but the flavour of the racing on the course has not changed quite so dramatically.

The big races of the 48-day season are held between the end of December and the beginning of March, with the feature races being the Queen's Plate, the J & B Met and the Cape of Good Hope Derby, all of which are Group 1 races. Both Flat and steeplechasing are conducted around the long left-handed course, but the jumping usually provides very much less of a diversion for the spectators.

The centre of the course has been left undisturbed since it is one of the very few remaining areas of the original Cape Flats and is the home of many varieties of flora and fauna particular to that habitat. This only adds to the natural beauty of the course, which is only ten miles from the city centre.

Crowds of around 10,000 are normal, whilst for the big Saturday events, like Derby Day and Met day, the richest of the season, the number of spectators rises up to 30,000.

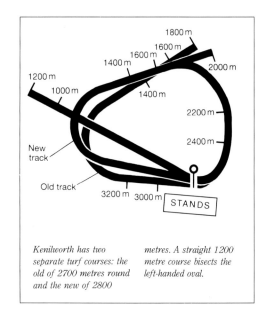

Kenilworth has two separate turf courses: the old of 2700 metres round and the new of 2800 metres. A straight 1200 metre course bisects the left-handed oval.

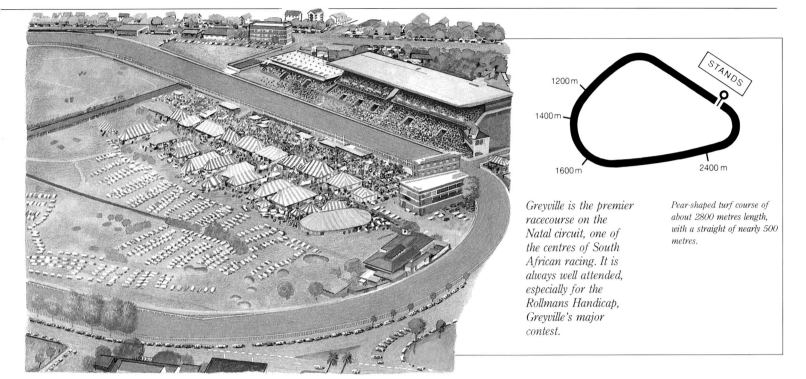

Greyville is the premier racecourse on the Natal circuit, one of the centres of South African racing. It is always well attended, especially for the Rollmans Handicap, Greyville's major contest.

Pear-shaped turf course of about 2800 metres length, with a straight of nearly 500 metres.

GREYVILLE

Situated close to the heart of Durban in Natal on a complex that also includes a championship golf course, Greyville is the most important of the courses in a state that boasts the best racing in South Africa. Together with neighbouring Clairwood and Scotsville, Greyville caters for the massive Summerveld training complex, which houses over 1,000 of the Natal-trained horses and can lay on some good competitive races.

Of those the most famous is the Rothmans July Handicap, the country's richest and most prestigious prize, which is always run on the first Saturday of the month. Like the Melbourne Cup, it is a two-mile handicap that will attract the best of the country's stayers and a large amount of the country's attention. Up to 60,000 people will turn up to witness the city's major summer social occasion, when the crowd will gamble up to 12 million rand on the outcome of the contest.

Other major races include the South African Guineas, which is run in May, the Game Gold Cup, the country's top weight-for-age staying race and the Miracle Mowers.

Both Greyville and Summerveld are administered by the Durban Turf Club, which has been calling the shots in the state since 1897, although there has been racing at Greyville since 1844.

The course itself is a right-handed round track of some 14 furlongs. A tight - some say too tight track - Greyville is considered to be very undulating by South African standards, though not when compared to some British tracks. The straight itself is only just over two and a half furlongs in length, which can lead to some scrimmaging at the death, but equally does ensure some close finishes.

OTHER NOTABLE COURSES

ENGLAND

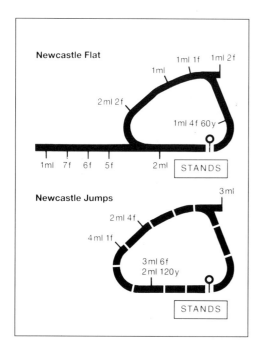

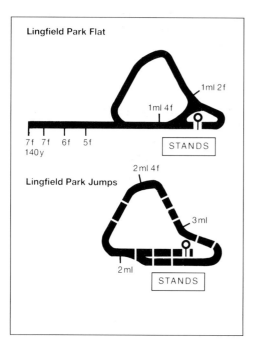

Newcastle

Five miles north of the city of Newcastle is the racecourse which is the home of the Northumberland Plate, a handicap better known as the Pitman's Derby. A mixed course, it attracts decent crowds to its bigger summer meetings.

Lingfield

This Surrey course is one of the most used in England, staging regular Flat and Jump meetings throughout the year and recent plans to build an all-weather course will only increase its use.

Salisbury

A delightful downland course, Salisbury has long been famous for the quality of its two-year-old races. A garden party atmosphere is ever present during the summer and the informality of its stands only adds to the racegoer's enjoyment of the sport.

Brighton

Although the days have gone when trainloads of punters would descend on the town for the summer meetings, Brighton still draws a decent crowd. The horseshoe-shaped course has been likened to Epsom on account of its undulations and turns.

Windsor

This Thameside course is packed throughout the summer for its Monday evening meetings; however, it would be difficult to find a course with worse viewing facilities and more decrepit stands.

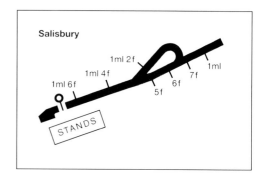

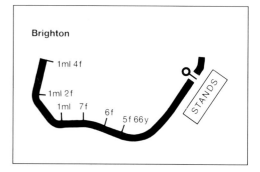

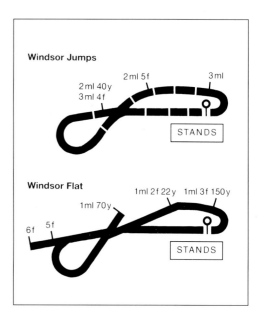

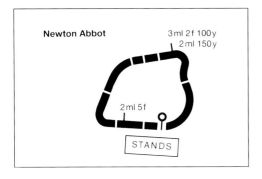

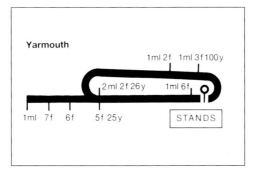

Newton Abbot

The biggest and best of the West Country racecourses, Newton Abbot sees in the start of the National Hunt season and stages some good chases during the season. A friendly and fun track that is very well worth a visit.

Yarmouth

Another seaside course that specialises in its summer meetings, Yarmouth is the schooling ground for many of Newmarket's better two-year-olds and in recent years Guineas and Derby favourites have been seen making their debuts at the Norfolk course.

IRELAND

Down Royal

Despite being the leading track in Northern Ireland, Down Royal is run by the Irish Turf Club rather than by the Jockey Club. The course boasts a rural charm, highlighted by the delay to the start of the 1988 Ulster Derby when a flock of sheep roamed on to the track.

Tipperary

A delightful country course in the south of the country, Tipperary stages both Flat and Jumps racing. Although it does not pretend to offer racing of Classic standard, there is plenty to enjoy in an afternoon's racing there.

Tralee

Tralee is another of the great Irish horse fairs and the six-day August festival is one of the centrepieces of the international Rose of Tralee Festival. The western course attracts both professionals and casual visitors to its gates.

Naas

Naas is situated almost exactly halfway between Dublin and The Curragh, an ideal spot for a racecourse. Although the track stages both codes of racing, it is much more renowned for its jumping.

Punchestown

Punchestown, which is a near neighbour of Naas, is one of the island's leading National Hunt courses. With races like the Tattersalls Gold Cup and the Guinness Champion Hurdle (for four-year-olds), Punchestown is a noted schooling ground for the Irish Cheltenham hopefuls.

BELGIUM

Ostend

Although the racing staged is predominantly trotting, Ostend stages a summer Flat festival that attracts runners from several European countries. The course and facilities are of a high standard and reaping the benefits of a recent promotional campaign.

SWEDEN

Taby

One of the premier Scandinavian courses, Taby is another course that doubles up thoroughbred racing with trotting. Home of the bulk of the country's top racing, though not the Derby or the Oaks, Taby's status is growing internationally.

FRANCE

Clairefontaine

Across the bay from Deauville, Clairefontaine is as enjoyable an experience as its more prestigious neighbour. With a similar summer season, Clairefontaine provides a delightful balance for the French holiday-maker.

Lyon-Parilly

One of the premier tracks on the French provincial circuit, Lyon-Parilly stages three or four races each season which are valuable enough to attract runners from the Chantilly stables, most notably the Grand Prix de Lyon.

Bordeaux-Arachon

This western course holds its big meeting in July when the Grand Prix d'Aquitaine is the major event, but Bordeaux also hosts one of few Group races to be staged away from Paris, the Andre Baboin, each October.

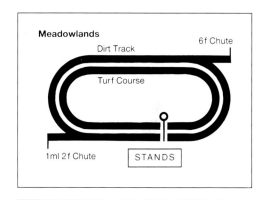

GERMANY

Dusseldorf

Home of one of Germany's richest races, the Grosser Preis von Berlin, Dusseldorf is also one of the country's most attractive tracks. Set in a hilly park known as the Grafenberg, Dusseldorf hosts quality meetings throughout the summer.

Gelsenkirchen-Horst

Though not the most beautiful of courses, Gelsenkirchen stages some good racing, notably the Aral-Pokal which has recently been opened up to horses from all countries. It is one of the seven tracks in the Nordrhein-Westfalen region where the bulk of the country's racing is staged.

ITALY

Pisa

Pisa is one of Italy's leading training centres, thanks to the region's temperate climate. Racing at the course starts early and the Premio Pisa in April is one of Europe's first Group races of the season.

Naples

Naples boasts a summer racing season that takes over from Milan and Rome when the weather has become too hot to continue in those cities. A seaside course of an acquired taste, the major race of the season is the Gran Premio Citta di Napoli.

NETHERLANDS

Duindigt

Dutch racing is a poor relation to most countries in Europe, but Duindigt, the country's major course, holds some decent Flat racing during the summer. Staffed by a large number of English ex-patriots and often English horses, there is a familar look to the proceedings.

SPAIN

Madrid

The most important of Spain's four racecourses, Madrid presides over the spring racing and is home to the country's Classics. Unfortunately the country's horses have been struck down by African Horse Sickness and the movement of horses in and out of the country has been halted for the forseeable future.

BARBADOS

Bridgetown

Affectionately known as Newmarket-by-Sea because of the large number of English trainers who spend their winters on the island, Barbados also boasts a fledgling racing industry. The course in Bridgetown stages regular competitive meetings which are well attended.

CANADA

Fort Erie

One of Canada's most picturesque tracks, Fort Erie is right on the border of Canada and the United States, close to Buffalo. The course's major event is the Prince of Wales Stakes, but even the field for that is often overshadowed by the thousands of flowers planted in the infield.

USA

Atlantic City

As one of the few legalised gambling centres in the country, Atlantic City has to have a racecourse. And it has a good one, which stages the UN Handicap, a major Group I prize, as well as other major races during the summer racing season.

Canterbury Downs

Canterbury Downs is one of the most modern courses in the States. Opened in 1985 to bring racing to the north Midwest, it has found immediate popularity; regular attendance figures of over 20,000 suggest that the course has a rosy future.

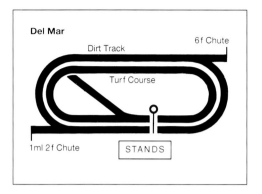

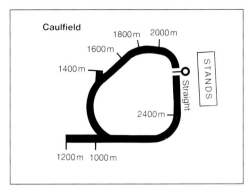

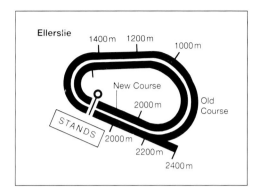

Meadowlands

Meadowlands is a New Jersey racecourse that specialises in night racing. Though outside New York, the track attracts big crowds and equine stars and holds several Group I races. It is sometimes regarded as Woody Stephens' personal racecourse beacuse year after year he chalks up major stakes victories here.

Sportsman Park

Chicago's second course, after Arlington, Sportman's Park has been one of the chief beneficiaries of the Arlington fire. For the last few years it has been doubling up its own meetings with those of Arlington and has enjoyed renewed popularity with the locals.

Philadelphia

Recently created out of the old Keystone racecourse, Philadelphia, with its park atmosphere, is a course which provides a family day out with racing thrown in. The facilities and racing are of a high standard.

Del Mar

Next door to the Pacific ocean in southern California is Del Mar, another racecourse which is closely associated with Hollywood. Bing Crosby was the first president of the course, and he helped engineer the growth of the course through its formative years.

Fair Grounds

The premier track of New Orleans, Fair Grounds has always had to battle to keep the interest of the city's inhabitants, for whom racing is not the biggest of draws. Notwithstanding, the course stages several Group I races and is run by Louis Roussel, owner of Risen Star, one of the Champions of the 1988 Flat season.

AUSTRALIA

Caulfield

One of Melbourne's three major courses, Caulfield stages major races like the Caulfield Guineas and the Caulfield Cup, important events in the Melbourne Spring Carnival. Close to the city centre the course regularly attracts a 10,000 plus crowd.

Tasmania

Tasmanian racing is definitely the poor relation of mainland Australian, with poor prize money, compared to the rest of the country, being competed for by poor horses. The two major tracks are Elwick in Hobart and Mowbray in Launceston.

Victoria Park

Adelaide's second oldest track, dating back to 1879, Victoria Park is close to the heart of the town. Major races staged at the course include the Adelaide Guineas and the Escort Cup, both run over a mile.

NEW ZEALAND

Ellerslie

Auckland's premier course and one of the four Grade A courses in the country, Ellerslie is home to the Auckland Cup, a major staying handicap on the lines of the Melbourne Cup, but one which has never thrown up a winner of that race.

INDIA

Calcutta

On the opposite side of the subcontinent from the other main racing centre, Bombay, Calcutta stages a regular season of racing but cannot match the quality of the Bombay circuit.

INDEX

Page numbers in *italic* refer to the illustrations and captions

Picture Acknowledgements

The publishers would like to thank the following organisations and individuals for their kind permission to reproduce the photographs in this book:

Action-Plus 23 bottom, 54, 65, 87 top, 124–5, 127 top, 181; Aintree Racecourse, Liverpool 52–3, 57, 59; AllSport 1, 12, 16, 25, 36, 37, 40, 71, 140–1; /David Cannon 80–1, 81, 202, 203; /Trevor Jones 32, 49, 66–7, 142; /Roger Labrosse 31; /Bob Martin 55; /Mike Powell 42, 120–1, 123, 128; /Steve Powell 44; /Pascal Rondeau 10 top, 13 bottom, 16–17, 35, 38 bottom; /Dan Smith 21, 177, 178, 179, 186 bottom; Arlington International Racecourse, Arlington Heights 143; Australian Jockey Club, Randwick 185, 186 top, 187; Bay Meadows Racecourse, San Mateo 157; P. Bertrand et Fils 8–9, 102, 105 bottom, 107, 108 top, 110, 112, 113, 115, 117, 118, 119; Peter Brauer 92, 93 bottom; Michael Burns Photo Ltd 164, 165; Čedok/Oldřich Karásek 85 top; /Jiří Šourer 84; Chepstow Racecourse 61; Churchill Downs, Louisville 126, 127; Colorsport 2, 4, 14, 15, 23 top, 27, 38 top, 56, 58, 63, 166, 198; Lupe Cunha 170, 172, 173; The Curragh Racecourse 70, 72; Pat Deasy 73; Lord Derby 29 bottom; Double J Photos 130–1, 132, 133, 146–7, 148, 149; Durban Turf Club 215; E. T. Archive 48 right; Mary Evans Picture Library 53, 68; Fairyhouse Racecourse, Ratoath 75; Hamburger Renn-Club e.V 93 top; Liam Healy 66, 74 top, 77, 78, 79, 80, 82; Hutchison Library/R. Ian Lloyd 199 left; Internationaler Club, Baden-Baden 88, 89, 90, 90–1; Irish Tourist Board 69; Japan Racing Association 6–7, 206, 208, 209; The Stewards of the Jockey Club 10 bottom, 26; Keeneland Association Inc. 138; William J. Kohm Inc. 145; Bob Langrish 86, 199 right; Moonee Valley Racing Club 188; Norsk Jockeyklub, Øvrevoll 83; N.Y.R.A. 134, 136, 137, 139, 144; Paddock Advertising and Marketing Consultants 74 bottom; Bernard Parkin 45, 64; Perrucci 94, 95, 96, 97, 98, 99, 100, 101; Phoenix Park Racecourse, Dublin 76–7; Popperfoto 30, 105 top, 106; Press Association 43; Queensland Turf Club, Eagle Farm Racecourse, Ascot (Queensland) 191, 192, 193; W.W. Rouch and Co. Ltd 29 top, 41; Royal Hong Kong Jockey Club, Happy Valley 174–5, 200, 201; Royal Western India Turf Club Ltd., Bombay 205; Alec Russell 18–19, 20, 46, 50, 51, 60; Schweizer Galopprennsport-Verband 87 bottom; George Selwyn 22, 34, 48 left, 109, 114; Société d'Encouragement pour l'Amélioration des Races de Chevaux en France 104; Société de Sport de France 111 right; South African Turf Club, Kenilworth Racecourse 214; South Australian Jockey Club Inc., Morphetville Racecourse, Adelaide 182; S.A. Stark 167, 168, 169; Santa Anita Park Archives/Steve Stidham 158; Steven J. Stidham 124, 129, 150, 151, 153, 154, 155, 156, 160, 161, 163; Sydney Turf Club 183; Times Newspapers Ltd 85 bottom; Turffontein Racecourse, Johannesburg 210, 212–3; Victoria Racing Club, Melbourne 180; Waikato Racing Club, Te Rapa Racecourse, Hamilton 194, 195, 196; The Wellington Racing Club Inc., Trentham Racecourse 197; The Western Australia Turf Club, Belmont 189.

The publishers would especially like to thank the following for their kind assistance in obtaining the illustrations for this book:
Paulo Benedetti, Blood Horse Magazine, Simon Cooper at the International Racing Bureau, Greg Magruder and Steve Stidham.
Picture Research: Jenny Faithfull

Many of the circuits, associated companies and photographers have also provided material for artwork reference, for which we are extremely grateful.